To Sue

for unselfishly giving
so much to so many

Contents

Study Guide for Motor Learning and Performance

Craig A. Wrisberg, PhD

Professor of Sport Psychology
Coordinator of Mental Training Services for Men's and Women's Athletics
University of Tennessee, Knoxville

Human Kinetics

Library of Congress Cataloging-in-Publication Data

Wrisberg, Craig A.
    Study guide for Motor learning and performance / Craig A. Wrisberg.
      p. cm.
    Includes bibliographical references.
    ISBN 0-7360-0000-3
     1. Schmidt, Richard A., 1941- Motor learning and performance.   2. Motor learning.   I.
    Title.

BF295.S2493 W75 1999
152.3'34--dc21   99-058645

ISBN: 0-7360-0000-3   20337019

Copyright © 2000 by Craig A. Wrisberg

Acquisitions Editor: Judy Patterson Wright, PhD; **Developmental Editor:** Anne Heiles; **Assistant Editor:** Laurie Stokoe; **Copyeditor:** Anne Heiles; **Proofreader:** Erin Cler; **Permission Manager:** Heather Munson; **Graphic Designer:** Robert Reuther; **Graphic Artist:** Kathleen Boudreau-Fuoss; **Photo Editor:** Clark Brooks; **Cover Designer:** Keith Blomberg; **Photographer (cover):** ALLSPORT; **Photographer (interior):** Tom Roberts, unless otherwise indicated; **Illustrators:** Accurate Art, Inc., Keith Blomberg, Mic Greenberg, Patrick Griffin, Mary Yemma Long, Tim Offenstein, and Paul To; **Printer:** Versa Press

Printed in the United States of America   10 9 8 7 6 5 4 3 2 1

Human Kinetics
Web site: http://www.humankinetics.com/

United States: Human Kinetics, P.O. Box 5076, Champaign, IL 61825-5076
1-800-747-4457
e-mail: humank@hkusa.com

Canada: Human Kinetics, 475 Devonshire Road Unit 100, Windsor, ON N8Y 2L5
1-800-465-7301 (in Canada only)
e-mail: humank@hkcanada.com

Europe: Human Kinetics, P.O. Box IW14, Leeds LS16 6TR, United Kingdom
+44 (0)113-278 1708
e-mail: humank@hkeurope.com

Australia: Human Kinetics, 57A Price Avenue, Lower Mitcham, South Australia 5062
(08) 82771555
e-mail: humank@hkaustralia.com

New Zealand: Human Kinetics, P.O. Box 105-231, Auckland Central
09-523-3462
e-mail: humank@hknewz.com

Acknowledgments

I would like to express sincere thanks to a number of people who helped me put this study guide together. Acquisitions editor Judy Wright, developmental editor Anne Heiles, and assistant editor Laurie Stokoe provided invaluable assistance. Judy offered many good ideas and frequent pep talks during the writing process; Anne provided helpful input regarding final choices for several activities and examples; Laurie furnished excellent editorial assistance. Craig Morrison and June Decker served as reviewers on earlier drafts of the manuscript and contributed many helpful suggestions. Finally, I am indebted to the students who inspired me to emphasize a problem-solving approach in my classes. The result has been a more stimulating learning environment for all of us.

The Benefits of Using This Study Guide

 **Introduction**

The field of motor learning and performance offers numerous concepts that are relevant to the work of movement practitioners in a variety of areas. An understanding of the way humans process information, plan and produce skilled movements, and adapt their movements to meet the demands of different sets of environmental conditions is important for practitioners in the areas of teaching, coaching, rehabilitation, and human factors. Formal motor skill instruction (i.e., teaching) can occur in the context of school physical education classes, specialized sport training centers (e.g., gymnastics, martial arts, swimming, etc.), public and private recreation centers, and performing arts studios. Specialized instructors also offer private lessons for individuals interested in skills like playing a musical instrument, horseback riding, and gourmet cooking.

Among their many other duties, coaches are required to provide skill instruction for athletes at all levels of competition. Younger athletes need help in learning the fundamental skills of their sport, while experienced athletes require assistance in refining their movements or in adapting them to meet the demands of different types of competitive situations.

Therapists and other individuals working in rehabilitation environments are called upon to provide assistance for patients trying to recover normal movement control after surgery or a job-related injury. Individuals with other sorts of handicapping conditions (e.g., cerebral palsy, stroke, etc.) require assistance in performing even the most routine, functional activities (e.g., walking, eating, climbing stairs, etc.).

Some movement practitioners assist individuals who want to learn skills involving the operation of machines or other equipment. In settings like this, practitioners must be mindful of the limitations of the human operator (i.e., human factors) and of the equipment being manipulated. A primary objective of human factors practitioners is to assist individuals in achieving optimal performance while minimizing the risk of injury to oneself or to others.

In order to provide the most effective instructional assistance, movement practitioners should have an

"OK, Howard. We'll play two more rounds using the training clubs, and, if all goes well, you'll play your first solo round on Wednesday."

understanding of the important theories of motor learning and performance and be able to adapt their instruction to meet the needs and goals of each individual learner. In the textbook, *Motor Learning and Performance: A Problem-Based Learning Approach*, you are introduced to the essential concepts and theories from the field of motor behavior. You are also given the opportunity to develop a problem-solving approach to instruction that you can use in assisting individuals who are trying to learn skills, relearn skills, or adapt the skills they have learned to meet the demands of new environments.

The Strength of Problem-Based Learning

In this present age of information, approaches to learning are shifting from the older traditions that emphasize the acquisition of subject matter to newer views that stress the importance of effective problem solving. Today's learners must to be able to accurately define problems and then sort out the available information they need to propose workable solutions. Sometimes individuals are required to solve problems without the benefit of all the necessary information—either because the available information does not suggest clear-cut answers as to how to proceed or because the facts are conflicting. A problem-based learning approach teaches individuals how to tackle problem scenarios in the most effective manner possible. It teaches them that there is usually no SINGLE correct answer to a problem but that the better solutions are the ones that are defensible and, wherever possible, supported by existing scientific evidence.

As Arthur Combs, the prominent humanist, suggests, "Effective problem solving is learned by confronting events, defining problems, puzzling with them, experimenting, trying, searching for effective solutions. Problem solving is using your brain and all the resources you can command to search for solutions. It is a creative process not tied to any particular subject. One can solve problems effectively in any area of human endeavor" (1981, p. 370).

For prospective movement practitioners, problem solving means asking the kinds of questions that are relevant to an instructional situation. Who is the learner? What is the individual's learning goal? What is the learning task? What are the cognitive, perceptual, and motor demands of the task? Where does the person want to be able to perform the task once he or she learns it? These are the kinds of questions you are going to be continually confronted with when completing the various activities in this book.

 ## Organization of the Chapters

This study guide is meant to accompany the textbook, *Motor Learning and Performance* (2nd ed.) by Schmidt and Wrisberg (2000). The activities contained in the study guide are designed to take you beyond the textbook assignments and give you additional opportunities to test your comprehension of the concepts you are learning. More importantly, the activities challenge you to apply this information to a variety of real-world problems and situations.

Each chapter corresponds to one chapter in the textbook (e.g., "Chapter 1: Getting Started"). The study guide chapters begin with a summary of the material covered in the textbook ("Key Concepts"). This summary contains a brief explanation of the key concepts in the chapter (and occasionally a few definitions to refresh your memory), discussion of how the concepts relate to each other, and practical examples or applications of the concepts. Understanding the "big picture" and the "bottom lines" of key concepts is essential to your development of a working knowledge of the field of motor learning and performance.

After the summary, there is a section ("Key Terms") that includes a list of key terms you will need to understand in order to complete the study guide activities. You can find the definitions of these terms in the running glossary in the textbook. Your ability to use these terms allows you to communicate with other professionals in the field and find solutions to problems within the available literature.

The remaining sections of the study guide include questions and exercises. The "Review Questions" cover several key concepts from the textbook and challenge you to come up with examples or illustrations of each concept. You must also provide an explanation of the appropriateness of each of your choices. For some of the questions, you are given an initial example (with supporting rationale) to help you get going. Coming up with concrete examples is one way you can evaluate your understanding of the concepts. If you can generate good examples, you are in a good position to apply your knowledge of motor learning and performance concepts to a variety of real-world situations.

The "Problem-Solving Exercises" enable you to practice putting the problem-solving approach to work. Each exercise begins with a description of an issue or problem, along with other relevant factual information. After this, there are two possible solutions and an evaluation of the quality of each. The evaluation pinpoints the relative strengths and weaknesses of the solution and offers suggestions as to how the solution might be improved. Then it's your turn to come up with a solution to the problem. To help you with this, you will find a highlighted worksheet you can use as a template to organize your answer. Once you have compiled the necessary information (including supporting rationale and, whenever possible, supporting experimental evidence), you should type your solution and proofread it for content and clarity (or, better yet, ask a classmate or friend to read the solution and give you some honest feedback). At that point you should be able to share your solution in class or turn it in to your professor. Knowing how to construct and support a logical solution to a real-world problem is the essence of the problem-based learning approach.

By completing each of the questions and problem-solving exercises in this study guide, you will be demonstrating your understanding of the key concepts and principles of motor learning and performance presented in the textbook. More importantly, you will be developing an effective approach to problem solving you can use in the future.

Best wishes.

References:

Combs, A.W. (1981). What the future demands of education. *Phi Delta Kappan, 62,* 369–372.

Schmidt, R.A., & Wrisberg, C.A. (2000). *Motor learning and performance* (2nd ed.). Champaign, IL: Human Kinetics.

CHAPTER 1

Getting Started

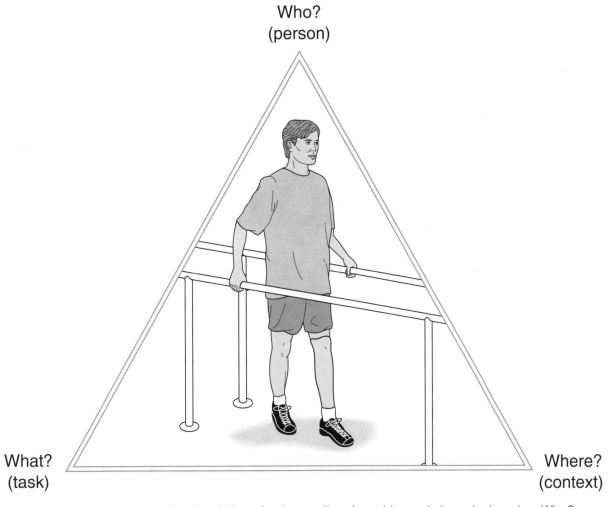

Movement practitioners continually ask three basic questions to assist people in motor learning: Who? What? and Where?

Key Concepts

The textbook begins by presenting several concepts that are foundational to understanding motor performance and learning. The first is the concept of motor skill, and we explain how the term *skill* can be viewed from the perspective of an act or motor task or from the perspective of observable characteristics of an individual's performance.

Considered *as tasks*, motor skills can be classified according to a number of prominent characteristics. One characteristic deals with how the movement is organized (e.g., as a single discrete action, as a series of discrete movements strung together in a particular order, or as a rhythmic repetition of basically the same action). A second characteristic concerns the relative importance of motor and cognitive elements to performance of the task. A third characteristic is the relative predictability of the environment in which the movement is performed. It is often useful to consider several dimensions of a skill when doing a task analysis. A good example of this approach is Gentile's (1987) two-dimensional classification system for physical therapy settings.

Viewing skill in terms of performance *proficiency* brings out other features. These include the degree of certainty of goal achievement, the relative amount of energy expenditure, and, in some cases, the time it takes to produce the movement. More-skilled individuals demonstrate higher levels of proficiency for these and other features of their movements.

We also define the terms *motor performance* and *motor learning.* These two concepts are related, yet distinct. Motor performance is observable movement behavior that is sometimes susceptible to temporary factors, such as fatigue and motivation. Motor learning is a more stable, internal process. A person's level of motor learning can only be estimated by observing the individual's motor performance. People demonstrate different performance characteristics at different stages of motor learning, and they are sometimes unaware of the reasons for their skill improvements.

Effective movement practitioners derive solutions to performance and learning problems by first asking the right questions. Once they obtain the answers to these questions, effective practitioners muster the best available rationale and supporting evidence for the solutions they come up with. The problem-based approach to motor performance and learning highlighted in the textbook is designed to help you develop a problem-solving technique for providing instructional assistance in a variety of situations (e.g., teaching, coaching, rehabilitation, and human factors).

Key Terms

In order to respond to the questions and complete the exercises in this chapter, you need a basic understanding of the following terms or concepts, which are explained in the textbook:

discrete skill

serial skill

continuous skill

motor skill

cognitive skill

open skill

closed skill

motor performance

motor learning

problem-based learning

Review Questions

Answer each of the following questions and *provide rationale for your answers.*

1. Classify *each* of the following tasks using the discrete-serial-continuous skill classification system, the motor-cognitive skill classification system, *and* the open-closed skill classification system.

    a. Eating spaghetti

    b. Line dancing

    c. Catching a ball

2. Indicate how differences in the following pairs of conditions might change the way you classify the task using each of the three classification systems.

    a. An individual eating spaghetti with chopsticks instead of with a fork and spoon

    b. A person line dancing with her arms interlocked with those of individuals on either side of her, as opposed to a person line dancing *without* physical contact with other people

    c. A person catching a ball that is bouncing toward him along an uneven surface instead of one that is rolling toward him along a smooth surface

3. Indicate how additional differences in the following pairs of conditions might again change the way you classify the task using each of the three classification systems.

    a. A food gourmet eating spaghetti with chopsticks, as compared with a fast-food fanatic eating spaghetti with chopsticks

    b. A person line dancing alongside familiar dance partners to the tune of a familiar song, as compared with a person line dancing alongside unfamiliar dance partners to the tune of an unfamiliar song

    c. A professional cricket player catching a ball bouncing toward him along an uneven surface, as compared with a novice game player trying to catch a ball bouncing toward him along an uneven surface

4. For *each* of the following tasks, indicate which of the three aspects of skill proficiency discussed in chapter 1 (i.e., certainty of goal achievement, energy expenditure, and movement time) would *most distinguish* the performance of beginning and advanced participants.

    a. Putting a golf ball

    b. Crutch walking

    c. Driving a car

    d. Beating an egg

 Problem-Solving Exercises

In the following exercises, you can demonstrate your comprehension of several concepts from chapter 1 of the textbook. In Exercise 1.1 you interview a beginning and advanced performer and ask each of them what they think about when they perform the task in question. Then you summarize and compare the thought patterns of these two people. In Exercise 1.2 you classify several skills by using Gentile's (1987) two-dimensional classification system, shown in table 1.4 of the textbook. In Exercise 1.3 you reflect on one of your own motor learning experiences. Then you describe the task, classify it, and explain five characteristics of the learning experience that for you particularly stand out.

Exercise 1.1

Examining the Cognitive Aspects of Motor Skill

The cognitive aspects of a motor skill change and sometimes diminish as individuals become better performers. To examine this issue in more depth, you need to interview (separately) two individuals who participate in the same motor activity (e.g., golf, tennis, skiing, sewing) but who differ with respect to their level of experience with the task. Ask each person to tell you what he or she "thinks about" *when performing the task* (you may need to identify a particular aspect of the task, such as executing a long putt in golf or hitting the serve in tennis). *Do not lead* the individuals in any particular direction! All you are interested in is what *they* are thinking, not what *you* think they *should* be thinking. Take notes, summarize the comments of each person, and then ask the individual to verify the accuracy of your summary. Then, you should finish with these steps:

1. Explain how you conducted the interviews.
2. Describe each individual and indicate why you think one is a beginner and the other is an advanced performer.
3. Discuss the differences in the quantity and quality of the thoughts of the two individuals.

Beth's Solution

The sport I am examining is soccer. First I interviewed Ira and then I interviewed Ben. Ira is a beginner and Ben is an advanced player. Ira says that all he thinks about when he plays soccer is the ball. When the ball comes to him, Ira thinks about not missing it and then getting rid of it as quickly as possible. Ben says that the ball is important to him as well, but that he doesn't spend all his time focusing on it. Ben also looks at his teammates and his opponents and thinks about what he will do with the ball when it comes to him. When Ben has the ball, he thinks about when and where to pass it or shoot it, depending on his own position on the field and on the position of his teammates and the opposing players.

Looking at the comments of these two players, I can see that Ben thinks about more things than Ira does and that the two players think about different things. Ira thinks about kicking the ball, period, and Ben thinks about what he will do with the ball when it comes to him.

Evaluation of Beth's Solution

Beth does not say much at all about the interview process, other than to indicate that she conducted two interviews. We don't know what it is she asked Ira and Ben to comment on, and we don't know whether those two people agree with Beth's summary of their comments. Beth gives no description of Ira and Ben except to say that one is a beginner and the other is an advanced player. Beth should provide more details when discussing how she conducted the interviews and the characteristics of the two individuals that make Ira a beginner and Ben an advanced player.

It appears that Beth asked Ira and Ben to tell her what each thinks about when he plays soccer. In order to determine the two individuals' thoughts when performing a particular soccer skill, Beth could ask them to focus on a specific task (e.g., trapping, passing, dribbling, heading). Ira's and Ben's comments pertain more to *strategies* they use *when playing soccer* than when performing a *skill*. Beth notes that the advanced player's (i.e., Ben's) strategies are greater in number and more varied than those of the beginner (i.e., Ira) but she doesn't discuss the differences in any depth.

In summary, Beth fulfills the minimum requirements of this exercise and nothing more.

Bonnie's Solution

I conducted two interviews with individuals who participate in Tae Kwon Do. Tae Kwon Do is a martial art that involves hand-to-hand combat. Each interview took place in my dorm room with no one present but me and the person I was interviewing. That way there were no interruptions during the interview. Both interviews lasted about 15 minutes. The question I asked each person was, "What do you think about when you perform the side kick?" After the person was finished talking, I read him or her what I had written in my notes to be sure that he or she thought it was accurate. I had to change a couple of things, but for the most part, both performers said my summary was accurate.

The name of the first person I interviewed is Dixie. Dixie is a 22-year-old graduate student who began taking Tae Kwon Do lessons one month ago. Dixie says that when she performs the side kick, she thinks about how awkward it feels and how difficult it is to maintain her balance (especially when she is trying to recover and return to the ready stance). Dixie says that she thinks about performing different parts of the movement, such as the correct hand position and the full extension of the leg. Dixie says she often gets confused and feels awkward because there are so many things to think about.

The name of the second person I interviewed is Brian. Brian is a 19-year-old undergraduate student who has participated in Tae Kwon Do since he was 11 years old. Brian says he thinks about the target he is trying to contact when executing the side kick. Brian does not think about the kick itself. He says his kicks seem more like reflexes; he feels the energy of the force he is applying but that's about all. Brian says he thinks more about what his opponent is doing and how he should attempt to counter his opponent's moves.

Looking at the comments of these two individuals, I see that Dixie thinks more about the execution of the movement, while Brian thinks more about hitting the target. Dixie thinks about a lot of things, while Brian thinks about one or two things.

Evaluation of Bonnie's Solution

Bonnie does a nice job describing the interview process and the two individuals she interviews. She should, however, provide a brief description of the side kick, since this is the skill the two individuals are commenting on. Bonnie describes the situation, the question she asks each person, and the way she obtains verification of her summaries. Bonnie indicates how long each person has been participating in Tae Kwon Do, suggesting that there is a difference in the skill levels of the two people. Bonnie does not say how often Brian trains or the rank he has achieved in the sport. Many people practice Tae Kwon Do for years but do not achieve a high rank because they are unable to perform the necessary skills.

Bonnie's summary of the comments of the two individuals is good. However, she does not discuss the differences to any great extent. Bonnie could say more about how the comments of the two people illustrate the kinds of changes that take place in the thoughts of individuals when they progress from early to more advanced levels of a motor skill. For example, more advanced performers like Brian do not have to think about the mechanics of their movements because they perform the movements almost automatically. On the other hand, beginners like Dixie are often unsure about how the movement is produced so they have to think more about the mechanical aspects of the task.

Your Solution to Exercise 1.1

Examining the Cognitive Aspects of Motor Skill

NAME_____ DATE_____

1. Definition of the problem:
2. Description of interview process:
3. Description of participants
   Beginner:
   Advanced performer:
4. Discussion of differences in the quantity and quality of participant's thoughts:

Exercise 1.2

Classifying Skills in Two Dimensions

Using Gentile's two-dimensional classification system (table 1.4 in the textbook), indicate the category you think each of the following skills belongs in:

1. Three consecutive attempts at throwing a Frisbee to a friend
2. Three consecutive attempts at catching a Frisbee thrown to you by an unskilled Frisbee player
3. Sculpting a ceramic bowl using a potter's wheel

Charlie's Solution

Three consecutive attempts of throwing a Frisbee to a friend belongs in the category dealing with no body transport, object manipulation, no regulatory variability, and no context variability.

Three consecutive attempts of catching a Frisbee thrown to me by an unskilled Frisbee player belongs in the category dealing with body transport, object manipulation, regulatory variability, and context variability.

Sculpting a ceramic bowl using a potter's wheel belongs in the category dealing with no body transport, object manipulation, regulatory variability, and context variability.

Evaluation of Charlie's Solution

Charlie indicates which categories of Gentile's (1987) two-dimensional classification system he thinks each of the skills belongs in, but he provides no supporting rationale or logic for any of his choices. For his solution to be acceptable, Charlie needs to explain *why* he thinks his choices are appropriate.

Jason's Solution

Throwing a Frisbee to a friend three consecutive times is a task that could fall into several of Gentile's (1987) classification categories. For simplicity purposes, let's say I decide to throw the Frisbee from a stationary position to a friend who is in a stationary position 20 feet from me. There would be no body transport on any attempt because I am stationary, but there would be object manipulation because I am throwing a Frisbee. There would be no regulatory variability and no context variability because I am throwing the Frisbee to a fixed target that is located in the same position on all three attempts.

Catching a Frisbee that an unskilled player throws to me on three consecutive occasions is a task that would be classified in the following way. Since I am catching a moving object, the task involves regulatory variability. Since the thrower is unskilled and therefore unlikely to produce the exact same throw on all three attempts, the task involves context variability. Since the thrower is unskilled, I am probably going to have to move my body to a position to catch the Frisbee. Therefore, the task involves body transport. Catching an object of any kind involves at least some object manipulation (e.g., closing the fingers around the rim of the Frisbee or cradling the Frisbee into the body).

Sculpting a ceramic bowl using a potter's wheel is a task that is usually performed by a person who is seated. Therefore, this task involves object manipulation but no body transport. The wheel is stabilized in a fixed location and spins in a predictable fashion. Therefore, there is little regulatory variability. There is some degree of context variability because the potter must move the bowl into different positions to create the desired shape.

Evaluation of Jason's Solution

Jason classifies the four tasks rather well. For the most part, he provides rationale for each of his choices. Jason points out that throwing a Frisbee can be classified in various ways depending on the circumstances. Theoretically, the same thing holds for the other tasks as well. Jason suggests that there is no context variability when throwing a Frisbee to a fixed target. However, the location of the target does not guarantee a consistent throw. If Jason's three throws travel different distances and in different directions, there is greater context variability—regardless of the position of his friend.

In his discussion of catching a Frisbee, Jason points out that the task involves regulatory variability because the Frisbee is in motion. He could also point out that regulatory variability is increased even more when the thrower is unskilled than when the thrower is skilled because the flight of the Frisbee is less predictable. Technically, Jason should discuss regulatory variability and context variability in terms of the degree of each. To say a task has regulatory variability or context variability does not say very much. The issue of variability is a relative one—that is, depending on task conditions, there is *relatively* more or less of each type of variability. This illustrates an important principle of communication: effective communication requires sufficiently *precise* language.

Classifying the sculpting of a ceramic bowl, Jason states that the potter's wheel is stabilized in a fixed position and spins in a predictable fashion, suggesting there is little or no regulatory variability. However, Jason might point out that unskilled potters would probably find the action of the spinning wheel to be less predictable than would skilled potters—making the act of sculpting more difficult.

Whenever you cite an article or book in one of your papers, you need to include the complete bibliographical reference at the end of the paper. Since Jason cites Gentile's (1987) classification system, he needs to include the following information:

Reference:

Gentile, A.M. (1987). Skill acquisition: Action, movement, and the neuromotor processes. In J.H. Carr, R.B. Shepherd, J. Gordon, A.M. Gentile, & J.M. Hind (Eds.), *Movement science: Foundations for physical therapy in rehabilitation* (pp. 93–154). Rockville, MD: Aspen.

Your Solution to Exercise 1.2

Classifying Skills in Two Dimensions

NAME_____   DATE_____

1. Definition of the problem:

2. Skill: Classification category:
   a.
   b.
   c.
   d.

Exercise 1.3

Reflecting on a Learning Experience of Your Own

By this time in your life, you have learned many different motor skills. Many of these skills you perform on a daily basis, whereas others you engage in only during occasional sport or recreational opportunities. Until now you have probably not thought much about how these skills might be classified or about the kinds of changes in your performance that took place as you moved from the beginning stages of practice to more advanced levels.

Reflect on one of your own experiences of skill learning. Think of a particular skill you have learned that took quite a while to master. Perhaps it is a skill you have still not mastered, but your performance is much better now than it was when you first began practicing the skill. Once you have selected the skill, provide the following information:

1. Briefly describe the skill, giving particular emphasis to the goal of the movement and the basic actions a person must produce to perform the skill.
2. Classify the skill using the three classification systems discussed in chapter 1.
3. List and describe *five* performance characteristics you remember from the beginning and later stages of your skill-learning experience. Refer to table 1.5 in chapter 1, but describe *in your own words* the characteristics you remember—don't merely parrot some of the characteristics listed in table 1.5.

Bob's Solution

The skill I want to talk about is baseball. The goal of baseball is to win games. The way you win games is to get a lot of hits and not make many errors. The basic actions required of performers are hitting, throwing, and fielding.

Baseball would be classified as a discrete skill, a motor skill, and an open skill. It's a discrete skill because most of the movements are brief and distinct in nature. It's a motor skill because movement execution is more crucial for performance than is thinking. It's an open skill because the environment is almost always in motion.

Now I will talk about five characteristics of my performance that I remember from my experience of learning to play the game of baseball. When I first started practicing, I was afraid of getting hit with the ball, I missed a lot of ground balls, and

I made a lot of bad throws. As I got better at the game, I knew what I was supposed to do when a ball was hit to me and I was able to hit the ball harder more often.

Evaluation of Bob's Solution

Bob chooses to discuss the game of baseball rather than a specific skill. This makes the entire assignment more difficult because it forces him to discuss generalities of the game rather than specific characteristics of individual skills. Before preparing his solution, Bob needs to read the assignment more carefully and perhaps ask his professor about the "skill" Bob wants to discuss.

Bob's skill classifications are oversimplified. For example, Bob says that baseball is an "open" skill because the environment is almost always in motion. This is perhaps true for the skills of batting and fielding but not so for pitching. Bob says that baseball performance does not depend on a lot of thinking. Certainly, players on defense must think about the game situation and what they are going to do with the ball if it is hit to them. Therefore, Bob should provide more rationale for his comment. (Note that it is more difficult for people to evaluate the things you *don't* say than the things you do say.)

Finally, Bob provides only vague descriptions of the characteristics he remembers from his learning experience. What does Bob mean by "a lot," "more," and "harder"? As Bob got "better," "what" is it he "knew" he was supposed to do? There are certainly more specific performance characteristics Bob could mention. Some of these characteristics are shown in table 1.5 in the textbook.

Kyle's Solution

I am going to discuss my experience of learning to shoot pool (i.e., billiards). The goal of the task is to strike a cue ball with a cue stick in order to propel the ball in the direction of a second ball. The cue ball must strike the second ball in such a way that the second ball rolls into one of the cue pockets on the billiards table. The basic actions required of this task are a smooth, steady arm movement and a stable base, or "platform," for the stick to rest upon. The arm action is produced by the hand holding the stick, while the opposite hand produces the platform.

The task of accurately striking a cue ball can be classified as a discrete task because the movement has well-defined beginning and end points. Once the player places the cue stick on the base, he or she begins the movement by pulling back on the stick and then pushing it forward so that the tip of the cue stick strikes the cue ball, propelling it in a forward direction. The forward movement of the stick ends shortly after contact with the ball.

Striking a cue ball is primarily a motor skill, but planning the shot requires some thought as well. If the cue ball is located in a more difficult position (e.g., resting against the side rail), the striking movement is more difficult to execute. In addition, more complex shots require more strategic planning than do simpler shots. Therefore, depending on the difficulty and complexity of the shot, striking the cue ball lies at various places along the motor skill–cognitive skill continuum.

The task is a closed skill because the environment is stationary when the movement is performed. The balls are stationary, the table is stationary, and the pockets of the table are stationary.

I remember several characteristics of my learning experience. Initially, I had difficulty forming a stable base and therefore my stick movements were quite variable. Since the cue stick also felt awkward in my hands, I found myself watching the stick rather than watching the cue ball. As a result, the stick would strike the ball in different places from one shot to the next, and sometimes it would miss the ball completely. As I became more accustomed to the feel of the stick and to the shooting motion, I began watching the cue ball better. Now I can strike the cue ball in about the same location on every shot. My shots are more accurate and consistent, and I am able to produce different types of shots that result in the target ball going into a pocket and the cue ball coming to rest in a good position for my next shot. When I look at the characteristics in table 1.5 in chapter 1, I see several terms that describe my own learning experience. Early on in learning my movements were "inaccurate, inconsistent, and rigid." Later on I experienced the characteristics of "more relaxed, more accurate, more consistent, more fluid, more confident, and more adaptable."

Evaluation of Kyle's Solution

Kyle's solution is clearly written and addresses each of the requirements of the problem in a detailed fashion. Another strength of Kyle's discussion is the supporting rationale he provides for his classifications. For example, Kyle indicates that billiards is a closed skill because the environment is stationary; he then goes on to list some specific stationary components of the environment. Kyle's description is particularly impressive in explaining the way motor skill and cognitive skill components of the task can vary for different types of shots. However, Kyle might provide contrasting examples of a simple shot and a more complex shot to illustrate how the cognitive demands are different in each.

Your Solution to Exercise 1.3

Reflecting on a Learning Experience of Your Own

NAME_____ DATE_____

1. Definition of the problem:
2. Description of the skill:
3. Classification of the skill:
   a.
   b.
   c.
4. Stage of learning: Performance characteristics:
   a.
   b.
   c.
   d.
   e.

CHAPTER 2

Individual Differences and Motor Abilities

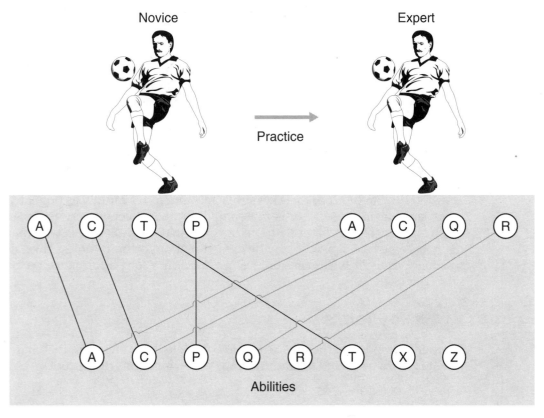

The underlying abilities necessary for success with a particular task change as the learner progresses from novice to expert.

Key Concepts

In chapter 2 we discuss some of the factors that make individuals different from one another and that play a role in determining which people eventually become the better performers of various motor tasks. Some of these factors are under the person's control (e.g., motivation, attitude, emotions) but others are not (e.g., inherited abilities, body type, cultural background).

The concept of motor abilities—those stable, genetically determined traits that individuals bring with them to performance and learning situations—is a primary focus of chapter 2. Individuals possess different patterns of abilities; they are stronger in some areas and weaker in others. Given a particular motor task, an individual fares better or worse depending, to some extent, on his or her unique patterns of abilities. For example, power lifting requires a great deal of strength, and a person who has high levels of static strength and dynamic strength usually performs better than an individual whose levels of those abilities are lower. However, the weaker power lifter may have higher levels of coordination and perceptual timing ability than his better power-lifting counterpart, allowing him to win more games of table tennis.

Abilities differ from skill in that abilities are fixed, inherited traits, whereas skill represents a level of performance proficiency that can be improved as a result of practice or rehearsal. A person's abilities determine his or her potential to achieve a particular level of skill on any task. For example, two individuals who want to learn how to shoot archery may differ with respect to the abilities important for archery performance. The person with higher levels of the important abilities has the greater potential to achieve success in this task. With practice, the person with lower levels of the important abilities is also going to improve his archery skill. However, an individual who possesses higher levels of the important abilities *and* who spends many hours practicing the task is usually the better archer.

It is difficult to predict an individual's future success on a motor task based on the person's *initial* performance. This is because the types of abilities that figure importantly in performing during the early stages of practice may be different from the types of abilities that are important for performance later on. In typing, for example, if aiming ability is important during the initial stages of practice (when individuals are trying to accurately position their fingers on the keys), people with a high level of aiming ability are going to demonstrate better performance than people with a low level of aiming ability. However, later in practice, it is likely that aiming ability is less important for performance; individuals now know the location of the keys and need to produce their keystroke movements as rapidly as possible. At this point, movement rate ability is more important for effective performance than is aiming ability. The problem with prediction is that the individuals who may eventually become best at a skill may be denied that opportunity unless they also possess high levels of whatever abilities are important for performance on an initial screening test.

Key Terms

In order to respond to the questions and complete the exercises in this chapter, you need to have a basic understanding of the following terms or concepts:

individual differences

abilities

skill

task analysis

 **Review Questions**

Answer each of the following questions and *provide rationale for your answers.*

1. For each of the following tasks, one factor is presented (from table 2.1 in the textbook) that might be expected to contribute to performance success. You should select *two* additional factors from table 2.1 and explain the role you think each might play in executing the task.

    a. Paddling a canoe in a swift-flowing river is a task that might be performed more effectively by someone with keen perceptual abilities—enabling the person to detect patterns of water current and the location of rocks and other obstacles.

Second factor:

Third factor:

    b. Building a boat dock is a task that might be performed more effectively by someone who has had prior experiences in construction—enabling the person to properly measure materials, obtain the appropriate materials, and operate the required tools and equipment.

Second factor:

Third factor:

    c. Performing a back handspring in gymnastics is a task that might be accomplished more effectively by someone who is stimulated by risk taking and the emotion of excitement—enabling the person to approach the task with a high level of energy and enthusiasm.

Second factor:

Third factor:

2. For each of the following tasks, one of the general abilities listed in table 2.4 or 2.5 is presented that might be expected to contribute to performance success. Select *two* additional abilities from either or both of these tables and explain the role you think each ability might play in executing the task.

    a. Performing a guitar piece is a task that might be accomplished more effectively by someone with high levels of multilimb coordination—enabling the person to produce intricate patterns of notes with both hands simultaneously.

Second ability:

Third ability:

    b. Performing dental surgery is a task that might be accomplished more effectively by a dentist who has high levels of arm-hand steadiness—enabling the person to position the hands in the proper places for executing the necessary surgical procedures.

Second ability:

Third ability:

    c. Hurling the discus is a task that might be performed more effectively by individuals with high levels of explosive strength—enabling them to maximize force in a brief period to project the discus as far as possible.

Second ability:

Third ability:

3. Four individuals, Mick, Mack, Mike, and Mooky, are interested in learning how to (a) drive a car, (b) perform a parallel bar routine in gymnastics, (c) cast a fishing lure, and (d) play the harp. Based on the stronger and weaker abilities of each person as outlined here, indicate which task (driving, parallel bars, casting, or playing harp) each individual has the *best* potential for achieving a *high* level of performance.

a. Mick has higher-than-average levels of finger dexterity and force control and lower-than-average levels of movement rate and speed of limb movement. The task Mick appears to be best suited for is:

b. Mack has higher-than-average levels of trunk strength and balance with visual cues and lower-than-average levels of stamina and perceptual timing. The task Mack appears to be best suited for is:

c. Mike has higher-than-average levels of reaction time and control precision and lower-than-average levels of explosive strength and gross body equilibrium. The task Mike appears to be best suited for is:

d. Mooky has higher-than-average levels of wrist-finger speed and aiming and lower-than-average levels of static strength and rate control. The task Mooky appears to be best suited for is:

4. Abilities that are important to task performance are sometimes different after extensive practice than during the early stages of practice. For each of the following tasks, indicate which of the corresponding pair of abilities might be more important for performance on the first day of practice and which might be more important after several years of practice.

a. Hitting a golf ball at a driving range—explosive strength and motor timing.

More important on the first day:

More important after several years:

b. Playing the drums—perceptual timing and force control.

More important on the first day:

More important after several years:

c. Hitting a jump serve in volleyball—speed of limb movement and multilimb coordination.

More important on the first day:

More important after several years:

 **Problem-Solving Exercises**

In Exercise 2.1 you reflect on your own life experience and discuss some of the factors you think contribute to your proficiency at a motor task you perform well. In Exercise 2.2 you discuss ways a person's abilities might influence the way the individual learns a motor skill. In Exercise 2.3 you evaluate a situation in which an individual's future performance opportunities are determined by the person's performance on a tryout test.

Each of us does some things better than other things. Mary may be a great soccer player but she has a tough time playing the piano. Li may be an accomplished woodworker but he struggles to even hit the target when throwing darts. While practice leads to improvements in everybody's performance, certain people are always going to be the better performers on particular tasks because of factors other than practice.

Think of a motor skill you perform rather well and how you became proficient at it. You probably achieved your present skill level as a result of many hours of practice or rehearsal, perhaps over a period of several years. However, in addition to the practice you put in, other factors have likely contributed to your proficiency on this task. Table 2.1 in the textbook lists factors that might contribute to individuals' movement performance and skill learning. Carefully review this list and then pick *four* factors that have contributed to your proficiency in performing the skill you picked. In your solution you should do the following:

- Describe the skill, emphasizing the goal of the movement and the basic actions to perform the skill.
- Discuss each of the four factors you select from table 2.1.
- Supply a rationale for *why* you think each factor is important for task performance.
- Explain *how* the factor contributes to skillful movement production.

Emily's Solution

The skill I have chosen is the forearm pass in volleyball. The goal of forearm passing is to direct the ball toward the setter so that she can effectively set the ball for the spiker. The basic actions of passing are stabilizing the body, clasping the hands, and contacting the ball on the forearms.

The factors I have selected from table 2.1 that I think contribute to my own performance of the forearm pass are attitude, emotions, prior experiences, and family. I have a good attitude about playing volleyball. It is an activity I want to be good at. I am an emotional person and emotions are important for a person who wants to be a good player. Prior experiences in other sports have also helped me be a good volleyball player. Finally, my family is an important factor because all of us enjoy participating in recreational activities.

Evaluation of Emily's Solution

Emily chooses to discuss the forearm pass in volleyball. She does a nice job of describing the goal of the movement and the basic actions required. However, a professor who doesn't know anything about the sport of volleyball may not understand some of the terms she uses, such as *setter* and *spiker*. Remember, it's always better to provide definitions and not need them than to need them and not provide them. In Emily's case, an uninformed professor would also benefit from seeing a diagram illustrating the basic actions of the forearm pass.

The factors Emily selects from table 2.1 appear to have the potential to contribute to her performance of the forearm pass. However, Emily needs to provide more precise discussion of *why* each factor is important and *how* each factor contributes to task performance. For example, Emily should explain why she thinks attitude is important to performance and how a good attitude influences performance. She should also explain why she thinks emotions are important and, more specifically, what *types* of emotions are beneficial. Joy, enthusiasm, grief, and anger are all examples of emotions—but are all these emotions beneficial for forearm passing? Emily also needs to describe the types of prior experiences and recreational activities she thinks contribute to effective passing performance—and *how* each experience or activity exerts an influence.

In short, Emily's solution needs a more detailed discussion of the factors she selects and a more precise explanation of how each factor contributes to her performance of the forearm pass.

Eduardo's Solution

I have played soccer for many years and am very adept at dribbling the ball. The goal of dribbling is to advance the ball along the ground with a series of nudging movements with either foot. The basic actions involved in dribbling are running and "nudging" (i.e., lightly tapping) the ball forward using the inside and outside surfaces of both feet. More advanced players can keep the ball under control at all times, protect the ball from opponents by using their legs and body, and use body feints to keep opponents off balance.

Several factors in table 2.1 contribute to my skill in dribbling. The first factor is "abilities," in particular those abilities labeled "motor" and "perceptual." People tell me that I have extremely quick feet and good balance while I'm dribbling on the run. These characteristics are similar to the abilities identified by Fleishman (1964) as "speed of limb movement" and "balance with visual cues." I always feel like I'm moving more quickly than everyone else while still maintaining contact with the ball and a good view of the field. These abilities are probably an advantage for people who have to perform tasks like dribbling a soccer ball quickly and accurately.

The second factor is "body type." I am stocky, strong, and built close to the ground. Being built closer to the ground allows me to be closer to the ball, and being stocky and strong allows me to protect the ball from opponents.

The third factor is "fitness." I train extensively, both in the weight room and on the track. In addition to the running I do during practices and matches, I do interval training and long-distance running on my own. This enables me to maintain my running speed throughout an entire match, while other players are getting tired and slowing down.

The final factor is "motivation." I want to achieve success in the sport of soccer, and I take particular pride in my dribbling skills. Whenever my team needs to advance the ball, my teammates expect me to do it. I love this challenge and devote all of my attention and energy to effective performance. In that way I can reward my teammates for their confidence in me.

Other factors in table 2.1 also contribute to my dribbling skill but the ones I have selected are probably the most influential. Writing out this solution has made me more aware of some of the factors that have made me the skilled dribbler I am today.

Reference:

Fleishman, E.A. (1964). *The structure and measurement of physical fitness.* Englewood Cliffs, NJ: Prentice-Hall.

Evaluation of Eduardo's Solution

Eduardo's solution is clearly written and addresses each of the requirements of the problem in a detailed fashion. He also gives a reference to related literature on the topic of individual differences and motor abilities, including a complete bibliographical citation of the Fleishman (1964) reference at the end of his solution. Eduardo's description of each of the factors he selects from table 2.1 and his explanation of the role each plays in his dribbling performance are excellent.

Your Solution to Exercise 2.1

Creating a Recipe for Skilled Performance

NAME_____ DATE_____

1. Definition of the problem:
2. Instructional situation (circle one):
   Teaching   Coaching   Rehabilitation   Human factors
3. Description of the skill:
4. Goal of the movement:
5. Basic actions required:
6. Contributing factors from table 2.1
   Factor: Why: How:
   a.
   b.
   c.
   d.

Exercise 2.2

Considering the Strengths and Weaknesses of Learners

Imagine that a person (e.g., friend, family member, therapy patient) has asked you to help him or her learn a particular motor task that you are adept at or familiar with. You can attribute any characteristics you want to this person. However, assume that the individual possesses the following strengths and weaknesses (see tables 2.4 and 2.5 for more complete descriptions of abilities):

- Strengths are multilimb coordination, rate control, motor timing
- Weaknesses are reaction time, response orientation, perceptual timing

In your solution you should do the following:

- Describe the learner (cite at least these characteristics: age, sex, sociocultural background, and handicapping condition, if any).
- Describe the learning task (including the goal of the movement and the basic actions required).
- Discuss the advantages and disadvantages this individual might bring to the learning situation as a result of his or her characteristics.

David's Solution

Description of the Learner:

Three months ago my friend Jeremy had arthroscopic knee surgery to repair a ligament he damaged while participating in gymnastics. While Jeremy is waiting for medical clearance to resume training and competition, he wants to learn how to hit the forehand and backhand tennis ground strokes. Jeremy is a 21-year-old black male from a middle-class background. For most of his life, Jeremy has participated in gymnastics and tumbling. Other than his knee injury, Jeremy has no other handicapping conditions.

Description of the Learning Task:

The goal of both the forehand and backhand ground strokes is to return a ball that is hit to you by an opponent. The task is called a ground stroke because the ball bounces once on your side of the net before you hit it. The basic actions required for producing effective tennis ground strokes, either forehands or backhands, are proper positioning of the body and feet, forward rotation of the shoulders and hips, a weight shift from back foot to front foot, a firm wrist during ball contact, and a pronounced follow-through.

Discussion of Possible Advantages and Disadvantages:

Jeremy's ability to coordinate the movements of a number of limbs simultaneously (multilimb coordination) should help him as he learns the mechanics of the two types of ground strokes. His ability to perform movements that are accurately timed (motor timing) should also be an advantage, since ground strokes must be executed within a certain time frame. Jeremy's ability to continuously adjust his movements in response to changes in the speed of a moving target (rate control) is probably less important. That is because with ground strokes, changes in the speed of the ball occur only when the ball happens to strike the net on its way over, causing it to slow down.

Jeremy's deficiencies in reaction time and response orientation should not cause him much of a problem. However, his deficiency in perceptual timing ability could give him some difficulty because he must be able to accurately judge the speed of the ball to hit effective ground strokes.

Evaluation of David's Solution

David's description of the learner is adequate. However, David should say more about Jeremy's present physical condition and level of mobility. His solution would be stronger with additional explanation of several comments and terms and with discussion of the role Jeremy's injury plays in the learning of the tennis ground stroke.

Depending on the severity of Jeremy's injury and resulting knee surgery, three months may not be sufficient time for complete healing to occur. Jeremy's injured condition could affect his learning of some components of the forehand and backhand ground strokes (e.g., the weight shift from back foot to front foot).

David provides a satisfactory description of the general mechanics of the ground stroke, but he should also distinguish between the mechanics of the forehand shot and the backhand shot. Those differences are important to a person recovering from knee surgery (e.g., there is a more pronounced weight shift for the backhand shot than for the forehand shot). David should also explain what he means by the terms "effective" and "proper." What are the characteristics of an "effective ground stroke"? What is "proper" positioning of the body or feet? David provides no information about the target context in which Jeremy hopes to be able to perform ground strokes in the future.

David describes the possible advantages and disadvantages of Jeremy's stronger and weaker abilities. He should provide more detailed explanation, however, of several points. For example, he might indicate more specifically *how* good multilimb coordination enhances Jeremy's learning the mechanics of basic ground strokes. He also could cite a few reasons *why* Jeremy's poor reaction time and response orientation do not cause him much of a problem in producing an effective ground stroke. David also entirely omits discussing the possible effects of Jeremy's injury on his learning of the tennis ground stroke.

Paula's Solution

Description of the Learner:

Averi is a 7-year-old Asian-American female who comes from a middle-class family of first-generation immigrants (from Vietnam) to the United States. Averi is the youngest of six children and has had limited exposure to many basic motor tasks (e.g., throwing, catching, jumping, climbing). She is 4 feet tall and weighs 75 pounds. She is extremely motivated to learn some of the activities her peers enjoy so that she will feel more confident and less self-conscious during play periods at school.

Description of the Learning Task:

The learning task is the horizontal ladder, an apparatus found at many children's playgrounds, community parks, and recreation centers. The goal of this task is to swing on the ladder while transporting the body from one end to the other without dropping to the ground below. This transporting movement is accomplished by grasping the sequence of rungs with alternate hands. Thus, the basic actions of the movement are alternate reaching and grasping of the hands and a rhythmical swinging of the body.

Discussion of Possible Advantages and Disadvantages:

Averi should be able to learn the horizontal ladder task without much difficulty. Her strong multilimb coordination and motor timing are definite assets, since the ladder movement consists of a repeating sequence of simultaneous and rhythmical (well-timed) hand and body movements. Unfortunately, Averi's exceptional rate control is not going to be of much help since the horizontal ladder is not moving— and therefore anticipatory adjustments are not needed. However, Averi's lesser abilities—her reaction time, response orientation, and perceptual timing—should not hurt her. The ladder-climb is a closed skill. It does not require rapid reactions to a suddenly presented stimulus, quick choices among a number of different stimuli, or accurate estimates of the timing of an external object or event.

In short, the horizontal ladder is an excellent choice of learning task for Averi. She has the motivation and some of the important abilities that should help her learn the task rather easily. This will enhance Averi's confidence in her motor abilities and make her feel more a part of her peer group.

Evaluation of Paula's Solution

For the most part, Paula does a good job describing the learner and the learning task. Paula might also provide a picture of the learning task to supplement her verbal description. Otherwise, she clearly defines the goal of the movement and the basic actions required. She also mentions the target context; that is, eventually Averi hopes to be able to perform the horizontal-ladder task in a school playground setting in the presence of other children.

Paula's solution is well-conceived and thorough. She makes her solution to the problem easier by developing a nice fit between the learner's characteristics and the demands of the task. Averi possesses strong multilimb coordination and motor timing, both of which should be assets to her in learning the horizontal-ladder task. Moreover, since the task is a closed skill, Averi's weaker abilities—all of which involve rapid responses to unpredictable environmental stimuli—are not a handicap.

Your Solution to Exercise 2.2

Considering the Strengths and Weaknesses of Learners

NAME_____   DATE_____

1. Definition of problem:
2. Instructional situation (circle one):
   Teaching   Coaching   Rehabilitation   Human factors
3. Description of the learner
   Age:
   Gender:
   Sociocultural background:
   Handicapping condition (if applicable):
4. Description of the learning task
   Goal of the movement:
   Basic actions required:
5. Discussion of advantages and disadvantages
   Advantages:
   Disadvantages:

Exercise 2.3

Predicting Future Performance Success

It is difficult for movement practitioners to predict an individual's later success on a task based on the person's level of achievement during early performance attempts. Unfortunately, practitioners in many applied settings (e.g., youth sports, performing arts, industry) routinely eliminate individuals from further participation based on evaluations of their initial performance. In this exercise, you are given the opportunity to examine in greater depth the process of performance prediction.

Consider the case of Ramon, who is an aspiring dancer. Ramon learns that a regional ballet company is holding a tryout at a theater near his home. Ramon decides to participate in the hope that he will be invited to join the company.

Description of Ramon:

Ramon is a 19-year-old male from a middle-class, Mexican-American family. During his youth, Ramon participated in a variety of sport and recreational activities with his family and friends (e.g., baseball, soccer, Latin dance). Ramon is 5 feet 9 inches tall, and he weighs 150 pounds. With respect to abilities, Ramon possesses the following strengths and weaknesses (see tables 2.4 and 2.5 in textbook).

- Strengths: explosive strength, dynamic strength, perceptual timing
- Weaknesses: extent flexibility, dynamic flexibility, force control

The person conducting the tryout says he is looking for the following performance characteristics:

- Flow, or smoothness of movement production
- Accurate timing of movements to music

- Vertical power (height and control of leaps)
- Balance and grace in movement
- Expression (i.e., gestures of arms, legs, hands, feet, fingers, toes)

Male ballet dancers who are selected for the company must eventually master the following tasks:

- Leaps (vertical and horizontal)
- Lifts (lifting and holding another dancer while in a stationary position or while moving)
- Throws (projecting another dancer into the air or toward a catcher)
- Catches (catching a dancer who has been projected into the air)

In this exercise, first discuss Ramon's prospects of performing successfully during the tryout. Then present your views regarding Ramon's chances of mastering the tasks required of male ballet dancers (whether or not he is invited to join the company). Although other factors could influence Ramon's performance (e.g., anxiety, motivation), in this exercise base your solution primarily on his *abilities*.

Your solution should address and discuss these issues:

- What aspects of ballet performance might give Ramon the most *success* during the audition?
- What aspects of ballet performance might cause Ramon the most *difficulty* during the audition?
- With what ballet tasks required of male dancers might Ramon eventually experience the most success?

Cal's Solution

Strengths of Ramon's audition:

Vertical power (i.e., height and control of leaps); timing of movements to music

Weaknesses of Ramon's audition:

Balance and grace in movement; expression (i.e., gestures of arms, legs, hands, feet, fingers, toes)

Tasks in which Ramon should succeed:

Leaps, lifts, throws

Evaluation of Cal's Solution

It is possible that Cal's solution to this exercise is defensible. Unfortunately, Cal provides so little explanation of and rationale for his choices that they are virtually impossible to evaluate accurately.

Sheri's Solution

Strengths of Ramon's audition:

Explosive strength is the ability to expend a maximum of energy in one explosive act. Ramon should do well on the vertical power component of the audition (i.e., height and control of leaps). Dynamic strength is the ability to repeatedly or continuously move or support the weight of the body. If the audition lasts for a long time, Ramon should be able to perform the movements without getting tired. Perceptual timing underlies tasks that require accurate judgments about the timing of perceptual events. Ramon's ability to accurately judge the rhythms of music should help him match his movements to those rhythms.

Weaknesses of Ramon's audition:

Extent flexibility is the ability to extend or stretch the body as far as possible in various directions. Dynamic flexibility is the ability to produce repeated, rapid movements involving muscle flexibility. Force control is important for tasks in which forces of varying degrees are needed to achieve the desired outcome. Ramon may not do as well on audition activities that deal with smoothness of movement.

Tasks in which Ramon should succeed:

Ramon should succeed in most of the tasks required of male dancers because he has high levels of explosive strength and dynamic strength—important abilities for leaps, lifts, and throws. Ramon's strong perceptual timing should also be helpful when he is performing catching tasks. Ramon's lack of flexibility can be improved with stretching exercises and his weakness of force control can be overcome by practicing the different dances he is going to be performing.

Evaluation of Sheri's Solution

Sheri provides definitions of each of Ramon's stronger and weaker abilities. Unfortunately, she does not include proper documentation of her definitions. This is a serious oversight because Sheri's definitions come from the works of other people (e.g., Fleishman, 1964; Keele, Ivry, & Pokorny, 1987). In the strictest sense, then, Sheri commits plagiarism. To "plagiarize" is "to steal and use (the ideas or writings of another) as one's own" (*Webster's Second New College Dictionary*, 1995, p. 841). It is permissible to cite the work of other people as long as you give those people credit for their work. Sheri needs to indicate the sources from which she "borrows" her definitions.

Sheri offers possible links between Ramon's stronger and weaker abilities and his dance performance—both at the audition and on the tasks required of male ballet dancers. However, she provides more detailed explanation of these links in some places than she does in others. For example, in one place Sheri makes the connection rather clearly by first defining perceptual timing ability and then by going on to say that "Ramon's ability to accurately judge the rhythms of music should help him match his movements to those rhythms." Later on, though, Sheri fails to make a clear connection between Ramon's ability and his performance when she simply states that "Ramon's strong perceptual timing ability should also be helpful when he is performing catching tasks." In this case, Sheri needs to explain more clearly how strong perceptual timing ability facilitates catching performance.

A possible drawback to the movement science perspective adopted by Sheri is that it doesn't consider the artistic side of dance performance. While, from a technical standpoint, Ramon might be able to demonstrate a strong perceptual timing ability during his audition, his movements could be devoid of the kind of artistic expression that is important to dance audiences. A more balanced solution might have included some mention of the artistic as well as the scientific dimensions of dance performance.

References:

Fleishman, E.A. (1964). *The structure and measurement of physical fitness.* Englewood Cliffs, NJ: Prentice-Hall.

Keele, S.W., Ivry, R.I., & Pokorny, R.A. (1987). Force control and its relation to timing. *Journal of Motor Behavior, 19,* 96–114.

Webster's second new college dictionary. (1995). Boston: Houghton Mifflin Company.

Your Solution to Exercise 2.3

Predicting Future Performance Success

NAME_____ DATE_____

1. Definition of problem:
2. Instructional situation (circle one):
    Teaching   Coaching   Rehabilitation   Human factors
3. Strengths of Ramon's audition:
4. Weaknesses of Ramon's audition:
5. Tasks in which Ramon should succeed:

CHAPTER 3

Processing Information and Making Decisions

In a hockey breakaway shot, the puck carrier must decide whether to shoot at the net or fake the shot and go to one side of the goalie before shooting.

◀◀◆ Key Concepts

In chapter 3 of the textbook, we describe the stages of processing that individuals use as they attempt to translate environmental information (i.e., input) into an effective motor response (i.e., output). The information-processing activities that take place in these stages include detecting and perceiving environmental cues (stimulus identification), choosing an appropriate action (response selection), and organizing the movement (response programming).

A good way to determine the speed with which individuals process information is to measure their reaction time. Factors that slow down processing speed (and thereby increase reaction time) include a greater number of stimulus-response alternatives (*Hick's Law*), a less-compatible relationship between the stimulus and the response, and less-predictable stimulus events. Individuals can speed up decision making by developing an anticipation of stimulus events. If performers can predict what is going to happen (*event anticipation*) and when it is going to happen (*temporal anticipation*), they can prepare their movements in advance and respond more quickly. Anticipation can be advantageous for performers when they anticipate correctly. However, when they anticipate incorrectly, it can cause their reaction times to be longer than if they had not anticipated at all.

Additional factors influence the quality of people's information processing, such as their arousal level, capacity for attention, and memory. It is important for individuals to identify and be able to achieve a level of arousal that produces the most effective performance of the target skill in the target context. Generally speaking, skills that require fine muscular control or more complicated decision making are performed better at lower levels of arousal, whereas skills requiring greater force production or lower cognitive involvement benefit from higher levels of arousal.

Humans have a limited attention capacity, which makes it difficult to process information. This limitation is clearly seen in situations calling for separate responses to two stimuli presented close together in time. The performer's delayed response to the second stimulus, termed the *psychological refractory period,* is presumably due to the individual's inability to execute the second response until after having completed the first one. This slower type of controlled processing is *serial* in nature, and it requires performers to shift their attention from one source of information to another from one moment to the next.

Limited attention capacity also makes the simultaneous control of two movements a difficult task, unless the temporal structure of the movements is similar. With practice, however, performers are sometimes able to produce more complex actions by using a form of automatic processing that relegates the control of subtasks to lower-level production units or that combines several movement components into a single response (output chunking).

Information processing also requires the use of memory systems that do the following:

- Briefly register sensory information in an ongoing fashion (short-term sensory store)
- Provide a temporary workspace for performing operations on the sensory information selected for processing and on stored information that is temporarily retrieved for use (short-term memory)
- Contain the previously stored information in a more permanent form (long-term memory)

Individuals who can effectively select, retrieve, rehearse, code, and store information enhance the quality of their information processing.

 **Key Terms**

In order to respond to the questions and complete the exercises in this chapter, you need to have a basic understanding of the following terms or concepts:

information processing

stages of processing

stimulus-identification stage

response-selection stage

response-programming stage

spatial (or event) anticipation

temporal anticipation

arousal

anxiety

trait anxiety

attention

open skill

closed skill

 **Review Questions**

Answer each of the following questions and *provide rationale for your answers.*

1. An example of the type of activity that might be expected to occur in each of the stages of information processing is provided in the first of the following four situations. See if you can provide your own examples of information-processing activity for the other three situations.

   a. A soccer goalie responds to a shot on goal.

Stimulus identification:

Since information about the approaching ball is important for task success, the goalie must estimate the speed and trajectory of the ball and estimate when and where it is going to arrive at the goal. In this example, the goalie estimates that the ball is traveling toward the lower left corner of the goal (i.e., low and to the goalie's right).

Response selection:

Although a variety of movements is possible, the goalie selects a kick save with the right foot because it is the closest limb to the estimated point where the ball is going to arrive at the goal.

Response programming:

A kick save with the right foot would involve a quick movement of the body to the right and a thrusting action of the foot in the direction of the estimated point of ball arrival.

   b. A tennis player returns an opponent's ground stroke.

Stimulus identification:

Response selection:

Response programming:

    c. A driver responds to a small animal that suddenly darts in front of her car.

Stimulus identification:

Response selection:

Response programming:

    d. A worker catches a lightbulb that is accidentally dropped by a colleague standing on a ladder.

Stimulus identification:

Response selection:

Response programming:

    2. For each of the following tasks, an example of spatial (where) anticipation and temporal (when) anticipation is given. Your challenge is to suggest an additional example of each type of anticipation and explain how you think such anticipation might affect performance of the task.

    a. Playing basketball.

Spatial anticipation:

Predicting where an opponent is going to pass the ball allows a defender to move quickly and intercept the pass.

Temporal anticipation:

Predicting the speed of an approaching pass allows a player to accurately time the ball-grasp response.

Spatial anticipation:

Temporal anticipation:

    b. Riding a bicycle.

Spatial anticipation:

Predicting that a dog is going to rush toward her bicycle from behind a fence allows the cyclist to increase speed as she approaches the fence or to steer a wider course around the fence.

Temporal anticipation:

Predicting the speed of a pedestrian crossing the street allows the cyclist to adjust her speed so that she passes safely behind the pedestrian.

Spatial anticipation:

Temporal anticipation:

    c. Couples dancing.

Spatial anticipation:

Knowing or anticipating the type of movement that her partner is about to make allows the dancer to prepare her own movement in advance.

Temporal anticipation:

Knowing the rhythm of a song allows the dance pair to maintain proper timing with the music.

Spatial anticipation:

Temporal anticipation:

   d. Playing volleyball.

Spatial anticipation:

Knowing the play that the opposing team is going to use enables the front line of a volleyball team to position its blockers in the proper place to defend the play.

Temporal anticipation:

A setter who is able to set the ball consistently at about the same speed enables her teammates to time their own hitting movements more effectively.

Spatial anticipation:

Temporal anticipation:

3. To estimate the level of arousal that promotes maximum performance, practitioners need to consider the trait anxiety level of the performer, the complexity of the task, and the demands of the target context. In the first of the following four scenarios, an example is given that shows how a person's arousal level might shift with a particular change in the performance situation and how this shift might be expected to influence the individual's performance. For the remaining three scenarios, indicate how and why you think the performer's arousal level might shift when a change occurs and what effect this shift might have on the person's performance.

   a. A basketball player with a moderate level of trait anxiety is shooting free throws alone in the gym and sinks 10 in a row. The coach walks into the gym and begins to watch the player. The player's anxiety level increases slightly because he knows the coach is watching him. This brings about an increase in the player's arousal level. Excessive arousal increases muscle tension and may result in a drop-off in performance.

   b. A gymnast with a high level of trait anxiety is attempting a complex floor exercise and is making numerous errors. The coach suggests that the gymnast select one component of the exercise and practice it in isolation.

   c. A power lifter with a low level of trait anxiety is attempting to exceed his previous maximum weight in the clean and jerk. Another competitor enters the room and begins to verbally taunt the individual.

   d. A moderately trait-anxious individual, Maria, is playing golf with three of her friends. They decide that the player with the most putts on the first nine holes will buy lunch for the others. Maria finishes with the lowest number of putts. After lunch, the friends play the back nine holes but no bets are placed.

4. As discussed in chapter 3, the simultaneous control of two different movements is difficult unless the movements possess a similar timing structure. An example of how control might be made easier is provided for the first of the following tasks. See if you can suggest a way that control might be made easier for each of the other three tasks.

   a. *Serving a tennis ball:* Coordinate the toss and the swing by starting the movements at the same time and then producing them at a similar speed. Synchronize (a) the release of the ball from the tossing hand with (b) the cocking of the wrist of the striking hand. Once the ball is in the air, two-hand coordination ceases, and all that is left is the discrete striking action of the hand holding the racket.

   b. *Playing the piano:*

   c. *Three-ball juggling:*

   d. *Tenpin bowling (coordinating the hands and the feet):*

 ## Problem-Solving Exercises

In the following exercises you are challenged to demonstrate your comprehension of several important concepts from chapter 3 of the textbook. In Exercise 3.1 you describe the information-processing activities that might take place in each of the stages of processing when a person is performing an open skill. In Exercise 3.2 you discuss ways that performers of open skills might better anticipate stimuli to speed up their decision making—or how to prevent an opponent's anticipation to slow down his or her decision making. In Exercise 3.3 you illustrate how a person might effectively manage his or her limited attention capacity during the performance of a motor skill.

Exercise 3.1

Information Processing During the Performance of an Open Skill

---

Review the three stages of information processing shown in figure 3.2 of the textbook. Then pick an open skill you are familiar with and give examples of the information-processing activities that might take place in each of the stages when someone performs the skill. Your solution should do the following:

- Describe the skill, emphasizing the goal of the movement and the basic actions that are required of the performer.
- Describe the person performing the skill, including personal characteristics that might affect the quality of the individual's information processing.
- Highlight an example of an information-processing activity that might take place in each of the stages.
- Identify one factor that might influence the speed of processing in each of the stages.

Stefan's Solution

The skill I have chosen is baseball batting. The goal of the batter is to hit the ball with the bat. The basic actions of the batter involve watching the ball, deciding whether to swing, and producing an effective swing (if the batter decides to swing).

The person performing the skill is a college baseball player who has 10 years of playing experience and good levels of the following abilities: response orientation, reaction time, wrist-finger speed, and perceptual timing.

An example of an information-processing activity performed in the stimulus-identification stage is identifying the pitch. An example of an information-processing activity performed in the response-selection stage is deciding whether to swing. An example of an information-processing activity performed in the response-programming stage is producing an appropriate swing.

One factor that could influence the speed of processing in the stimulus-identification stage is the batter's vision. One factor that could influence the speed of processing in the response-selection stage is the pitch count. One factor that could influence the speed of processing in the response-programming stage is the location of the pitch.

Evaluation of Stefan's Solution

Stefan selects an appropriate open skill for this exercise (baseball batting), but his solution lacks precision. He does not explain his answers and presumes that the professor guesses the rationale for each. For example, Stefan does not define what abilities the batter possesses nor does he indicate how each might contribute to the processing of information. Presumably Stefan "borrowed" the abilities from tables 2.4 and 2.5 in the textbook but he fails to provide proper documentation of that information (Schmidt & Wrisberg, 2000; or he might have found the original material in Fleishman, 1964, and cited that). Stefan's examples of information-processing activities and the factors that might affect the speed of processing in each stage may be appropriate. However, he should explain *what* he means by "identifying the pitch" and "producing an appropriate swing." He should describe *how* and *why* the batter's vision, the pitch count, and the location of the pitch could influence the speed of processing in the stimulus-identification stage, the response-selection stage, and the response-programming stage, respectively.

Reference:

Fleishman, E.A. (1964). *The Structure and measurement of physical fitness*. Englewood Cliffs, NJ: Prentice-Hall.

Schmidt, R.A., & Wrisberg, C.A. (2000). *Motor learning and performance* (2nd ed.). Champaign, IL: Human Kinetics.

Tina's Solution

The skill I have chosen is the forward dive. The goal of the movement is to perform the dive in such a way that the starting position, takeoff, flight, and entry into the water conform to the judging criteria. The basic actions of the forward dive are the arm swing, knee bend, takeoff, flight (the body must not be bent at the knees or hips, the feet must be together, and the toes must be pointed), and entry (the body must be near vertical and in a completely straight position with the hands together, feet together, and toes pointed).

The person performing this skill is a 12-year-old girl who has had two years of gymnastics experience and now wants to learn how to dive. The girl has several abilities listed in table 2.4 in the textbook, which could be an advantage for her when she attempts the forward dive. These abilities are multilimb coordination (the ability to coordinate the movement of a number of limbs simultaneously), explosive strength (the ability to expend a maximum of energy in one explosive act), extent flexibility (the ability to extend or stretch the body as far as possible in various directions), and gross body equilibrium (the ability to maintain total body balance in the absence of vision).

An example of an information-processing activity in the stimulus-identification stage is identifying the start position on the diving board. An example of an information-processing activity in the response-selection stage is deciding to produce the forward dive. An example of an information-processing activity in the response-programming stage is determining how to perform the forward dive (i.e., thrust the arms down and up; bend the knees and use the legs to explode off the board; keep the body straight, knees together, hands together, and toes pointed).

Evaluation of Tina's Solution

Tina's solution is a "good news, bad news" scenario. For example, she describes the basic actions of the forward dive well, but unfortunately the forward dive is not an open skill (which is what the exercise called for). Tina lists and defines several abilities that the performer in her example has that could help her produce the forward dive. She mentions that the abilities come from table 2.4 in the text, but she neither includes as a reference the textbook (i.e., Schmidt & Wrisberg, 2000) nor the primary source from which the table originated (i.e., Fleishman, 1964). It is better to cite the *primary source* of information (e.g., Fleishman, 1964) rather than a secondary source if you can locate the source to read. However, a citation of *some* kind is better than no citation at all. Finally, Tina fails to indicate *how* each of the abilities might be helpful in the performance of the front dive.

Tina's description of the information-processing activities in the response-programming stage is quite good. She points out the various components of the forward dive that the performer must consider when she is programming the movement. Tina's examples of information-processing activities in the other two stages suggest that the forward dive demands little in the stimulus-identification or response-selection stages. This is not surprising, since diving is a closed skill. The primary demands of closed-skill performance are in the response-programming stage.

Unfortunately, Tina either runs out of ideas or overlooks the last requirement of the exercise. In any case, she provides no examples of factors that might affect the speed of processing in each of the three stages. If she had, Tina might have realized why students were instructed to select an *open skill* for this exercise. Processing speed in the stimulus-identification and response-selection stages is much more crucial for open skills than it is for closed skills. In open skills—like soccer, basketball, or cricket—individuals must be able to identify a wide variety of environmental stimuli and select the most appropriate response, usually in a very short time. In closed skills—like diving—performers can take time to identify the stimulus and select the response. In most cases they are able to perform both of these activities without much difficulty.

Your Solution to Exercise 3.1

Information Processing During the Performance of an Open Skill

NAME_____ DATE_____

1. Definition of problem:
2. Instructional situation (circle one):
   Teaching   Coaching   Rehabilitation   Human factors
3. Description of the skill
   Goal of the movement:
   Basic actions required:
4. Description of the performer:
5. Examples of processing activities
   Stimulus-identification stage:
   Response-selection stage:
   Response-programming stage:
6. Examples of factors affecting processing speed
   Stimulus-identification stage:
   Response-selection stage:
   Response-programming stage:

Exercise 3.2

Speeding Up and Slowing Down the Process of Decision Making

An open skill requires performers to make rapid decisions in brief periods of time. Performers can speed up their decisions by developing anticipation for various aspects of the stimulus environment. Two types of anticipation (see chapter 3) are spatial and temporal. Pick a sport you are familiar with that is an open skill. You are to discuss one spatial and one temporal component of the task for which performers might develop their anticipation and speed up their decision making—or diminish an opponent's anticipation and slow down the opponent's decision making.

Your solution to this exercise should include the following:

- A brief description of the skill, giving particular emphasis to the goal of the movement and the basic actions required of the person performing the skill
- A brief description of the person performing the skill, including personal characteristics that might influence the quality of the individual's information processing
- One *spatial component* of the task for which anticipation might be developed or prevented and an example of how this might be done
- One *temporal component* of the task for which anticipation might be developed or prevented and an example of how this might be done

Kelly's Solution

Description of the skill:

The skill I have chosen is table tennis. The goal of table tennis is to hit the ball with a paddle so that the ball travels over a small net and onto the table surface on the opposite side. The opponent must then contact the ball between the first and second bounce, sending it back across the net. This sequence is repeated until one of the players misses the ball, hits the ball into the net, or hits the ball so that it lands off the opposing player's table surface. The basic actions of table tennis include watching the ball and then striking it with the paddle, using a rapid movement of the arm, wrist, and hand.

Description of the performer:

The performer is a 25-year-old male who has suffered partial amputation of his right forearm as a result of a work-related accident. The man wears a prosthetic device and uses a table tennis paddle that has been modified to fit onto the end of the prosthesis. Prior to his accident, the individual participated in badminton and tennis. Because it takes this player longer to decide what to do and how to program his response, it is important for him to be able to anticipate what his opponent is doing and to prevent his opponent from anticipating what he is doing.

Spatial component of the skill and strategy for developing anticipation:

One spatial (or event) component of the skill of table tennis deals with the number of different shots that players can hit. If players produce a variety of shots, it makes their opponent's prediction of their shots more difficult and therefore slows down the speed of their opponent's decision making. The player in this example could develop anticipation for the type of shot his opponent is likely to hit by observing the spatial pattern of his opponent's swing. If the paddle movement originates at a point below the opponent's waist and finishes at a point above the opponent's waist, the opponent is hitting the ball with topspin. Conversely, if the paddle movement originates above the opponent's waist and finishes below the opponent's waist, the opponent is hitting the ball with underspin. By knowing in advance what type of spin the opponent is using, the player can prepare his response more quickly.

Temporal component of the skill and strategy for preventing anticipation:

One temporal component of the game of table tennis is the timing of a player's service motion. The service is performed by gently tossing the ball into the air and then hitting it before it bounces. One way to prevent an opponent from anticipating the timing of the service motion is to vary the height with which the ball is tossed each time. The more variable the interval of time, the more difficult it is for the opponent to anticipate the moment of ball contact.

Evaluation of Kelly's Solution

Kelly appears to have a good knowledge of the game of table tennis and is able to relate the concepts of spatial and temporal anticipation to table tennis performance. She also notes that the performer in her example is an individual who is required to use a prosthetic device and an adapted paddle due to a partial amputation. Kelly correctly points out that the person's physical condition makes it imperative for him to be able to predict as much as possible about his opponent's movements and prevent as much as possible his opponent from anticipating his movements.

Kelly offers interesting examples of the spatial and temporal components of the game of table tennis and ways a player might anticipate the opponent's shot (event anticipation) and prevent his opponent's anticipation of the timing of his service motion (temporal anticipation). She does not document her discussion of table tennis rules or strategies with a bibliographical reference, and therefore the professor must assume that Kelly is speaking from personal experience. Nevertheless, it would be better for Kelly to provide a bibliographical reference for a table tennis book the professor could use to confirm the validity of Kelly's statements. Kelly also does not provide any descriptive information about the performer other than that dealing with the nature of his handicapping condition and the fact that he has had previous experience with other racket sports. Thus, the professor must assume that the individual is capable of developing the type of event anticipation and of preventing the (opponent's) type of temporal anticipation that Kelly mentions in her solution.

Kevin's Solution

The open skill I have chosen to discuss is racquetball. The goal in racquetball is to win points. This happens when a player who is serving hits a shot in which the ball bounces twice before the opponent can return it or when the player's opponent hits a shot in which the ball strikes the floor before it contacts the front wall (Kozar & Catignani, 1997). The basic actions required in racquetball include watching the ball and striking the ball with the racquet using a whip-like arm action.

The performer is a male college student who possesses an intermediate level of skill and who has played racquetball competitively for two years. One *spatial aspect* of the skill is the direction that a player hits the ball. If a player hits the ball in about the same direction each time, the player's opponent can develop spatial anticipation for the shot and prepare his or her response more quickly.

One *temporal aspect* of the skill is the speed with which a player hits the ball. If a player hits the ball with varying amounts of force from shot to shot, the ball will approach the opponent at different speeds. Seeing the ball approaching at different speeds makes timing the ball's arrival more difficult for the opponent. This in turn makes the timing of the opponent's response to the approaching ball more difficult.

Reference:

Kozar, A., & Catignani, E. (1997). *Beginning racquetball.* Winston-Salem, NC: Hunter Textbooks.

Evaluation of Kevin's Solution

Kevin's choice of sport is appropriate because racquetball is, for the most part, an open skill. However, he does not discuss the characteristics of racquetball that make it an open skill. Instead he mentions the rules of the game that are not particularly relevant to this exercise. To his credit, Kevin documents the source from which he obtained the rules that he mentions. He could have provided a more detailed description of the basic actions of the racquetball shot. He might also have indicated how a "whip-like arm action" is important for the performance of this skill.

Kevin characterizes the player's skill level as "intermediate", but he could have discussed some of the relevant characteristics of an intermediate-level performer, rather than assuming a reader knows these. He might also have said more about the type and frequency of the performer's competitive experiences (e.g., recreational competition, tournament competition, the level of opponents' skill, frequency of competition per week, frequency per month).

Kevin's description of the spatial and temporal aspects of racquetball skill is adequate, and his suggestions for promoting spatial anticipation and preventing temporal anticipation are appropriate. Here, too, Kevin could have improved his answer with a more detailed description of each of these components, and an explanation of why they are crucial for effective racquetball performance.

Your Solution to Exercise 3.2

Speeding Up and Slowing Down the Process of Decision Making

NAME_____ DATE_____

1. Definition of the problem:
2. Instructional situation (circle one):
   Teaching   Coaching   Rehabilitation   Human factors
3. Description of the skill
   Goal of the movement:
   Basic actions required:
4. Description of the performer:
5. Spatial (or event) aspect of the skill and how to speed up or slow down spatial anticipation:
6. Temporal aspect of the skill and how to speed up or slow down temporal anticipation:

Exercise 3.3

Managing Attention During Motor Performance

The attention capacity of humans is limited, a phenomenon that people clearly experience when they try to attend to too many things at the same time. In many performance situations, several sources of information compete for a person's attention. Attention demands, for example, can come from the environment, from the process of decision making, and from the act of performing the movement.

In this exercise you are to consider how a person might manage his or her limited attention capacity when performing a motor skill. Your solution should do the following:

- Explain the concept of limited attention capacity in terms that a person who has not read the textbook might understand.

- Describe a performance situation in which several types of information might compete for a person's attention (for each source of information, indicate whether the demand is primarily on the process of stimulus identification, response selection, or response programming).
- Discuss how the person might manage his or her limited attention capacity during performance.

Jamie's Solution

Attention can be thought of as a more focused type of consciousness. The reason we have to focus our consciousness is because we can't deal with a lot of information at one time. Think about how difficult it is to listen to a radio program, talk to a friend on the telephone, and complete a calculus assignment all at the same time. Sometimes we can do several things at once as long as those things don't require a lot of attention. For example, most adults can walk, talk, and chew gum at the same time. A skilled basketball player can even dribble the ball, listen to the coach, and watch the movements of defenders at the same time. The more familiar we are with a task, the less attention we need to devote to it during performance.

One performance situation in which there is competition for a person's attention is grocery shopping, particularly when the store is full of customers. The shopper must watch out for other people while trying to locate a grocery item on the shelf (stimulus identification). Occasionally the shopper must decide whether to move the cart, stop the cart, or check the price of an item (response selection). When the aisles are crowded, the shopper must be able to adjust the speed and direction of control movements (of the hands, arms, and feet) to maneuver the cart safely (response programming).

One way a shopper can reduce the attention demands of stimulus identification and response selection is to compile a shopping list and know in advance where grocery items are located. This reduces the demands of stimulus identification because the shopper does not have to do an exhaustive visual search for each item. It reduces the demands of response selection because the shopper can decide in advance when to stop the cart and when to reach for an item. Because less of the shopper's attention is required for stimulus identification and response selection, more attention is available for effectively operating the cart (response programming) and avoiding collisions.

Evaluation of Jamie's Solution

Jamie does a nice job explaining the concept of limited attention capacity in simple terms. However, he could have mentioned the point that the amount of attention capacity is relatively fixed. Therefore, if the attention demands of a task exceed this fixed capacity, individuals must decide which sources of information to attend to and which to ignore. Jamie does state that the more familiar a person is with a task, the less attention the individual needs to devote to performing the task. This means that the person has more capacity available for other things (e.g., identifying environmental information, adding creative aspects to the movement).

While grocery shopping is not usually thought of as a demanding performance situation, James uses it creatively to illustrate the attention demands of stimulus identification, response selection, and response programming. He also proposes a strategy for a shopper to reduce the demands of stimulus identification and response selection; by reducing the demands in these two information-processing stages, the shopper can devote more attention to response programming. By relating attention demands and the various stages of processing in this way, Jamie demonstrates a good comprehension of the concept of attention and its potential role in the performance of motor skills.

Roger's Solution

We humans have only a certain amount of attention capacity, and can devote our attention to only so many things at one time. An example is driving a car. Some people can talk on a cell phone, smoke a cigarette, listen to a song on the radio, and still operate the car safely. Others have a difficult time driving the car when all they are doing is driving the car. So what's the difference? The attention capacity of these two types of people may not be that different but the amount of attention each person must devote to the task of driving is different. In the first case, the person is so skilled at driving (which might be considered the primary task) that he doesn't need to use very much of his attention capacity for driving. Therefore, the person can drive the car and do other things (e.g., talk, smoke, listen to the radio) at the same time. In the second case, the person is not very skilled at driving so he must devote more of his attention capacity to the task of driving.

Even skilled performers can experience attention demands that exceed their available attention capacity. For example, a skilled driver may have to operate the car at night in a rainstorm on a busy highway. Such a situation increases demands on stimulus identification because the driver has to watch the road more carefully and observe the movements of other drivers. This situation would also increase the demands of response selection: the driver may have to quickly decide whether to accelerate, brake, or steer in a different direction. Response programming could also be more demanding because the driver needs to perform more precise control movements to keep his car in the proper lane and avoid collisions with other vehicles.

Two ways the driver might reduce stimulus-identification demands in this situation would be to turn off the radio and hang up the cell phone. By doing so, the driver reduces the amount of stimulus information competing for his attention. The driver could also reduce response-selection demands by steering his car into the outside lane and *remaining* there. At least the driver would eliminate one possible response decision: to pass other vehicles. By reducing his speed to a constant level and maintaining greater distance between his car and the vehicle in front of him, the driver could also reduce response-programming demands. By reducing the number of possible movements that accompany steering (e.g., steering while periodically applying the brakes, accelerator, and—if driving a standard transmission vehicle—the clutch and gear shift), the driver would have more attention (and time) to devote to steering the car.

Evaluation of Roger's Solution

Roger's description of the concept of limited attention capacity is simple but thorough. Although he doesn't use the word *fixed,* Roger indicates that individuals have a "certain" amount of attention and that this amount is limited because we "can devote our attention to only so many things at one time." He explains how individuals who are more skilled at a task require less attention during performance (e.g., driving a car) and therefore are able to engage in additional activities at the same time (e.g., talking on a cell phone, smoking, listening to the radio). However, Roger's use of the term *primary task* would be lost on the average person.

Roger nicely illustrates how even skilled performers may exceed their available attention capacity if the demands of the task are sufficiently increased. Another positive aspect of Roger's answer is his explanation of how a driver might voluntarily diminish attention demands by eliminating two sources of environmental information (i.e., hanging up a cell phone and turning off a radio), positioning the vehicle in the outside lane, reducing vehicle speed, and increasing following distance. Roger then describes how each of these choices would reduce the attention demands of stimulus identification, response selection, and response programming.

Your Solution to Exercise 3.3

Managing Attention During Motor Performance

NAME_____ DATE_____

1. Definition of problem:
2. Instructional situation (circle one):
   Teaching   Coaching   Rehabilitation   Human factors
3. Explain the concept of limited attention capacity:
4. Describe an attention-demanding performance situation
   Stimulus-identification demands:
   Response-selection demands:
   Response-programming demands:
5. Discuss a strategy for managing attention
   Effects on stimulus identification:
   Effects on response selection:
   Effects on response programming:

Sensory Contributions to Skilled Performance

A skier can voluntarily adjust the amplitude of the M2 response to match environmental demands, making the knees supple and yielding to sudden bumps.

◆ Key Concepts

Chapter 4 of the textbook discusses some of the ways people use sensory information to control their movements. Sensory information can come from environmental sources *(exteroception)* as well as from sources within the performer's body *(interoception)*. The closed-loop system is a useful way to conceptualize how people control slower, discrete actions or continuous tracking movements. This system for motor performance includes a mechanism for making decisions about the desired movement *(executive)*, a mechanism for carrying out the movement (the *effector*), a feedback loop for conveying information about the present state of the movement, and a mechanism for comparing feedback about the present state of the movement with the expected feedback of the desired state of the movement (the *comparator*).

Closed-loop control systems that involve the three stages of processing (introduced in chapter 3 of the textbook) operate rather slowly. They allow no more than three to five corrections per second, but they are flexible, adaptable, and effective for controlling deliberate or slow, continuous actions (such as tracking movements). Other closed-loop systems operate much more rapidly because they do not involve the processing stages. However, the reflex-like responses produced by these systems (e.g., *M1 and M2 responses*) are relatively inflexible.

Perhaps the key determinant of the number and type of feedback loops available for motor control is the duration of a movement, or *movement time.* The longer the movement time, the greater the number of feedback loops that can contribute to movement control. The most rapid movements allow few if any feedback-based corrections, but as movement time lengthens, more feedback loops are utilized, beginning with the fastest reflex reaction (M1 response) and progressing hierarchically to the slowest feedback loop that involves the stages of processing (M3 response).

A special type of closed-loop control incorporates the activity of the two visual systems. *Focal vision* is used to identify objects in the center of the visual field and to make feedback-based corrections in movements using the slower stages of processing. *Ambient vision,* on the other hand, contributes to motor control in a more rapid, nonconscious fashion. Ambient vision uses optical flow patterns that inform the system about the relationship of eye position or the position of objects in the environment (or both). In this way ambient vision provides performers with several types of information about their movements in the environment (e.g., stability, balance, and time to contact between the performer and an object). The faster feedback loop that carries optical flow information produces minor adjustments in the programmed action without involving the stages of processing (e.g., modifications in the balance of a figure skater during a sit-spin maneuver).

◆ Key Terms

In order to respond to the questions and complete the exercises in this chapter you need to have a basic understanding of the following terms or concepts:

exteroception

interoception

proprioceptive feedback

kinesthetic feedback

visual proprioception

closed-loop control

stages of processing

movement time

passive guidance procedure
focal vision
ambient vision

 **Review Questions**

Answer each of the following questions and *provide rationale for your answers.*

1. An example of one type of exteroceptive information and one type of interoceptive information individuals might use during skill performance is given for the first of the following four tasks. For the remaining three tasks, you should add examples of each type of information and suggest how a performer might use it.

　　a. A potter shaping a ceramic bowl.

Exteroceptive information:

The potter would use vision, seeing the changes she was making to the bowl in order to smooth out the rough spots and ultimately achieve the desired shape.

Interoceptive information:

The potter might use proprioception from her arm and hand movements to alter forces and pressures being applied to the bowl.

　　b. A jeweler engraving a person's initials on a bracelet.

Exteroceptive information:

Interoceptive information:

　　c. An artist painting a picture.

Exteroceptive information:

Interoceptive information:

　　d. A person walking up a flight of stairs in the dark.

Exteroceptive information:

Interoceptive information:

2. For the first of the following three tasks, you can read an example of how a performer might use the *stages of processing* to make feedback-based adjustments in the movement. Now you describe how a performer might use closed-loop control in performing the other two tasks.

　　a. Knitting a sweater.

A performer would use the executive (containing the stages of processing) to determine the desired knitting pattern. The commands for the movements intended to produce this pattern would be sent to the muscles. A copy of the feedback associated with the desired movements and the results of the movements (e.g., expected visual feedback from the evolving pattern of the object being knitted and about the position of the yarn and the needles, expected proprioceptive feedback from the hands and fingers) are sent to the comparator. There the information is compared to feedback from the actual movements. If there is a difference between the expected feedback and the actual feedback, an error signal is produced. This signal is then sent to the executive, and corrections in the movements are made using the three processing stages. This cycle is repeated until the person decides to stop knitting or until the object the person is knitting is successfully completed.

Here's how this type of closed-loop control might function: The knitter receives an error signal indicating that a loop in the yarn is larger than intended. The error signal is identified and a response is selected that calls for a tightening of the loop. This response is programmed to produce hand and finger movements that create a loop that is the desired size.

b. Riding a bicycle.

c. Tying a necktie.

3. The duration of a movement, or movement time, is a primary determinant of *how* and *when* a performer is able to use the stages of processing to make feedback-based corrections. Four scenarios follow, the first of them having an example of how and when the performer might use the stages of processing to make corrections in a movement. For the remaining three scenarios, you are to provide your own examples.

a. Hitting a golf ball.

Since the backswing in golf is relatively slow, the performer is able to use proprioceptive feedback *during* the movement to achieve the desired stopping position at the top of the backswing. The golfer does this by comparing the expected feedback of the desired position to the actual feedback of arm and hand position and then making changes (using the processing stages) until no discrepancy exists between the two feedback states. Since the downswing is relatively rapid, the performer is unable to use visual or proprioceptive feedback during the movement—but the player can use this feedback *after* the swing to make changes in the downswing of the next shot. He does this by noting the visual and proprioceptive feedback of the downswing and comparing it (after the downswing is completed) to the expected visual and proprioceptive feedback. If a difference is detected, the error signal is sent to the executive, and corrections for the next downswing are made using the stages of processing.

b. Writing your signature on a letter to a friend.

c. Pushing a wheelbarrow through a vegetable garden.

d. Operating a jigsaw to cut a piece of wood in the shape of a teardrop.

4. Focal vision and ambient vision provide performers with different types of information for controlling their movements. Each of the following tasks already has one example of how these two sources of visual information might contribute to movement control. See if you can come up with an additional example of each type of vision and describe how it might contribute to the performer's movement control.

a. Returning a ground stroke in tennis.

- A tennis player might use *focal vision* to determine the trajectory of the approaching ball. With focal vision the player might be able to estimate the position she needs to move to in order to achieve the proper hitting position for a return shot.

- Ambient vision might enable the player to preserve body stability as she moves to meet the approaching ball.

- *Focal vision:*

- *Ambient vision:*

b. Running and jumping over a hurdle.

- A person running and jumping over a hurdle might use *focal vision* to estimate the takeoff position in front of the hurdle.

- *Ambient vision* might enable the player to estimate the time of arrival as he approaches the takeoff position.

- *Focal vision:*

- *Ambient vision:*

c. Tenpin bowling (coordinating the hands and the feet).

- A bowler might use *focal vision* to determine the target he is aiming for.

- *Ambient vision* might enable the bowler to detect the relationship of his own movement to the position of the foul line as he makes his approach.

- *Focal vision:*

- *Ambient vision:*

 ## Problem-Solving Exercises

The next exercises challenge your comprehension of several important concepts from chapter 4 of the textbook. In Exercise 4.1 you consider the possible advantages and disadvantages of passive guidance during a person's motor performance. In Exercise 4.2 you identify some of the relevant sources of feedback that performers might use in controlling their movements. In Exercise 4.3 you examine the possible role of vision during the performance of a motor skill.

Exercise 4.1

Advantages and Disadvantages of Passive Guidance During Skill Performance

Passive guidance procedures often produce different kinesthetic sensations than those associated with active movement. Nevertheless, movement practitioners sometimes find it necessary to use passive guidance to assist individuals during the early stages of skill learning or to assist therapy patients in recovering some form of voluntary motor activity.

Each motor skill usually has a particular feel associated with it. Given the fact that the feel of active movement (i.e., an action produced *by the performer*) and the feel of passive movement (i.e., a performer's action that is guided or assisted *by the practitioner*) are different, what might be the relative advantages and disadvantages of passive guidance procedures?

Think about some ways that passive guidance provided by a practitioner might enhance or diminish the learner's or patient's understanding of the desired movement and of the kinesthetic cues associated with unassisted task performance. It is a good idea to pick a skill you are familiar with and, if possible, experience the passive guidance procedure yourself in order to identify some ways it might alter the kinesthetic sensations associated with unassisted movement. Your solution should include the following:

- A brief description of the skill, emphasizing the goal of the movement and the basic actions required of the performer

- A brief description of the person performing the skill, including personal characteristics that might affect the quality of the individual's processing of kinesthetic feedback

- An example of a passive guidance procedure that a practitioner might use to assist the person in acquiring or reacquiring the skill

- A discussion of one possible advantage and one possible disadvantage of the passive guidance procedure for skill acquisition

Ted's Solution

The skill I have chosen is downhill snow skiing. The performer's goal is to maintain stability, control, and correct body position while gliding over the snow. The basic actions include flexion of the legs, control movements of the hands and arms (using ski poles to preserve balance and stability), and the rotation of the feet to achieve desired direction and to brake forward movement. Vision is important for detecting obstacles and changes in the snow's surface and for decision making.

The person performing the skill is a 15-year-old male with a mild case of cerebral palsy. The individual has moderate to good functioning in the hands and legs but overall muscular weakness. He is highly motivated to learn to ski and has good vision and hearing.

Since it is usually recommended that beginning skiers not use ski poles (Adams & McCubbin, 1991), a passive guidance procedure could be used in which the learner skis in tandem with another person. This is accomplished by positioning the learner directly in front of the instructor, with both individuals facing forward. The learner's feet are positioned in parallel and between the feet of the instructor. The instructor places his arms around the waist of the learner for postural support and enhanced stability. This technique allows the learner to experience the sensation of moving rapidly without the fear of falling.

An advantage of this procedure is that it allows the learner to process visual information associated with the experience of downhill skiing, such as changes in the snow's surface and potential obstacles. The learner might also feel the kinesthetic sensation of slight knee flexions and extensions in response to hills and troughs in the skiing surface. However, as Schmidt and Wrisberg (2000) mention in chapter 4, some sensations that a learner experiences with passive guidance probably differ from those accompanying unassisted movement. One such sensation could be appropriate balance. With passive guidance, the learner is supported by the ski instructor and therefore may not experience the kinesthetic sensations of balance that accompany unassisted skiing.

References:

Adams, R.C., & McCubbin, J.A. (1991). *Games, sports, and exercises for the physically disabled* (4th ed.). Philadelphia: Lea & Febiger.

Schmidt, R.A., & Wrisberg, C.A. (2000). Motor learning and performance (2nd ed.). Champaign, IL: Human Kinetics.

Evaluation of Ted's Solution

Ted selects an appropriate skill for the exercise and provides a good description of the goal of the movement and the basic actions involved. He might have documented his explanation of the skill using a standard, more specific manual on downhill skiing. He adequately describes the learner but could add more about the individual's ability to maintain postural balance in a standing position.

Ted nicely describes a possible passive guidance procedure, offering documentation for its use during the beginning stages of learning. Although he does not mention having experienced the guidance procedure himself, Ted offers a pretty good explanation of its possible advantages and disadvantages. If Ted had experienced skiing with and without passive assistance, he might have been able to discuss his suggestions with more confidence.

Amy's Solution

I chose hitting a golf ball off the tee using a driver as a skill. The goal of the movement is to move the club head through the ball in such a way as to achieve maximum distance and accurate placement. The basic actions of driving a golf ball include using the hands, arms, and shoulders to slowly take the club back while allowing the weight to shift to the back foot. After a brief pause at the top of the backswing, the downswing begins with a weight shift of the hips and legs back toward the front foot, followed in close proximity by the shoulders, arms, hands, and club head. The follow-through of the hands and arms should continue until they are in a position high above the head (Seward, 1986).

The performer is a 40-year-old woman who wants to learn to play so that she can enjoy golfing with her friends. The woman played softball in college and demonstrates good levels of multilimb coordination, aiming ability, and explosive strength. She has no obvious handicapping conditions.

To help her learn the proper mechanics of the swing, the woman's husband uses a passive guidance procedure that is sometimes used by golf instructors. With both individuals facing the ball, the man stands behind his wife and places the palms of his hands on the backs of her hands as she grips the club. The man tells his wife to "just relax" as he moves her hands and arms backward and forward in an attempt to produce the swing. In essence, he is doing the swinging and she is "along for the ride."

A possible advantage of this procedure is that the woman may acquire a general idea of the spatial path the club should take during the backswing and downswing. However, having experienced this procedure myself, I know that the feel of the swing when another person is moving my arms is very different than when I am swinging the club myself. I notice the presence of the person behind me and the pressure of his chest against my back. It is distracting! I would not recommend an instructor using this passive guidance procedure for teaching the golf swing.

Reference:

Seward, J. (1986). Golf. In B.M. Edgley & G.H. Oberle (Eds.). *Physical education activities handbook* (pp. 83–97). Winston-Salem, NC: Hunter Textbooks.

Evaluation of Amy's Solution

Amy selects the task of driving a golf ball using a full swing. She describes the task well and documents a reference she uses to write her description. Amy mentions several characteristics of the learner that could be important for successful performance of the golf swing, but she does not document the source of this information, which she presumably borrowed from table 2.4 in the textbook listing Fleishman's (1964) grouping of abilities.

Amy's description of the passive guidance procedure is good and she even adds a touch of humor. The fact that Amy has experienced the procedure herself lends weight to her explanation of its possible adverse influence on learning the unassisted swing. Amy could improve her solution by discussing some other problems with this procedure in light of the limitations of closed-loop control addressed in chapter 4. For example, she could point out that since the downswing of the golf drive is performed in a very short time, any procedure that draws a performer's attention to feedback *during* that movement may inadvertently cause the performer to try to control the movement in a closed-loop fashion. That attempt at control would likely result in a slow, awkward, and ineffective swing.

Your Solution to Exercise 4.1

Advantages and Disadvantages
of Passive Guidance During Skill Performance

NAME_____ DATE_____

1. Definition of the problem:
2. Instructional situation (circle one):
   Teaching   Coaching   Rehabilitation   Human factors
3. Description of the skill
   Goal of the movement:
   Basic actions required:
4. Description of the performer:
5. Performer characteristics that might affect the quality of kinesthetic feedback processing:
6. Description of passive guidance procedure:
7. Possible effects of the procedure on skill acquisition
   Advantage:
   Disadvantage:

Exercise 4.2

Identifying Relevant Sources of Feedback
for Effective Motor Performance

Having read chapter 4, you know that the control of movements is slower if the participant or patient uses feedback to make adjustments while performing a movement (i.e., with closed-loop control). People may choose to emphasize various types of sensory information during skill practice (e.g., a golfer could swing with eyes closed to highlight the *feel* of the movement). Further, if a person pays too much attention to movement-produced feedback, the quality of the individual's performance may suffer (the so-called "paralysis by analysis").

In this exercise you are to identify some relevant sources of sensory information that a person might attend to during motor performance. Then discuss how a person's attention to feedback during performance might enhance or diminish movement quality. Your solution should do the following:

- Describe the skill, emphasizing the goal of the movement and basic actions required for performing it.
- Describe the person performing the skill, including personal characteristics that might influence how the individual processes feedback.
- Give one source of exteroceptive feedback the performer might attend to.
- Give one source of interoceptive feedback the performer might attend to.
- Explain the possible positive or negative effect of each source of feedback on the individual's performance.

Jacob's Solution

Description of the skill:

The skill is hitting a croquet shot. The goal of a croquet shot is to hit a wooden ball with a wooden mallet in order to propel the ball accurately along the ground toward and through small iron hoops. The performer stands over the ball and positions one foot slightly forward and the other slightly back. The basic actions of the movement include a backward and forward motion of the hands. The hitting surface of the mallet contacts the ball at the bottom of the pendulum-like swing.

Description of the performer:

The performer is a 12-year-old male who is hearing impaired. Except for this impairment, the boy has no other handicapping conditions and he is in good physical condition. He has had little previous experience playing ball sports but does have several abilities that might be important for croquet performance: these include control precision, manual dexterity, arm-hand steadiness, and aiming ability (Fleishman, 1964).

Exteroceptive feedback:

One source of exteroceptive feedback the boy might attend to during the croquet swing is the ball. By fixating visually on the ball, he could benefit from ambient vision giving information about the direction of arm and mallet movement relative to the position of the ball (Schmidt & Wrisberg, 2000).

Interoceptive feedback:

One source of interoceptive feedback the boy might attend to during the movement is kinesthesis, arising from the motion of the backswing, or proprioception of the position of the hands at the end of the backswing (Schmidt & Wrisberg, 2000). Since the backswing is performed slowly, the boy might be able to use the kinesthetic feedback to make several adjustments in arm motion or he might be able to use the proprioceptive feedback to achieve the desired position of the mallet at the end of the backswing.

References:

Fleishman, E.A. (1964). *The structure and measurement of physical fitness.* Englewood Cliffs, NJ: Prentice-Hall.
Schmidt, R.A., & Wrisberg, C.A. (2000). *Motor learning and performance* (2nd ed.). Champaign, IL: Human Kinetics.

Evaluation of Jacob's Solution

Jacob's good points start with his describing the skill and explaining the basic actions. However, he could have provided a reference that explains croquet in greater detail for a reader who may not be familiar with the game. Although the basic description of the performer is good, Jacob does not mention how the boy's hearing impairment might influence performance. On the other hand, Jacob lists several of the boy's abilities that may be helpful for task performance and provides appropriate documentation. He could improve his answer by explaining each ability more precisely and describing its potential contribution to croquet performance.

Jacob suggests sources of both exteroceptive and interoceptive information that a performer might use during the croquet shot. He further points out that by looking at the ball during arm movement the boy might benefit from optical array patterns coming from the ambient visual system. He goes on to note the potential usefulness of kinesthetic and proprioceptive feedback during the boy's slow backswing motion. One deficiency in Jacob's discussion is that he seems to assume that an inexperienced player (such as this boy) is able to effectively use kinesthetic and proprioceptive feedback to detect and correct errors in the pattern of the swing or the position of the mallet. This may not be a valid assumption.

Gina's Solution

The skill I have chosen is archery. The goal in archery is to shoot arrows at a target from different distances. The basic actions include a firm extension and fixed placement of the arm holding the bow and a slow pulling action of the bowstring by the fingers, hand, and arm of the opposite side of the body. The archer performs this task in a standing position with the feet spread shoulder-width apart and the body aligned at approximately 90 degrees to the line of arrow flight.

The archer is an 18-year-old female who has been competing in the sport for 5 years and has won numerous awards for her performance.

An example of exteroceptive feedback the archer might attend to is visual information about the spatial relationship of the bow sight and the point of aim, which differs according to the distance the arrow must travel to the target. One source of interoceptive feedback the performer might attend to is proprioceptive information concerning joint position and muscle tension.

Both sources of feedback should help the archer in drawing the bowstring. Because the drawing movement is produced in a deliberate fashion, the performer can control the action in a closed-loop fashion (Schmidt & Wrisberg, 2000). The archer uses visual feedback to align the bow sight and proprioceptive feedback to achieve the desired draw position or tension. The archer does this by comparing actual feedback with expected feedback for both information sources and then making the necessary adjustments until the expected and actual feedback from each source are perceived to be the same.

Reference:

Schmidt, R.A., & Wrisberg, C.A. (2000). *Motor learning and performance* (2nd ed.). Champaign, IL: Human Kinetics.

Evaluation of Gina's Solution

Archery is a good choice of skill for this exercise because it involves movements that are controlled in a closed-loop fashion. As you learned in chapter 4, performers can make feedback-based corrections during the course of a movement using the stages of processing as long as the movement time is sufficiently long. The adjusting of aim and pulling of the bowstring in archery are good examples of such movements. Gina's description of the basic action of pulling the bowstring is thorough, but she provides no documentation for this information.

Although Gina's description of the performer is brief, it seems sufficient. Because the individual is an accomplished archer, the reader can assume that the person possesses the requisite abilities for success and is skilled in using exteroceptive and interoceptive feedback to make the necessary adjustments in the sighting and bowstring pulling actions.

Gina offers nice examples of exteroceptive and interoceptive feedback during the bowstring pull. She also points out that it is the slow time of this action that allows the archer to control the movement in a closed-loop fashion. She describes how the archer does this by comparing expected and actual feedback from each source (i.e., exteroceptive and interoceptive) and then making necessary adjustments until no discrepancy between expected and actual feedback exists for either source. Gina also provides appropriate documentation for her discussion of the type of closed-loop control being used by the performer.

Your Solution to Exercise 4.2

Identifying Relevant Sources of Feedback for Effective Motor Performance

NAME_____ DATE_____

1. Definition of problem:
2. Instructional situation (circle one):
   Teaching   Coaching   Rehabilitation   Human factors
3. Description of the skill
   Goal of the movement:
   Basic actions required:
4. Description of the performer:
5. Performer characteristics that might influence feedback processing:
6. Possible source of exteroceptive feedback:
7. Possible source of interoceptive feedback:
8. Positive or negative effect of attention to each feedback source:

Exercise 4.3

Exploring the Role of Vision in Movement Control

Vision is an important source of sensory information for controlling many types of movements. In this exercise you'll examine the possible contributions of visual information to motor performance by manipulating the availability of vision before, during, and after the movement. You can do this by simply asking a person to perform the task with full vision and then perform the same task under various conditions of restricted vision (i.e., they can close their eyes at different times). Your solution should do the following:

- Describe the skill, including the goal of the movement, basic actions required, and the measure(s) you are using to assess performance.

- Explain the visual conditions of performance you are examining (i.e., the different ways you manipulate the availability of vision before, during, or after the movement).

- Discuss your results for each of the visual conditions.

- Discuss the possible role of focal and ambient visual systems in controlling the movement.

Tami's Solution

Description of the skill:

I examined the ball-in-cup task. A small wooden ball (1 inch in diameter) is attached to a string that is connected to a wooden device with a small cup at the top (1⁺-inch inside diameter), a neck, and a handle (total length is 10 inches). The performer holds the device by the handle. The goal is to swing the ball in an arc and catch it in the cup. The basic actions required are a forward motion of the arm that propels the ball into the air, visual tracking of the moving ball, and adaptive movements of the hand and arm to move the cup to a final fixed position. I measured performance by calculating the number of successful catches, the number of times the ball hit the cup but bounced off, and the number of times the ball missed the cup completely.

Explanation of the visual conditions:

The person who performed the skill is my roommate. She performed the task 10 times for each of the following visual conditions.

1. *Vision throughout.* Her eyes were open at all times prior to, during, and after movement completion.
2. *Vision early.* Her eyes were open prior to and during ball movement but were closed when the ball was within an inch or two from the rim of the cup.
3. *Vision late.* Her eyes were closed prior to and during the early phase of ball movement. She opened her eyes when she heard me say "Open" (at the time the ball was about 6 inches from the rim of the cup).
4. *No vision.* Her eyes were closed at all times prior to, during, and after movement completion.

Discussion of the results:

For each vision condition, I totaled the number of times the ball landed in the cup, hit the rim of the cup, and missed the cup completely. The totals are shown in the following table.

Table 4.1
Ball-in-Cup Task Results

	NUMBER OF TIMES		
Condition	Landed in cup	Hit the rim of cup	Completely missed
1	3	6	1
2	1	3	6
3	2	3	5
4	0	0	10

My roommate performed best when she had full vision and performed worst when she had no vision. The results of the partial vision conditions (#2 and #3) are similar, suggesting that it doesn't matter too much whether she could see the ball early or late in ball flight, as long as she was able to see it during some part of its flight.

Possible role of focal and ambient visual systems:

Clearly, vision is important in the control of this skill. Removing vision entirely produced poor performance. The best performance occurred when vision was available prior to, during, and after the movement. When vision was not available early or late in the movement, performance was not as good. Prior to the movement, vision is probably not that important unless the performer is using focal vision to imagine how high she might want to project the ball. During ball flight, ambient vision is probably used to detect the movement of the ball and the positioning of the limb. This combined use of visual and proprioceptive information might be an example of visual proprioception (Lee, 1980).

My roommate's inability to catch the ball successfully on every attempt is probably due to her relative lack of practice and experience with the task. It may also be due to the fact that last-moment corrections (i.e., during the final 200 ms of ball flight), based on focal visual information, are unlikely to occur due to the lack of time needed to consciously process this feedback (e.g., Keele & Posner, 1968). Any corrective movements during the last 200 ms of ball flight are probably made using the quicker, nonconscious ambient system.

References:

Keele, S.W., & Posner, M.I. (1968). Processing of visual feedback in rapid movements. *Journal of Experimental Psychology, 77,* 155–158.
Lee, D.N. (1980). Visuo-motor coordination in space-time. In G.E. Stelmach & J. Requin (Eds.), *Tutorials in motor behavior* (pp. 281–285). Amsterdam: North-Holland.

Evaluation of Tami's Solution

Tami's answer is organized and written well. She has followed the requested format in describing the skill, explaining the approach she used to manipulate visual information, presenting the results, and discussing the findings in the light of concepts discussed in chapter 4 that deal with the role of vision in movement control.

Tami points out that ambient vision is probably used during ball flight to estimate the movement of the ball and the movement of the responding limb. She suggests that this interaction of visual and proprioceptive information may be an example of "visual proprioception" and provides documentation of this notion. However, Tami might also have pointed out that ambient vision provides information about time *before* contact (i.e., tau) between the performer and the object. Tami does suggest that even if focal vision is being used in the control of this task, its potential function as error-correction information is reduced during the last 200 ms of ball flight, citing Keele and Posner's (1968) study in support.

Jon's Solution

My task is blocking a hit in volleyball. The goal of this task is to keep the ball from coming over the net onto my side of the court. Vision is very important in this task. The use of vision to control the movement starts when the opposing setter is setting the ball. The blocker has to read the setter to see where he is going to place the ball— right, left, or middle. This means that the blocker must watch the setter and his position on the court and must also watch the ball. A good set from the middle of the front court will look the same, regardless of whether it is going to be a front set or a back set. Middle sets are very quick and not very high, so there isn't much time for the blocker to react before the hit. Fortunately for the blocker, middle sets require perfectly timed passes by the setter to the hitter. If the setter has to run to another part of the court to set the ball, it is easier to tell where the setter is going to place the ball. When the ball reaches the outside hitter, the blocker should concentrate on watching the hitter's shoulders. The hitter's shoulders will always face in the direction that he intends to hit the ball. Therefore, by watching the hitter's shoulders, the blocker should be able to position his body to deflect the hit. If the hitter's shoulders are pointing straight, the hit will be down the line. If the shoulders are at an angle, the hit will be crosscourt. For a down-the-line hit, the blocker must position himself directly across the net from the hitter. For a crosscourt hit, the blocker must position himself closer to the center of the court, opposite the inside shoulder of the hitter.

When vision is removed from this situation, blocking is impossible. The blocker's not seeing the setter is not as detrimental as the blocker's not seeing the hitter's shoulders. As long as the set is a high set and the blocker has time to get to the correct side of the court, vision of the setter is not necessary. However, if the setter and his middle hitter want to run what is called a "quick," which is a very short set

and a very fast hit, vision of the setter's position is crucial. When the view of the hitter's shoulders is taken away, the blocker has no way of telling where to position himself to deflect the ball. He might look at the hitter's feet, but looking down could cause him to miss the hit altogether. There is really no need for the blocker to see the hitter's face. The blocker can judge when the hitter is going to contact the ball by the hitter's approach. The blocker must see the ball. The ball and the shoulders are the two pieces of visual information that are necessary for a successful block.

Closed-loop control of the block occurs right up until the moment the hit is executed and the blocker jumps. After the blocker leaves the ground, he may be able to adjust his arms and hands a bit, but not much.

Evaluation of Jon's Solution

Jon offers a detailed description of the possible visual cues used by a skilled volleyball player to perform the block. Presumably, Jon's comments are based on his own experience as a volleyball player. Jon should add definitions of some of the sport-related terms he uses (e.g., setter, hitter, front set, back set) and probably a reference to a book on the techniques of volleyball. This way a reader who is not acquainted with the sport would have a better idea of what Jon is talking about.

Jon does not describe the basic actions required of a blocker. Moreover, it does not appear that Jon made any attempt to manipulate vision in a controlled fashion to determine its possible role in the control of the blocking movement. Jon also provides no discussion of the possible roles of the focal and ambient visual systems in controlling the blocking movement. In summary, then, while Jon's solution is well written and makes rather interesting reading, it fails to comply with the requirements of the exercise.

Your Solution to Exercise 4.3

Exploring the Role of Vision in Movement Control

NAME_____ DATE_____

1. Definition of the problem:
2. Instructional situation (circle one):
   Teaching   Coaching   Rehabilitation   Human factors
3. Description of the skill
   Goal of the movement:
   Basic actions required:
4. Measurement of performance:
5. Explanation of the visual conditions of performance
   Full vision:
   Restricted vision:
6. Discussion of results
   Full vision:
   Restricted vision:
7. Possible role of visual systems
   Focal system:
   Ambient system:

CHAPTER 5

Movement Production and Motor Programs

In quick, forceful actions, movement behavior is largely controlled in an open-loop fashion, without much feedback involvement.

◀◀◆ Key Concepts

Sometimes people perform movements so rapidly they are unable to use feedback and the stages of processing to make corrections during the action. For these types of movements, performers use a different form of control than the slower type of closed-loop control discussed in chapter 4. When performers have insufficient time to process feedback from the movement and then make corrections, they must plan their movements in advance so that they can execute them with little need for feedback. This type of movement control is called *open-loop control*.

Chapter 5 of the textbook presents a mechanism called the *motor program* that people might use to control their movements in an open-loop fashion. Experimental evidence for the existence of motor programs comes from several lines of research. First, there is evidence that performers take longer to react to a stimulus when they are producing complex movements than when they are producing simple movements. One interpretation of this result is that it takes the system longer to assemble and execute a complex program than it does to assemble and execute a simple program. Second, there is evidence from studies of animals that demonstrates that relatively effective movements can be produced when sensory information from the moving limb is completely eliminated. Presumably the animals use some form of motor program that allows them to produce voluntary movements in the absence of sensory feedback. Third, there is evidence that the pattern of muscular activity that exists during the first hundred milliseconds or so of a rapid limb movement remains the same even when the limb is unexpectedly prevented from moving. One interpretation of these results is that when a motor program is activated and a pattern of activation is forwarded to the muscles, the system attempts to produce the movement until it is clear that motion is impossible.

Although the motor program determines the primary elements of a movement pattern, its effectiveness in carrying out the desired action is sometimes determined by lower-level sensory processes. These processes generate rapid corrections in the movement when unexpected disturbances occur. For example, reflex mechanisms (like those discussed in chapter 4) can produce immediate increases in muscle activation that allow a movement to be completed in the face of sudden resistance (e.g., when the club head unexpectedly strikes the ground during the downswing of a fairway shot in golf).

The current view is that people use programs that are more generalized in nature when producing variations of a class of movements (e.g., throwing, catching, striking, jumping). These generalized motor programs have invariant features, such as the relative timing pattern of the movement, that preserve the "signature" of the particular movement class. Generalized programs also contain variable parameters that allow performers to adjust the movement in order to achieve different environmental outcomes (e.g., throwing with more or less force to propel an object different distances). Three variable parameters of the generalized motor program are movement time, movement amplitude, and (in some cases) the effector used to produce the movement (e.g., throwing with the right hand or the left hand). With considerable practice, the invariant features of a generalized motor program become engrained, and performers become adept at adjusting parameter values so that they can produce a variety of movement outcomes with the same program.

An alternative to motor program theory is *dynamical systems theory*. Proponents of this theory argue that the motor program notion places too much emphasis on the central organization of movements. Dynamical systems theorists believe that a good deal of motor activity is nothing more than the system's attempt to achieve stability, a phenomenon they call self-organization. They propose that whenever instability exists (e.g., during the transition from walking to running), the system adjusts the dynamics of limb action (i.e., it self-organizes) using the simple mechanical properties of the muscles and gravitational forces. While dynamical systems theory appears to accurately *describe* some forms of movement control (particularly rhythmic and cyclical actions), it does not as yet thoroughly *explain* motor performance or learning. For now, the concept of the motor program is the most viable theoretical account of how people control their movements.

 **Key Terms**

In order to respond to the questions and complete the exercises in this chapter you need to have a basic understanding of the following terms or concepts:

closed-loop control
open-loop control
motor program
generalized motor program
invariant features
parameters
parameterization
parameter values
stages of processing

 **Review Questions**

Answer each of the following questions and *provide rationale for your answers.*

1. As skill level improves, closed-loop control is sometimes replaced by open-loop control. An example of this type of shift in control is given for the first of the following four tasks. For the remaining three tasks, discuss how a shift from closed-loop control to open-loop control might take place.

　　a. *Typing:* A beginner uses closed-loop control by watching the fingers and the keys to be sure that the fingers strike the correct keys each time. Performance is slow as the individual employs visual feedback and the stages of processing to guide the positioning of the fingers. With practice, the person learns the location of all the keys as well as the correct finger combinations. Once this is done, the typist need only orient the hands in the proper position above the keys in order to produce long sequences of rapid and accurate keystroke movements. The individual uses open-loop control to produce these sequences and corrects any errors after the sequences are completed.

　　b. Handwriting:

　　c. Dribbling a basketball:

　　d. Dancing the waltz:

2. When individuals shift the control of their movements from closed-loop to open-loop control, they devote less attention to producing the actions themselves. Therefore, performers are able to shift attention to other dimensions of the task or the environment. Using the skill examples listed in the previous question, discuss one aspect of the task or environment that a performer might attend to once he or she is able to use open-loop control to produce the movement. An example is again provided for the first skill, and you are to suggest an example for each of the remaining skills.

   a. *Typing:* Once the typist can use open-loop control to produce keystroke movements, he can devote more attention to the content and phrasing of the sentences he is composing. If the typist is reproducing material from another document, he can devote more attention to the structure and meaning of that material.

   b. Handwriting:

   c. Dribbling a basketball:

   d. Dancing the waltz:

3. One parameter of the generalized motor program is *movement time*. Sometimes a change in the environmental goal requires performers to adjust this parameter (i.e., the speed with which the movement is produced). At other times changes in the environmental goal require no adjustments in movement time. Read the following example of a situation in which a change in the environmental goal might require the performer to adjust the movement time parameter and of a situation in which a change in the environmental goal would require no movement time adjustment. Then suggest an example of each type of situation for the other three skills.

   a. *Hitting a golf ball:* A situation calling for an adjustment of movement time would be putting a golf ball a distance of 20 feet and a distance of 5 feet. Assuming that the distance of the putting stroke is the same for both putts, the golfer would need to program a shorter movement time (i.e., faster swing) for the longer putt and a longer movement time (i.e., slower swing) for the shorter putt. A situation calling for no adjustment of movement time would be hitting a golf ball a distance of 150 yards and hitting a golf ball a distance of 160 yards. No adjustment of movement time would be needed as long as the golfer uses different clubs for the two shots (e.g., a 7 iron for the 150-yard shot and a 6 iron for the 160-yard shot).

   b. Jumping over a fence:

A situation calling for an adjustment of movement time would be:

A situation calling for no adjustment of movement time would be:

   c. Paddling a canoe:

A situation calling for an adjustment of movement time would be:

A situation calling for no adjustment of movement time would be:

   d. Shoveling dirt:

A situation calling for an adjustment of movement time would be:

A situation calling for no adjustment of movement time would be:

4. As discussed in chapter 5, movement control often involves a combination of open-loop and closed-loop processes. In each of the following four movement scenarios, an example of open-loop control and an example of closed-loop control are provided. You are to suggest an additional example of each type of control for the other scenarios.

   a. *Riding a bicycle to the store:* An example of *open-loop control* is kicking the kickstand into the upright position. This is performed with a rapid, discrete movement of the foot. An example of *closed-loop control* is steering the bicycle along a winding sidewalk. This is accomplished by using visual feedback from the position of the bicycle and the boundaries of the sidewalk to make periodic handlebar control movements with the arms and hands.

Open-loop control:

Closed-loop control:

b. *Preparing breakfast:* An example of *open-loop control* is flipping a pancake with a spatula. This movement is performed by a rapid flick of the wrist in order to project the pancake into the air. An example of *closed-loop control* is spreading jam on toast using a table knife. This movement is performed by using visual information about the edges of the toast and about the position of the jam to control adjustments of the fingers and hand. These adjustments continue until visual feedback indicates that the jam is covering the entire piece of toast in a smooth fashion.

Open-loop control:

Closed-loop control:

c. *Playing with a kitten:* An example of *open-loop control* is tossing a ball of yarn on the floor. This action is performed with a gentle flick of the wrist. An example of *closed-loop control* is pulling a rubber mouse on a string so that it remains just out of the reach of the kitten. This slow hand movement requires using visual feedback from the kitten's stalking movements and the position of the mouse to determine how and when to pull the string.

Open-loop control:

Closed-loop control:

d. *Moving furniture:* An example of *open-loop control* is unplugging the television. The finger and hand movement needed for this task is performed by grasping the plug and, in a single brief action, pulling it from the socket. An example of *closed-loop control* is moving a small table from the dining room to the kitchen. The control of this movement requires visual information about the location of potential obstacles and about the dimensions of the table. With this information, the mover is able to adjust motion of the arms and hands and avoid collisions with the walls, doorway, or other objects until the table is safely delivered to the desired destination.

Open-loop control:

Closed-loop control:

 Problem-Solving Exercises

The following exercises challenge you to demonstrate comprehension of several important concepts presented in chapter 5 of the textbook. In Exercise 5.1 you consider what aspects of a rapid movement might be planned in advance and produced in an open-loop fashion. In Exercise 5.2 you discuss how individuals might parameterize a generalized motor program for controlling their movements. In Exercise 5.3 you describe the possible contribution of closed-loop and open-loop control processes during the performance of a motor skill.

Exercise 5.1

Advance Planning and Open-Loop Control of Rapid Movements

Some movements are produced so rapidly that performers lack the time to make feedback-based corrections until after the action is completed. The performer must plan the entire movement in advance so as to produce it effectively without feedback-based modifications.

Consider a movement that a person might control in an open-loop fashion. Pick a skill you are familiar with and then, if possible, attempt the movement several times before formulating your solution. As you do this, consider those aspects of the action that you must plan in advance to achieve the movement goal. Your solution should do the following:

- Briefly describe the skill, particularly emphasizing the goal of the movement and the basic actions required of the performer.

- Briefly discuss *two* aspects of the movement that a performer might have to control in an open-loop fashion.

- Succinctly describe a performance situation in which the performer might have to produce the movement.

- For each of the two aspects of the movement you discussed previously, indicate one feature the performer might plan in advance.

Tim's Solution

I have chosen the skill of side kicking used in self-defense. The goal of this movement is to discourage the advance of an attacker. The side kick is a powerful kick, usually aimed at the shin or knee. The basic actions are performed from the standard defensive position, which involves standing with one side turned toward the attacker. The feet are about shoulder-width apart, and the hands are closed or slightly open. The arm nearer the attacker is bent at the elbow, and the hand is used to protect the face. The other arm is also flexed at the elbow, with the hand positioned over the solar plexus. From this position, the performer shifts the weight to the rear foot, bending the front leg and lifting it to thigh height (so that it is parallel to the ground). She then quickly kicks out sideways and drives the heel or side of the foot into the attacker's shin or knee, then quickly returns the foot to the starting position (Peterson, 1989).

Two aspects of the side kick that must be controlled in an open-loop fashion are lifting the front leg and the kick itself. A typical self-defense situation for using the side kick is when a person is attempting to unlock a parked car in an isolated and poorly lit location. As soon as a potential attacker approaches, the person should assume the defensive stance.

Advanced planning of the leg lift must occur first because the potential kicker must be ready to initiate the lift quickly if attacked. Advanced planning of the kick should occur next and should include the location of a possible target on the attacker's legs. With these types of advanced planning, the person should be able to defend herself (or himself) by executing the side kick rapidly and effectively.

Reference:

Peterson, S. (1989). *Self-defense.* Englewood, CO: Morton Publishing.

Evaluation of Tim's Solution

Tim selects an appropriate skill for the exercise. He describes the goal of the movement and the required basic actions pretty well and offers a supporting reference.

He does not indicate why open-loop control is needed to perform the leg lift and the kick. Presumably time constraints are a determining factor, but Tim does not mention this issue. He may not have tried performing the side kick prior to compiling his solution.

Tim offers an adequate description of a possible performance situation but does not discuss the reasons a person might need to engage in advance planning of the movement. Tim fails to mention one feature of the leg lift that could be planned in advance. With respect to the kick itself, Tim states that target location needs to be planned in advance, but he does not explain how the person would go about doing this.

In summary, Tim's solution lacks important details in a number of places. When in doubt, it is usually better to add more details to your solutions.

Barry's Solution

Description of the skill:

The skill I am selecting for this exercise is the sequence of gear shift, clutch, and accelerator movements a person uses to operate a standard transmission automobile. The goal of this movement sequence is to perform the proper hand and foot movements in a synchronized fashion to achieve smooth transition through the gears and forward progress of the vehicle. The basic actions required of this task involve several repetitions of the following sequence of hand and foot movements: depression of the clutch with the left foot, right-hand movement of the control lever to the desired gear position, simultaneous depression of the accelerator with the right foot and release of the clutch with the left foot, simultaneous release of the accelerator and depression of the clutch, movement of the control lever to the next desired position, and so on.

Two aspects of the movement requiring open-loop control:

According to Schmidt and Wrisberg (2000), people use open-loop control when they must produce movements that are brief in duration and performed in stable and predictable environments. Two aspects of the sequence of movements used to operate a standard transmission car seem to match this type of control. Those aspects are depressing the clutch pedal and releasing the accelerator pedal with the left and right foot, respectively. Both actions require foot movements that are relatively brief in duration.

Description of performance situation requiring advance planning:

One situation calling for advance planning of clutch and accelerator movements is a drag race. In this sport, performers must watch the illumination of a sequence of several lights. When the "go" light is illuminated, they must rapidly accelerate the car and quickly perform the shifting sequence to move the vehicle from the start line to the finish line in the shortest time possible.

Examples of advance planning of the two movement aspects:

Advance planning of initial accelerator depression is needed to execute the movement at the precise moment that the "go" light is illuminated. Advance planning of simultaneous accelerator release and clutch depression movements is needed to execute them at the precise moment of maximum engine revolutions in each gear. In both cases the movement features that must be planned in advance are simple foot flexion (when releasing the pedal) and extension (when depressing the pedal). In both cases, however, high levels of explosive force must be programmed in order to produce the action in as short a time as possible. Compounding the challenge is the gear shift action of the hand, which occurs in the instant between the release and depression of the accelerator. The shifting action must also be planned in advance to occur at the precise moment of accelerator release. A key feature of this action is the target location of the desired gear—the performer must know the location and be able to move the control lever to that position in the shortest time possible.

Reference:

Schmidt, R.A., & Wrisberg, C.A. (2000). *Motor learning and performance* (2nd ed.). Champaign, IL: Human Kinetics.

Evaluation of Barry's Solution

Barry's solution is clearly written and nicely organized. He describes the goal of the skill and gives a detailed list of the basic actions. Barry offers persuasive rationale for the use of open-loop control in the performance of foot movements to operate the clutch and accelerator. While he mentions nothing about practicing the task before compiling his solution, Barry appropriately uses supporting literature as a basis for his decisions.

Barry provides a great description of a performance situation in which advance planning of clutch and accelerator movements is essential for effective vehicle operation. In addition he mentions that a high level of explosive force would need to be programmed to achieve the desired movement speed. As a finishing touch, Barry discusses the importance of advance planning of hand movement to achieve rapid and accurate repositioning of the control lever that must occur in the brief time between accelerator release and depression. He suggests that target location of the desired gear might be an important feature the race driver considers when programming the hand movement. All in all, Barry's solution is quite interesting and innovative.

Your Solution to Exercise 5.1

Advance Planning and Open-Loop Control of Rapid Movements

NAME_____ DATE_____

1. Definition of problem:
2. Type of instructional situation (circle one):
   Teaching   Coaching   Rehabilitation   Human factors
3. Description of the skill:
4. Goal of the movement:
5. Basic actions required:
6. Two aspects of movement requiring open-loop control
   First aspect:
   Second aspect:
7. Description of performance situation requiring advance planning:
8. Examples of advance planning of the two movement aspects
   First aspect and possible movement feature:
   Second aspect and possible movement feature:

In chapter 5 you learned about the concept of the generalized motor program, a mechanism people might use to produce variations of a particular class of movements (e.g., throwing, kicking, jumping, striking). Depending on the requirements of a performance situation, the individual adjusts parameters of the generalized motor program to achieve the desired goal. Some of the parameters that might be adjusted include the duration of the movement (i.e., movement time), the magnitude of force required, and, in some cases, the limb that is used to produce the action.

Consider a movement that a performer might control using a generalized motor program. Think of parameters that the performer would adjust to achieve a movement goal that changes from time to time. Your solution to this exercise should do the following:

- Briefly describe the skill, particularly emphasizing the goal of the movement and the basic actions required.
- Discuss two parameters of the generalized motor program that a performer might adjust to produce the movement.
- Give an example of how the performer might adjust each parameter to promote goal achievement.

Michelle's Solution

The skill I have chosen is the deep serve in badminton. The goal of the deep serve is to hit the shuttlecock in a high arc toward the back of the opponent's court. The basic stance in the deep serve is to place the feet approximately shoulder-width apart, turning the body so that the forward hip, shoulder, and foot point in the general direction of the opponent's court. The wrist holding the racket is cocked so that the racket points to the rear of the server. The server holds the shuttlecock in the forward hand by gripping the cork base with the fingers. The action begins when the server drops the shuttlecock. Without moving the feet, the server shifts the weight to the forward foot and accelerates the racket head downward with a sweeping arm motion. Contact between the racket and the shuttlecock occurs with a rapid flexion of the wrist. The follow-through of the swing carries the racket to a final position above the head.

Two possible parameters of the generalized motor program for this skill are force and angle of the racket face at the point of contact. The server can produce different speeds of wrist flexion by adjusting the amount of force and can produce different contact angles by fixing the wrist in various positions of lateral rotation.

During a game situation, a server might adjust the force and angle parameters of the deep serve to achieve slightly different goals. On one serve the server could program greater force (producing a more rapid wrist flexion) and rotate the wrist slightly clockwise to project the shuttlecock with a high vertical trajectory to the deep outside corner of the opponent's court. On another serve the performer might program less force and rotate the wrist counterclockwise to project the shuttlecock with a moderate vertical trajectory toward the center of the opponent's court.

Evaluation of Michelle's Solution

Michelle does a rather thorough job describing the skill and explaining the basic actions. However, she presumes some knowledge of the sport of badminton on the part of the reader and does not document her description of the skill with any supporting reference.

Michelle suggests two parameters that a performer might adjust when attempting the deep serve. She needs to first discuss the basic concept of the generalized motor program (with a supporting reference) and explain its potential relevance to the control of this skill. Michelle's examples are interesting and appear quite plausible. If a reader is unfamiliar with the sport, however, he would want a simpler explanation of what the server is trying to do or perhaps a figure illustrating how the adjustments the performer is making in the serving action produce the two different outcomes.

Ryan's Solution

I chose the skill of casting a fishing lure. The goal of casting is to project the lure different distances to a variety of targets. The basic casting motion involves a flexion and extension of the elbow and wrist in rapid succession. This action is similar to the one some people use when they throw a baseball. The two-phase movement causes the point of the fishing rod to travel backward and then forward. The other important component of the casting movement is the release of the reel button. The fishing reel is the device that contains the fishing line. When a person depresses the reel button, it causes the fishing line to remain in the reel. Releasing the button allows the line to unwind and come out of the reel. When casting a lure, the person must release the reel button sometime during the forward motion of the rod.

In chapter 5 of the book by Schmidt and Wrisberg (2000), there is a discussion of the concept of the generalized motor program. The generalized motor program is a mechanism that allows people to perform variations of a particular movement (such as throwing) by adjusting certain parameters (such as movement time or movement amplitude). Assuming that casting a fishing lure requires a motion that is similar to throwing a baseball, it seems possible that people could use the generalized motor program for throwing whenever they are attempting to cast a fishing lure. Two parameters of the program that might be adjusted from one cast to the next are movement time and the moment of reel-button release. The shorter the movement time, the faster the rod would travel and the farther the lure would be projected. The earlier in the forward motion of the rod that the reel button is released, the higher the arc that the lure would travel on its way to the target. Schmidt's and Wrisberg's (2000) book mentions that movement time is one parameter of the generalized motor program. No mention is made of a parameter like the moment of reel-button release. However, it seems that reel-button release qualifies as a parameter since it is something that the performer can adjust to produce different outcomes with the same generalized motor program.

If a person casts from the bank of a river, he needs to project the lure different distances while watching out for tree limbs overhead. Let's say that a person attempts two casts under the following sets of circumstances. In the first situation, the target is 50 feet away and the person is standing in a position on the riverbank that is clear of trees. In the second situation, the target is 25 feet away and the person is standing under a big tree with low-hanging limbs. For the first situation, the person would have to program a combination of force and moment of button release that produces a casting movement that projects the lure the required distance. For the second situation, the person might need to program the moment of button release later in the forward motion of the rod. In this way the lure would travel in a more direct path to the target and be less likely to get caught in the low-hanging limbs. A decreased force level might also be programmed because the target is closer to the riverbank.

Reference:

Schmidt, R.A., & Wrisberg, C.A. (2000). Motor learning and performance (2nd ed.). Champaign, IL: Human Kinetics.

Evaluation of Ryan's Solution

Ryan selects an interesting activity for his solution, describing the goal of casting a fishing lure and providing a nice explanation of the basic actions. He might have added a reference to a book on fishing for inexperienced readers. A figure illustrating the action of the cast (i.e., backward and forward motion) might also be useful. A good rule of thumb for including a figure or photo is to add it only when it illustrates a concept more clearly than does a verbal description.

Ryan provides a nice background discussion of the generalized motor program concept along with appropriate documentation. He suggests the interesting possibility that the generalized program for throwing a ball might also be useful for a person who is casting a fishing lure. Ryan's choice of parameters is appropriate, and he makes a compelling case for choosing the moment of reel-button release as one of the parameters. According to the theory of generalized motor programs, parameters are components that performers adjust in order to achieve different environmental goals. Ryan points this out and cleverly argues that the moment of reel-button release seems to satisfy this criterion.

Ryan presents practical examples of situations that would require a performer to adjust the generalized motor program to accomplish slightly different goals. Casting a fishing lure a greater distance with no overhead obstacles calls for a level of force and moment of button release that is likely different than the force and moment of release needed to cast a lure a shorter distance while standing under a tree with low-hanging branches. Ryan's discussion of the possible parameter adjustments for these two situations is quite reasonable.

Your Solution to Exercise 5.2

Parameterization of the Generalized Motor Program

NAME_____ DATE_____

1. Definition of problem:
2. Type of instructional situation (circle one):
   Teaching   Coaching   Rehabilitation   Human factors
3. Description of the skill:
4. Goal of the movement:
5. Basic actions required:
6. Description of two parameters of the generalized motor program
   First parameter:
   Second parameter:
7. Description of situation requiring parameter adjustments:
8. Examples of how the performer might adjust each parameter to achieve the movement goal
   First parameter:
   Second parameter:

Exercise 5.3

Using Closed-Loop and Open-Loop Control During Motor Performance

Individuals use various combinations of closed-loop and open-loop control to produce many movements. The task for you here is to consider the relative contribution of closed-loop and open-loop control processes during the performance of a goal-directed movement. Your solution to this exercise should do the following:

- Describe the skill, including the goal of the movement and the basic actions required.

- Give an example of one component of the movement that a person might control in a closed-loop fashion using the stages of processing.

- Give an example of one movement component that the person would most likely have to control in an open-loop fashion.

- Give an example of a performance situation in which *both* types of control might be evidenced.

Celia's Solution

The skill I have chosen for this exercise is canoeing. The goal of canoeing is to navigate the canoe in all types of water conditions and achieve various destinations in a safe and effective manner. The basic actions of canoeing primarily involve the operation of the paddle using the arms and hands. A canoeist propels the boat forward with a pulling motion and steers the boat's course by placing the paddle blade in the water at various angles.

Closed-loop control is often used when steering the boat. The canoeist places the blade of the oar in the water and slowly rotates the handle, causing the blade to act like a rudder. Using visual information about the position of the boat in the water, the canoeist rotates the handle and guides the boat in the desired direction. Open-loop control is used in situations requiring rapid movements of the oar, such as when the canoeist wants to increase boat speed or must paddle against a swift current.

An example of a situation in which both types of control are needed is when the canoeist is operating the canoe in rapidly flowing water. As the canoe moves quickly downstream, the canoeist uses the oar as a rudder to steer clear of rocks lying at or near the water's surface. If the canoeist saw a tree limb blocking the path, she would need to perform a series of rapid oar pulls to navigate the boat away from the obstacle.

Evaluation of Celia's Solution

Celia selects an interesting skill for this exercise. However, she needs to explain more fully the basic actions required of the canoeist and add a description of proper hand position on the oar. A supporting reference or visual illustration might also help the reader.

Celia's discussion of the way closed-loop control and open-loop control might be used by a canoeist seems logical. However, she provides no theoretical background dealing with the differences between the two types of control. Celia also fails to provide any supporting literature for her discussion.

Celia's examples of how closed-loop and open-loop control might be used in a particular canoeing situation are consistent with her earlier discussion. The examples would be more understandable for people not familiar with canoeing if Celia provided a more precise description of the activity in her introduction.

Jason's Solution

The skill I chose for this exercise is figure skating. The goal of figure skating is to propel the body along the ice while producing a variety of jumps, spins, steps, and other linking movements (Diagram Group, 1974). The figure skater must execute most free-skating routines with only one foot in contact with the ice. The legs perform the basic actions, while the hands and arms are used for leverage and balance. Figure skating is one of the few sport activities that combines both power and grace.

Schmidt and Wrisberg (2000) contend that closed-loop control can be used for movements that are produced more slowly because there is sufficient time for the performer to use feedback from the movement (and the stages of processing) to make any needed adjustments. On the other hand, the authors point out that open-loop control is needed for rapid actions because the movement is completed too quickly for feedback modification. In these quickly moving situations, the performer must plan the entire action in advance. A figure skater might use closed-loop control whenever he is gliding on one foot in preparation for a jump or spin. Open-loop control would be needed for very rapid actions, such as jumps or spins.

Compulsory figures are slow tracing movements performed on one foot at a time without pause, and they would require closed-loop control (Diagram Group, 1974). Three compulsory figures have been required in major championships. Two of these involve the tracing of two adjoining circles and one involves the tracing of three adjoining circles. To perform these movements the skater uses visual feedback of the figure being traced and proprioceptive feedback from the ongoing action to adjust blade position and maintain balance, flow, and tracing accuracy.

A skating movement that might be performed using open-loop control is the "double lutz" jump (The Diagram Group, 1974). In preparation for this jump, the skater glides in a rearward direction, balancing on the left foot with the right foot extended back. From this position, the skater leaps upward and performs two complete 360-degree revolutions of the body in a counterclockwise direction before landing again on the right foot.

This action is completed in such a short time that it is probably necessary to plan the entire jump in advance. When preparing for the jump, the skater probably uses a form of closed-loop control to produce the gliding movement that stabilizes the body prior to takeoff.

References:

Schmidt, R.A., & Wrisberg, C.A. (2000). *Motor learning and performance* (2nd ed.). Champaign, IL: Human Kinetics.

The Diagram Group (1974). *The rules of the game.* New York: Paddington Press Ltd.

Evaluation of Jason's Solution

Jason provides a general description of the goal of figure skating and the basic actions involved. He could add more detail to explain some of the actions, but he does mention a reference on the specifics of figure skating for the reader to examine. Presenting figures or photos to supplement his discussion would have made the reader's task of understanding compulsory figures and the double lutz jump much easier.

Jason offers an excellent discussion of the theoretical basis for closed-loop and open-loop control along with supporting documentation. He then mentions two categories of movements (i.e., gliding and jumps or spins) that might require each type of control. His examples of performance situations requiring each type of control are clearly described. Jason offers a nice illustration of the way the act of skating shifts between closed-loop and open-loop control by mentioning the gliding action that precedes takeoff for the double lutz jump. The former is controlled using closed-loop processes and the latter is controlled in an open-loop fashion.

Using Closed-Loop and Open-Loop Control During Motor Performance

NAME_____ DATE_____

1. Definition of problem:
2. Type of instructional situation (circle one):
   Teaching   Coaching   Rehabilitation   Human factors
3. Description of the skill:
4. Goal of the movement:
5. Basic actions required:
6. Example of a movement component requiring closed-loop control:
7. Example of a movement component requiring open-loop control:
8. Example of a performance situation requiring both closed-loop and open-loop control:

CHAPTER 6

Principles of Motor Control and Movement Accuracy

A batter selects movement time and prepares the swing to coincide with the ball's arrival.

© Robin Rudd/Unicorn Stock Photos

 **Key Concepts**

Many movements have features that remain essentially the same anytime the movement is produced. These features are called *invariant features*, and they represent the deep structure, or "fingerprint," of the movement. Perhaps the most prominent invariant feature of movements is their *relative timing structure*, which is the relative duration of the various temporal intervals in the action. Another way to conceptualize the phenomenon of relative timing is to think of it as the rhythm of the movement.

In chapter 5 you learned about the *generalized motor programs* that people probably use when performing different classes of movements, such as throwing. Generalized motor programs exist for a variety of movement classes (e.g., throwing, kicking, running, galloping), with each program possessing its unique pattern of relative timing and other invariant features (e.g., its spatial blueprint). In addition to invariant features, generalized motor programs contain parameters (e.g., movement time, movement amplitude, overall force) that performers can adjust to achieve different environmental outcomes (e.g., throwing with more or less force to propel an object longer or shorter distances). Whereas the parameter values may change from one situation to the next, the invariant features of the program (e.g., relative timing) remain the same. For example, the "fingerprint" of the throwing action is always the same—regardless of the changes a performer makes in the amount of force used to produce different types of throws.

In chapter 6 we discuss several principles of movement *accuracy*. Most of these principles concern the speed-accuracy trade-off that exists whenever individuals attempt to produce rapid, accurate movements. For continuous aiming movements (e.g., tapping back and forth between two targets as quickly as possible), increases in movement speed or decreases in movement time usually result in diminished spatial accuracy. This relationship between speed and accuracy, described by Fitts' Law, has been shown to hold true for the control of numerous types of continuous aiming movements.

For discrete aiming movements (i.e., a single rapid movement to a target), several additional principles seem to apply. *As the force* that is used to produce the movement *increases* (up to about 70 percent of maximum), spatial *accuracy decreases* in a nearly linear fashion. These increased errors are presumably due to low-level processes in the spinal cord and muscles that produce contractions slightly different from the ones originally intended. This force-accuracy relationship, sometimes referred to as the *linear speed-accuracy trade-off*, holds for many discrete aiming movements. However, two other principles of movement accuracy present "violations" of the speed-accuracy trade-off. For extremely rapid aiming movements, spatial accuracy seems to stabilize or even improve as the amount of force is increased beyond 70 percent of maximum. For movements that must be produced in a particular time, temporal accuracy improves as the speed of the movement is increased (i.e., faster movements are timed more accurately than slower ones).

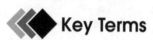 **Key Terms**

In order to respond to the questions and complete the exercises in this chapter you need to have a basic understanding of the following terms or concepts:

    generalized motor program
    invariant features
    parameters
    parameterization
    parameter values

relative timing
speed-accuracy trade-off
linear speed-accuracy trade-off
Fitts' Law
continuous skill
discrete skill
spatial accuracy
temporal accuracy

 ## Review Questions

Answer each of the following questions and *provide rationale for your answers.*

1. An important invariant feature of the generalized motor program is relative timing. One way to think of relative timing is in terms of the relative speeds of different components of a movement. You'll find an example of the basic action and relative speeds of the components of one movement pattern below. You are to discuss the basic action and suggest the relative speeds of components for each of the other patterns. (Hint—attempt each movement several times at different speeds before formulating your answer.)

a. The swinging action in the tennis serve:

Basic action:

This task involves an extension of the wrist, forearm, and upper arm in a throwing type of motion. The goal of the movement is to move the racket at a particular velocity in order to impart a particular force to the ball.

Upper arm:

The upper arm moves the slowest because it serves as the foundation for the actions of the other swing components.

Forearm:

The forearm moves faster than the upper arm but slower than the wrist.

Hand:

The hand moves the fastest and is the component that imparts most of the velocity to the racket.

b. Kicking a stationary ball for distance:

Basic action:

Plant foot:

Upper leg of kicking foot:

Lower leg of kicking foot:

c. Dribbling a basketball:

Basic action:

Upper arm:

Lower arm:

Hand:

    d. Hopping on one foot:

Basic action:

Upper leg:

Lower leg:

Foot:

    2. Different generalized motor programs have different relative timing structures. Sometimes two different classes of movements appear to be quite similar, yet they possess subtle differences in their structures of relative timing. An example of subtle differences between the relative timing structure (i.e., relative speeds of the movement components) of two different actions is provided for the first pair of movements given below. You are to suggest possible differences in relative timing structure for each of the other pairs of movements.

    a. Walking and running (compare the relative speed of the upper leg, lower leg, and foot):

Walking:

In walking, the upper leg moves slower than does either the lower leg or foot, which seem to move at approximately the same speed. The lower leg is extended at a faster speed than the upper leg, and the foot seems to be "carried along" at the speed of the lower leg.

Running:

In running, the upper leg, lower leg, and foot all seem to move at about the same speed. Thus, the relative timing of the three movement components appears to be more similar for running than for walking.

    b. Throwing a dart and throwing a ball (compare the relative speeds of the upper arm, lower arm, and hand):

Throwing a dart:

Throwing a ball:

    c. Forehand ground stroke in tennis and forehand shot in racquetball (compare the relative speeds of the upper arm, lower arm, and hand):

Forehand ground stroke in tennis:

Forehand shot in racquetball:

    d. The healthy leg and the injured leg of a person walking with a sprained knee:

Healthy leg:

Injured leg:

    3. Fitts' Law describes the speed-accuracy trade-off that occurs when people perform continuous aiming movements. For the first of the following four skills, an example is provided of a continuous aiming movement for which a change in the environmental goal or the requirements of the task might cause a shift in the performer's emphasis on speed and accuracy. You are to suggest an example of a change in either the environmental goal or the requirements of the task that might cause a shift of speed-accuracy emphasis for the other three skills.

 a. Continuous movement: Walking on a paved sidewalk.

Change in environmental goal or the requirements of the task:

Walking on a balance beam.

Effect on the speed-accuracy trade-off:

Because the size of the walking surface is reduced, the performer might need to reduce the speed of the movement in order to preserve accuracy. In other words, the stricter demands on accuracy for walking on a balance beam as compared to a paved sidewalk might require a decrease in movement speed.

 b. Continuous movement: Swimming alone in a lap pool.

Change in environmental goal or the requirements of the task:

Effect on the speed-accuracy trade-off:

 c. Continuous movement: Paddling a canoe through a shallow stream containing rocks and other obstacles.

Change in environmental goal or the requirements of the task:

Effect on the speed-accuracy trade-off:

 d. Continuous movement: Running in the rain through a field with numerous puddles of water.

Change in environmental goal or the requirements of the task:

Effect on the speed-accuracy trade-off:

 4. For discrete, rapid aiming movements, spatial accuracy decreases with increases in movement speed, up to about 70 percent of maximum speed. Beyond that, spatial accuracy remains the same or even improves as movement speed increases. In the first of the following four scenarios, the importance of spatial accuracy for goal achievement is discussed and a suggestion for maximizing task performance is provided. You are to discuss the importance of spatial accuracy and suggest how task performance might be maximized for the other scenarios.

 a. Kicking a field goal in American football

Importance of spatial accuracy:

The goal of field-goal kicking is to project the ball from its position on the ground upward and over the crossbar and between the uprights of the goal posts. The ball is approximately 6 inches in diameter. The crossbar is parallel to and a distance of 10 feet from the ground. The distance between the vertical uprights of the goal post is 18 feet 6 inches. Spatial accuracy is important to goal achievement, particularly for longer kicks. The farther the ball is positioned from the goal post, the narrower the target angle.

How task performance might be maximized:

Since the ball is the primary target of the kicker's movement, it is important to strike the ball as close to its center as possible on every kick. To achieve the greatest spatial accuracy and consistency, the kicker should move the leg at close to maximum speed each time, particularly for longer kicks. For the kicker to compensate for spatial errors during contact with the ball, he should attempt to direct the kick toward the midpoint of the area between the uprights.

 b. Throwing darts

Importance of spatial accuracy:

How task performance might be maximized:

 c. Serving a tennis ball

Importance of spatial accuracy:

How task performance might be maximized:

 d. Breaking a board with a karate kick

Importance of spatial accuracy:

How task performance might be maximized:

Problem-Solving Exercises

The following exercises challenge you to demonstrate comprehension of several important concepts presented in chapter 6 of the textbook. In Exercise 6.1 you describe the possible pattern of relative timing for a movement you are familiar with. In Exercise 6.2 you discuss possible differences in the generalized motor program or the relative timing pattern for two similar-appearing movements. In Exercise 6.3 you explain ways a performer might improve the spatial or temporal accuracy (or both) of a rapid aiming movement.

Exercise 6.1
Relative Timing Characteristics of a Familiar Movement

Relative timing is an important invariant feature of the generalized motor program for a class of movements. This means that regardless of the adjustments a performer makes in the parameters of the movement (e.g., movement time, movement amplitude, overall force, limb used), the pattern of relative timing remains approximately the same.

Pick a skill you are familiar with and then attempt to perform the skill several times before formulating your solution. Consider the possible pattern of relative timing of the movement. One way of discovering the pattern of relative timing is to perform the movement at slightly different speeds or amplitudes or with different limbs. As you do this, try to identify the relative speeds of several components of the movement (i.e., compare the speed of one component with that of another). Your solution should do the following:

- Describe the skill, emphasizing the goal of the movement and basic actions required of the performer.
- Discuss how you attempted to discover the pattern of relative timing of the movement.
- Describe the relative timing pattern (i.e., relative speeds of movement components) for at least *three* components of the action.

Matt's Solution

The skill I have chosen for this exercise is wheelchair shuffleboard. The goal of shuffleboard is to slide a wooden puck down a smooth surface toward a target. A player receives points for any puck that stops entirely within the boundaries of the target zone. Different point values are assigned to different target zones. If two individuals are competing, they alternate shots until each has attempted four shots. Sometimes players attempt to bump their opponent's pucks outside of the target zones.

While the basic action is the same for all shots, players use different amounts of overall force for different types of shots (e.g., bumping an opponent's puck out of a target zone or gently sliding one of their own pucks into a target zone). The shuffleboard shot begins when the player places the shuffleboard stick on the ground behind the puck. Once this is done, the player extends the hand and arm, pushing the puck with the stick in the direction of the target. Wheelchair players must generate most of the force for their shots from the arm and hand since their feet are immovable.

I have a friend who is paralyzed from the waist down. Since this person enjoys playing shuffleboard, I decided to watch her play a game to see if I could detect the pattern of relative timing she used to produce her shots. During the game my friend attempted shots requiring different levels of force. Therefore, I was able to observe the relative speeds of different components of her movement under different force conditions. In particular, I watched the relative speeds of her forearm, upper arm, and trunk.

What I observed was a pattern of motion characterized by slower movement of the trunk than of the upper arm or forearm. It was difficult for me to detect much difference in the speed of the upper arm and forearm, but I would guess the forearm was moving faster, particularly near the end of the movement. My friend began each movement with her arm flexed at the elbow and her hand positioned near her right hip (she is right-handed). From this position she extended her hand in the direction of the target so that her arm was almost perfectly straight when she completed the movement. Near the end of the movement, she flexed at the waist so that her trunk moved slightly forward during the follow-through.

Evaluation of Matt's Solution

Matt describes the goal of the movement and the basic actions required adequately. He might have mentioned that there is flexion of the humerus at the shoulder joint, extension of the elbow, and ulnar flexion of the wrist as part of the arm action. And since the trunk is included in his final analysis, Matt should have included it in the initial description of the shot. In his discussion of how he determined the pattern of relative timing, Matt might have provided more details about his method of observation—such as where he was standing relative to the performer (e.g., behind her, to the side of her). He mentions that he focused on the movement of the trunk, upper arm, and forearm, but he doesn't indicate whether he attempted to observe all three components at the same time.

Matt's discussion of the pattern of relative timing he observed is vague. He says that his friend's trunk appeared to be moving slower than her forearm and upper arm, but he says little else about the relative speeds of the different movement components. Although he describes the mechanics of his friend's movements, Matt might indicate how these mechanics relate to the issue of relative timing. Finally, Matt cites no related literature to support the notion of invariant relative timing and the generalized motor program for the shuffleboard action.

Chris's Solution

The skill I am selecting for this exercise is the chest pass in basketball. The goal of the chest pass is to propel the ball quickly and accurately toward a teammate. The starting position for the chest pass is usually with the feet spread apart, one foot slightly in front of the other. The hands are used to grip the ball on its opposite sides. The ball is held closely to the chest, with the elbows flexed and tucked in near the passer's waist. The basic action is a rapid forward extension of the arms and hands and then a slight outward rotation of the hands during the release of the ball.

Schmidt and Wrisberg (2000) state that an important invariant characteristic of a class of movements is relative timing. One way to consider relative timing is to think of the speeds with which different components of a skill are moving in relation to each other. In other words, which components are always moving the fastest, which are always moving the slowest, and which are moving at speeds that are somewhere in between? Regardless of the overall speed with which a person produces the chest pass, relative timing (or the relative speeds of the various movement components) should remain approximately the same.

To determine the relative timing pattern of the chest pass, a friend and I passed a basketball back and forth. Sometimes we passed the ball fast (i.e., using more force) and sometimes we passed it slowly. Sometimes we made chest passes that bounced once before reaching the other person (i.e., bounce passes). The more passes my friend and I made to each other, the more I began to notice the relative speeds of our hands, forearms, and upper arms.

It seemed to me that the hands, forearms, and upper arms always moved at about the same speed. However, near the end of the chest pass when the ball was being released, it appeared that the hands moved a bit faster than the forearms and upper arms. This increased hand speed appeared to be the result of a wrist snap that the passer used to add a last bit of force to the ball. Some critics doubt whether relative timing is perfectly invariant when performers change the overall speed or duration of a movement (Gentner, 1987). My observations (based on seeing my partner's passes and the feel of my own) indicated that the relative timing of the chest pass is quite invariant for different speeds of movement.

References:

Gentner, D.R. (1987). Timing of skilled motor performance: Tests of the proportional duration model. *Psychological Review, 94,* 255–276.

Schmidt, R.A., & Wrisberg, C.A. (2000). *Motor learning and performance* (2nd ed.). Champaign, IL: Human Kinetics.

Evaluation of Chris's Solution

Chris could improve his description of the chest pass by documenting it and providing a photo or figure depicting the movement sequence. Nevertheless, he provides an excellent discussion of the theoretical background for the concept of invariance of relative timing for a class of movements. Citing Schmidt and Wrisberg (2000), Chris explains how the relative timing of movement components remains the same regardless of the overall speed with which the movement is produced. He then offers a description of the technique he used to discover the possible relative timing pattern of the chest pass. While Chris doesn't indicate the number of passes he and his friend attempted, he does mention that each person varied not only the speed of his passes but also the type of chest pass he performed (e.g., both air passes and bounce passes).

Chris's discussion of the relative timing pattern he observed is quite clear. Chris concludes that the chest pass seems to possess a distinct pattern of invariant relative timing consistent with the prediction of generalized motor program theory. He correctly acknowledges, moreover, that his conclusion is limited to his interpretation of the visual and proprioceptive feedback he obtained from his brief experience of passing the ball with his friend. Chris balances his discussion by pointing out that the notion of perfect invariance of relative timing is not without its critics (i.e., Gentner, 1987).

Your Solution to Exercise 6.1

Relative Timing Characteristics of a Familiar Movement

NAME_____ DATE_____

1. Definition of problem:
2. Type of instructional situation (circle one):
   Coaching   Teaching   Rehabilitation   Human factors
3. Description of the skill:
   Goal of the movement:
   Basic actions required:
4. Technique to discover the relative timing pattern:
5. Discussion of the relative timing pattern:

Exercise 6.2

Differentiating Generalized Motor Programs for Two Classes of Actions

The pattern or structure of relative timing is an important distinguishing characteristic of generalized motor programs. For a movement to be controlled by a particular generalized program, it must possess the relative timing pattern unique to that program. Sometimes similar-appearing movements consist of slightly different patterns of relative timing. They therefore are controlled by different generalized motor programs.

Think about two similar classes of actions that might be controlled by different generalized motor programs. You might perform each movement several times (perhaps at different speeds) before formulating your solution. If you do this, you should be able to achieve a rough approximation of the pattern of relative timing for each movement (i.e., the relative speeds with which different components of the movement are produced). In addition you should be able to detect obvious differences in the two patterns. Your solution to this exercise should do the following:

- Describe the two skills, emphasizing the goal of each movement and the basic actions required.
- Discuss the technique(s) you used to determine the relative timing patterns of the two types of movements.
- Summarize the differences you observed in the relative timing patterns of the two types of movements.

Lori's Solution

I compared the back dive and the inward dive from the pike position (see the figures on the following page). The goal of springboard diving is to perform the required components of each dive according to standard form criteria (e.g., during entry into the water the body must be straight and in a vertical position with the toes pointed). Both dives begin with the diver facing the board, with his back to the water and his arms extended to the front at shoulder height and parallel to the board. However, the basic actions are different. For the back dive, the performer arches his back and thrusts his arms to the rear as he slowly rotates to an upside-down position and enters the water. For the inward pike dive, however, the performer's first move is to spring upward from the board and immediately flex at the waist so that he touches his fingers to his toes. From this position, the diver slowly extends from the waist, with his hands and arms extending directly over his head and his legs extending directly beneath his hips. Entry into the water should be vertical, with the entire body in a straight line with arms extended.

For this exercise I decided to compare the relative timing of the arms, trunk, and legs for these two dives. I attempted both types of dives 6 times each. On the first two attempts of each dive, I focused on the relative speed of the arms and the legs. On the second two attempts, I focused on the relative speed of the arms and the trunk. On the last two attempts, I focused on the relative speed of the legs and the trunk.

I noticed the following patterns of relative speeds for the two dives. For the back dive, the legs and trunk seemed to be moving at nearly the same speed as they essentially remained in a fixed extended position throughout the dive. The arms moved fastest during the initial takeoff, as I extended them to the rear to achieve the back

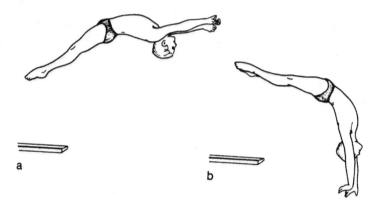

Reprinted, by permission, from R. O'Brien, 1992, *Ron O'Brien's diving for gold* (Champaign, IL: Human Kinetics), 30.

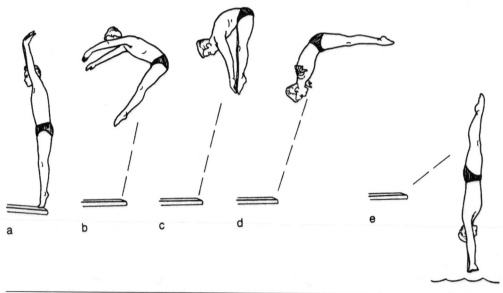

Reprinted, by permission, from R. O'Brien, 1992, *Ron O'Brien's diving for gold* (Champaign, IL: Human Kinetics), 37.

layout position. Then I slowly moved them to an extended position directly over my head for entry into the water.

For the inward pike dive, the legs and trunk moved fastest during the initial take-off as I flexed at the waist and extended my legs. From the point of toe touch, all components of the movement seemed to move at about the same speed as I slowly extended the legs, trunk, and arms to achieve a straight-body position for entry into the water.

Before I attempted this assignment, I knew that the back dive and inward pike dive looked different and felt different, but I had never thought much about differences in the relative timing pattern of the arms, trunk, and legs. The clear differences I experienced in the pattern of relative timing of the two dives could be interpreted to mean that different generalized motor programs are used to produce them.

Evaluation of Lori's Solution

Lori ably describes the goals and basic actions of the two skills she is comparing in this exercise. To help the reader conceptualize the two dives more clearly, Lori also includes a figure depicting the sequence of movements for each, but she doesn't document the source of the descriptions of the dives! Not doing so is a serious oversight (i.e., plagiarism). It is acceptable to use other people's ideas in writing a paper, but it is essential to acknowledge the people who came up with those ideas (or did the research) with an appropriate bibliographical citation.

Lori clearly explains her technique for discovering the patterns of relative timing for the two dives. She indicates how many dives she attempted and that she focused on the relative speeds of just two movement components at time. She should add some sort of rationale for these decisions.

After a good description of the relative timing patterns she observed for both dives, Lori mentions that she learned a lot from her experience with this exercise. It would have been even more impressive if Lori had related her findings to some of the literature dealing with the notion of generalized motor programs and the concept of invariance of relative timing.

Keith's Solution

The two skills I have chosen for this exercise are putting the shot and throwing a baseball. The goal of the shot put is to project a heavy metal sphere (16 pounds for males) as far as possible while maintaining body balance. The goal of throwing a baseball, in contrast, is to project the ball different distances to a variety of targets. Thus, the demands of the shot put (i.e., maximum force and balance) are slightly different than those of throwing a baseball (i.e., optimal speed and accuracy).

The technical requirements of the shot put state that the performer must begin in a stationary position, use only one hand to put the shot, not let the hand drop below its starting position during the action, and not bring the shot in front of the line of the shoulders during the movement (The Diagram Group, 1974). For a right-handed performer, the action begins with the shot being held in the flexed hand in a position under the chin. To produce the movement, the performer coils the body so that the weight is balanced over the right foot; takes several hops forward; plants the left foot and rotates the hips, trunk, and shoulders in a counterclockwise direction; rapidly extends the arm and hand to release the shot; and then maintains balance following release (see the figure on the next page).

The basic action of the baseball throw involves flexing and extending the elbow and wrist in rapid succession. The ball is released at various points during wrist extension, depending on the desired velocity and trajectory of ball flight. For a right-handed thrower, the action is preceded by a forward step with the left foot and an extension of the throwing shoulder to the rear.

Reprinted, by permission, from G. Carr, 1999, *Fundamentals of track and field*, 2nd ed. (Champaign, IL: Human Kinetics), 201.

The slightly different goals of these two actions suggest that they would be produced using different generalized motor programs. According to Schmidt and Wrisberg (2000), different generalized motor programs should have different patterns of relative timing. To determine whether this might be the case for the shot put and the baseball throw, I observed the performance of two university athletes. One is a member of the track team, and the other is a pitcher on the baseball team. Since the shot put and baseball throw both involve coordinated arm motion, I decided to focus on the pattern of relative timing of the hand, forearm, and upper arm during each movement. I observed 10 performance attempts by each person. Because the shot put requires near-maximal force, I asked the baseball pitcher to perform 10 pitches with near-maximal force.

I observed clear differences in the pattern of relative motion for these two skills. For the shot put, the hand, forearm, and upper arm seemed to travel at nearly the same speed in propelling the shot. However, for the baseball pitch, the hand appeared to move faster than the forearm, and the forearm appeared to move faster than the upper arm. The pattern of the shot put action appeared to be more of a "thrusting" motion (rotation of the shoulder and extension of the arm) while the pattern of the throwing motion appeared to be more "whip-like" (progressively more rapid extension from the upper arm to the forearm to the hand). Based on my limited observations, I must conclude that performers probably use different generalized motor programs to control the shot put and the baseball throw.

References:

Carr, G. (1999). *Fundamentals of Track and Field* (2nd ed.). Champaign, IL: Human Kinetics.
Schmidt, R.A., & Wrisberg, C.A. (2000). *Motor learning and performance* (2nd ed.). Champaign, IL: Human Kinetics.
The Diagram Group (1974). *Rules of the game.* New York: Paddington Press Ltd.

Evaluation of Keith's Solution

Keith selects an interesting pair of skills for this exercise. He notes that while the actions of the shot put and baseball throw appear similar in several respects, there are enough key differences to suggest that the two movements might be controlled by different generalized motor programs. Keith provides an excellent description of the shot put action along with a figure depicting the movement sequence. He also provides appropriate documentation for both the skill description and the figure.

Keith's description of the basic action of the baseball throw is not as thorough as the one he offers for the shot put, and he provides no figure to illustrate the throwing sequence. Even though baseball is a more familiar sport, Keith's presentation would have been more balanced if he had devoted similar attention to his discussion of the throw as he did to his discussion of the shot put. Moreover, Keith's statement that the shot is held in a flexed hand position under the chin is incorrect; the wrist is extended. The hand is flexed at the moment of release.

Keith provides good theoretical rationale and documentation for the possibility that the shot put and baseball throw might be controlled by different generalized motor programs. He also describes his methodology well, discussing how he attempted to determine the relative timing patterns of the two movements. An interesting aspect of Keith's procedure is the fact that he instructed the baseball pitcher to produce throws with near-maximum force, making the force requirements more similar to those of the shot put. Unfortunately, Keith does not offer any particular theoretical rationale for doing this.

Keith clearly describes his findings, but he does not connect them in any way to the literature on generalized motor programs or to that dealing with the concept of invariant relative timing.

Your Solution to Exercise 6.2

Differentiating Generalized Motor Programs for Two Classes of Actions

NAME_____ DATE_____

1. Definition of problem:
2. Type of instructional situation (circle one):
   Teaching   Coaching   Rehabilitation   Human factors
3. Description of the skills
   First skill:
       Goal of the movement:
       Basic actions required:
   Second skill:
       Goal of the movement:
       Basic actions required:
4. Technique(s) to identify the relative timing patterns of the two movements
   First movement:
   Second movement:
5. Description of the relative timing patterns of the two movements
   First movement:
   Second movement:

Exercise 6.3

Improving the Accuracy of a Rapid Skill

The spatial and temporal accuracy of rapid, discrete aiming movements can be influenced by the time, distance, and speed of the movement. In this exercise you are to pick a rapid skill you are familiar with (*except for baseball batting!*) and discuss ways an individual might improve the spatial or temporal accuracy (or both) of performance. Your solution should do the following:

- Describe the skill, including the goal of the movement and the basic actions required.

- Discuss the demands for spatial accuracy, temporal accuracy, or both spatial and temporal accuracy in the performance of the movement.

- Specify and explain two things a performer might do to improve the spatial-temporal accuracy of performance.

Andrea's Solution

The skill for this exercise is passing a moving soccer ball using the inside of the foot. The goal of passing is to direct the ball to a teammate who may or may not be moving. In preparation for the kick, the passer watches the approaching ball and runs to the estimated interception point. The basic action starts by placing the nonkicking foot about 5 to 6 inches alongside and away from the ball and pointing it in the intended direction of the pass. The kicking leg is turned outward from the hip, and the sole of the kicking foot is parallel to the ground. The passer moves from the hip so that the kicking leg swings easily and contact with the ball is made near the instep of the foot. To keep the ball on the ground, the passer should contact the ball near its center. To put the ball in the air, the passer should aim for just below the center of the ball. Just prior to contact, the passer stiffens the kicking leg to provide additional power. The passer should attempt to "push" the ball, rather than stabbing at it (Erdogan, 1986, p. 142).

Passing a moving ball demands both spatial and temporal accuracy. Spatial accuracy is needed so that the foot contacts the ball in the best spot. Temporal accuracy is needed so that the foot arrives at the interception point at the proper time (i.e., not too early or too late).

To improve spatial accuracy, the passer needs to watch the ball carefully to be sure that she contacts it in the right place. To improve temporal accuracy, the passer needs to start the kicking motion slightly before the ball arrives so that the foot arrives at the interception point at the same time as the ball does.

Reference:

Erdogan, S. (1986). Soccer. In B.M. Edgley & G.H. Oberle (Eds.), *Physical education activities handbook,* 2nd ed. (pp. 134–189). Winston-Salem, NC: Hunter Textbooks.

Evaluation of Andrea's Solution

Andrea selects an interesting skill for this exercise and gives it a thorough description. Adding a figure or photo of the action sequence would add further help. You may have noticed that, in addition to the name of the author and the publication year of the source she documents, Andrea lists a page number in her citation. Technically speaking, she is only required to include the page number if she directly quotes from the source. If, in fact, Andrea did this, she should have put the sentences she directly quoted in quotation marks. A rule of thumb in scientific writing is that direct quotes should be used only sparingly. Most of the time you should paraphrase (i.e., put in your own words) what you read from an article or book.

Because Andrea's description of the spatial and temporal accuracy demands of the soccer pass seems simplistic and commonsensical, she probably is speaking from her own experience. Likewise, her suggestions for improving the spatial and temporal accuracy of the soccer pass are superficial. Sometimes the solution to applied problems can only be based on our experience or intuition. However, the strongest solutions are based on sound theoretical rationale and, whenever possible, concrete scientific evidence. When it comes to the factors influencing the spatial and temporal accuracy of rapid aiming movements, the supporting literature exists (see chapter 6 for examples), and at the very least, Andrea should have referred to the discussion in the textbook to substantiate her suggestions.

Dawn's Solution

The skill I have chosen for this exercise is the drop shot in the game of squash rackets. The goal of the drop shot is to hit the ball softly so that it strikes low on the front wall and drops short in the front part of the court. The drop shot is a touch stroke and, when struck with deception, it can result in a clean winner. The shot is performed using the same grip, as well as the same feet and body position, used for the other squash strokes. However, the basic action of the drop shot requires a backswing and follow-through that are shortened to reduce racket speed. The racket is held with the racket's head up and the player's elbow flexed and close to the side of the body. During the backswing, the shoulders are turned and the wrist is flexed so that the racket head moves from a position in front of the face to one behind the shoulders. From this position the racket is brought forward and down, and contact with the ball is made at a position slightly in front of the body. A high to low swing, along with wrist extension and rotation, imparts underspin to the ball (Varner & Bramall, 1967).

The primary accuracy demands of the drop shot are temporal rather than spatial. Since the ball is much smaller than the face of the racket, there is only a minimal demand for spatial accuracy (as long as the player is watching the ball!). The biggest challenge of the drop shot is to strike the ball in such a way that it travels toward the front wall at a slow speed.

As Schmidt and Wrisberg (2000) discuss in chapter 6, there are several ways that temporal accuracy can be improved for timing tasks such as the drop shot. One way is for the performer to shorten the movement time of the swing. Schmidt (1969) conducted an experiment to explore the characteristics of timing movements and found that both the consistency of initiation time and the movement time itself were better when the movement time was shorter than when it was longer. Fortunately for squash players, the drop shot requires a shorter swing than the drive shot. Therefore, it should be possible for a player to produce the shot in a relatively short movement time. By shortening movement time the player also gains the advantage of being able to watch the ball for a slightly longer time. Increased viewing time should improve the quality of visual information processing, because the player can obtain a bit more information about the approaching ball (e.g., flight path, velocity, spin) before executing her shot. Watching the ball a bit longer should enhance the player's anticipation of the time and place of interception.

References:

Schmidt, R.A. (1969). Movement time as a determiner of timing accuracy. *Journal of Experimental Psychology, 79,* 43–47.

Schmidt, R.A., & Wrisberg, C.A. (2000). *Motor learning and performance* (2nd ed.). Champaign, IL: Human Kinetics.

Varner, M., & Bramall, N. (1967). *Squash rackets.* Dubuque, IA: W.C. Brown.

Evaluation of Dawn's Solution

Dawn could amplify her general description of the goal of the drop shot. Her discussion of the basic actions of this skill is more thorough and includes appropriate supporting documentation. A figure depicting the action sequence might help readers visualize the shot.

Dawn suggests that the primary accuracy demands of the drop shot are temporal rather than spatial in nature, giving a logical rationale for this suggestion based on the description she provides of the skill itself. She also offers excellent rationale and documentation for her suggestions for improving temporal accuracy. Particularly impressive is Dawn's use of both primary and secondary supporting references. Primary sources are those that report information obtained through direct observation. The experiment by Schmidt (1969) is an example of a primary source. Secondary sources are those in which the authors attempt to summarize the work of others. Textbooks are good examples of secondary sources.

Your Solution to Exercise 6.3

Improving the Accuracy of a Rapid Skill

NAME_____ DATE_____

1. Definition of problem:
2. Type of instructional situation (circle one):
   Teaching   Coaching   Rehabilitation   Human factors
3. Description of the skill
   Goal of the movement:
   Basic actions required:
4. Demands for spatial-temporal accuracy:
5. How a performer might improve spatial-temporal accuracy (two suggestions):
   a.
   b.

CHAPTER 7

Preparing for the Learning Experience

A child leaping between rocks can transfer skills developed in performing the broad jump.

◀◀◆ Key Concepts

People's learning experiences occur in many different ways. Movement practitioners who supervise an individual's learning experience must first identify the skill or skills the person wants to acquire (i.e., target skills) and the situation(s) in which the individual wants to be able to perform those skills (i.e., target contexts). Once this is done, the practitioner can assist the learner in setting goals that represent the road map for skill achievement. Goals are more effective when they are challenging, attainable, realistic, and specific (i.e., CARS). Goals are also helpful for assessing personal improvements in the learner's performance (i.e., performance goals), improvements in the desired target behaviors (i.e., process goals), and the achievement of external performance standards (i.e., outcome goals).

Transfer of learning is an important concept practitioners need to keep in mind when providing instructional assistance. This concept concerns both the role of prior experiences on the performance or learning of the target skill and the effect of practice of the target skill on its later performance in the target context. Practitioners can encourage the first type of transfer by reminding learners of the similarities of previous movement experiences to the target skill. Practitioners can also facilitate the second type of transfer by structuring learning experiences that lead to successful performance of the target skill in the target context.

Learners differ in the levels of motivation, abilities, previous experiences, and stage of learning they bring to a performance situation. Although the basic principles of motor control and information processing (discussed in chapters 3–6 and summarized in the conceptual model of human performance) apply to most people, practitioners sometimes need to modify the learning environment to meet the needs and interests of individual learners.

Assessing the progress of learners is an important component of the skill acquisition process. When evaluating improvements in an individual's performance, practitioners should consider process and outcome measures that assess the desired target behavior(s) and represent the person's level of goal achievement. Process measures reflect the quality of various aspects of the learner's movements (e.g., proper body lean in sprinting, desired hip and shoulder rotation in the discus throw, efficient swing mechanics in the golf shot). Outcome measures indicate the level of achievement of various external standards of performance (e.g., time in the 100-meter dash, distance the discus travels, number of strokes for a round of golf).

◀◀◆ Key Terms

In order to respond to the questions and complete the exercises in this chapter you need to have a basic understanding of the following terms or concepts:

    goal setting
    stages of learning
    performance goals
    process goals
    outcome goals
    transfer of learning
    near transfer
    positive transfer
    target skill
    target behavior
    target context

outcome measures

process measures

 **Review Questions**

Answer each of the following questions and *provide rationale for your answers*. If you are not familiar with the skill or activity in a particular scenario, you may discuss the skill or activity with an expert or consult a book or training manual to obtain an informed explanation or description.

1. Goal setting is an important component of the skill-learning process. The best goals are challenging, attainable, realistic, and specific (CARS). The first of the following scenarios has an example of a process goal, a performance goal, and an outcome goal provided, along with a brief discussion of how the goals meet the CARS criteria. You are to provide examples of the three types of goals and discuss how they meet the CARS criteria for the remaining scenarios.

    a. Scenario—an 8-year-old girl with no handicapping conditions wants to learn how to play soccer. On the first day of team practice, the learner's coach introduces her to one of the most basic skills of the game of soccer: the push pass. A player performs the push pass by kicking the ball with the inside of the foot. Soccer players use the push pass to direct the ball accurately over short distances (10–20 feet) at a moderate pace.

Process goal:

Place the nonkicking foot 5 to 6 inches alongside the ball and allow enough room for the kicking leg to swing freely 5 out of 10 times.

Performance goal:

Improve the number of times from 2 out of 10 successful passes to 5 out of 10 successful passes that the player passes the ball directly to a partner standing in a stationary position a distance of 10 feet away.

Outcome goal:

Break the team record for most consecutive successful push passes (now 8) by a beginning player on the first day of practice.

How the goals meet the CARS criteria:

These goals meet the CARS criteria because they represent modest (attainable and realistic) and specific targets for performing a soccer skill that is basic yet challenging for a beginning player (Pronk & Gorman, 1991).

Reference:

Pronk, N., & Gorman, B. (1991). Soccer everyone. Winston-Salem, NC: Hunter Textbooks.

    b. Scenario—a 16-year-old boy who has played golf for eight years wants to try out for the varsity golf team at his school. The area of his game that he is least happy with is his putting. Currently, he averages 2.5 putts per hole.

Process goal:

Performance goal:

Outcome goal:

How the goals meet the CARS criteria:

c. Scenario—a 50-year-old male wants to learn to swim so that he can compete in triathlons. An accomplished distance runner and cyclist, the man must learn the freestyle stroke to enter triathlon competitions. He has had no prior formal swimming instruction but is "drownproofed."

Process goal:

Performance goal:

Outcome goal:

How the goals meet the CARS criteria:

d. Scenario—a 70-year-old female with arthritis in her hands wants to learn to play the piano so that she can use it as a therapeutic activity. The woman has been a regular member of her church choir for 30 years and reads music easily. She was an accomplished seamstress until her arthritic condition forced her to give up that activity.

Process goal:

Performance goal:

Outcome goal:

How the goals meet the CARS criteria:

2. Another important component of the learning process is identifying target skills, behaviors, and contexts. Each of the following four scenarios describes a hypothetical learner, movement activity, and target context. The first scenario includes three appropriate target skills and three target behaviors plus supporting rationale for each. You are to provide three target skills and three target behaviors (with supporting rationale) for the remaining scenarios.

a. Scenario—a 12-year-old male wants to learn to play ice hockey recreationally with his friends. The boy, an accomplished skater, has also played organized baseball for the past five years. However, he has had neither experience nor instruction in the sport of ice hockey.

Three target skills (American Sport Education Program, 1996).

1. Skating backward—when retreating to defend the forward rush of an opponent, a player must be able to skate backward with little or no difficulty.
2. Stick handling while skating—a major demand of ice hockey is the simultaneous performance of skating and stick handling (i.e., using the hockey stick to control the puck).
3. Passing the puck—to interact successfully with teammates, a player must be able to pass and receive the puck in a controlled fashion.

Three target behaviors:

1. Skating backward—a player must be able to maintain body balance and control with the eyes focused on the puck or on other players.
2. Stick handling while skating—a player must be able to maintain control of the puck and keep the eyes focused on other players while skating.
3. Passing the puck—a player must be able to deliver the puck to a teammate so that the teammate can receive it and control it easily without breaking stride.

Reference:

American Sport Education Program. (1996). Coaching youth hockey. Champaign, IL: Human Kinetics.

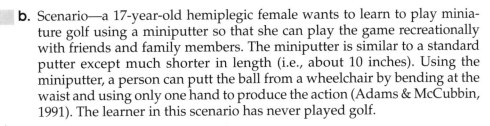

　b. Scenario—a 17-year-old hemiplegic female wants to learn to play miniature golf using a miniputter so that she can play the game recreationally with friends and family members. The miniputter is similar to a standard putter except much shorter in length (i.e., about 10 inches). Using the miniputter, a person can putt the ball from a wheelchair by bending at the waist and using only one hand to produce the action (Adams & McCubbin, 1991). The learner in this scenario has never played golf.

Three target skills:

1.

2.

3.

Three target behaviors:

1.

2.

3.

Reference:

Adams, R.C., & McCubbin, J.A. (1991). *Games, sports, and exercises for the physically disabled* (4th ed.). Philadelphia: Lea & Febiger.

　c. Scenario—a 60-year-old male wants to learn social dancing so that he can dance with his wife at a local dance club. The man has not had experience or instruction in social dance, but he is an accomplished pianist and he competed in gymnastics during his years in college.

Three target skills:

1.

2.

3.

Three target behaviors:

1.

2.

3.

　d. Scenario—a 15-year-old female wants to improve her softball skills to compete for a position on the community slow-pitch softball team. Her throwing skills are excellent, but her batting lacks power; she makes contact with the ball, but does not hit it as hard as she would like. The woman is physically fit and has played softball for seven years. However, she has had no formal instruction in the sport.

Three target skills:

1.

2.

3.

Three target behaviors:

1.

2.

3.

3. Acquiring a motor skill often involves learning the conceptual, perceptual, and movement elements of a task (see table 7.4 in the textbook). For the first of the following four skills, you'll see an example of and supporting rationale for a conceptual element, a perceptual element, and a movement element. You are to provide an example of each type of element and give supporting rationale for the remaining skills.

    a. Hitting a chip shot in golf.

Conceptual element:

The chip shot is an appropriate shot for golfers to hit when they are close enough to the green to hit a shot that travels in the air and, after it hits the ground, rolls slowly toward the hole (Owens & Bunker, 1995). Conceptually, the golfer needs to understand those situations for which the chip shot is most appropriate (e.g., chipping over a sand bunker and onto the green).

Perceptual element:

When hitting the chip shot, the golfer must be able to accurately identify the environmental conditions of the shot. Perceptually, the golfer must recognize features such as the length of the grass, its thickness, and the slope of the ground on which the ball is lying. Accurate perception of environmental conditions enables the golfer to determine appropriate modifications to make in the swing.

Movement element:

When hitting the chip shot, the golfer must keep the wrists firm and move the shoulders, arms, and hands as a single unit, taking the club straight back and then moving it straight through the ball. By keeping the swing firm, the golfer is able to produce the shot in a more controlled fashion.

Reference:

Owens, D., & Bunker, L.K. (1995). *Golf: Steps to success.* Champaign, IL: Human Kinetics.

    b. Hitting a defensive lob shot in tennis.

Conceptual element:

Perceptual element:

Movement element:

    c. Hitting a "z" serve in racquetball.

Conceptual element:

Perceptual element:

Movement element:

    d. Driving a car on an icy road.

Conceptual element:

Perceptual element:

Movement element:

4. When assessing an individual's performance improvements, practitioners should consider examining both movement outcomes and processes. For the first of the four activities listed in the previous question, two outcome measures and two process measures are provided along with supporting rationale for each. You are to suggest two examples of each type of measure (with supporting rationale) for the remaining activities.

   a. Hitting a chip shot in golf (Owens & Bunker, 1995).

Outcome measures:

1. Distance from the hole; obviously, the closer the ball stops to the hole, the better the shot. Outcome is measured to the nearest foot.

2. Location of the ball relative to the hole (when the green is sloped); uphill putts are usually easier to make than downhill putts. Therefore, if the green is sloped near the hole, chip shots are better when the ball stops on the downhill side of the hole than when it stops on the uphill side of the hole. Outcome is measured as a plus one (if ball stops downhill) or a minus one (if ball stops uphill).

Process measures:

1. Degree to which shoulders, arms, and hands move as a single unit during the swing; the firmer the swing, the more controlled the swing. The swing process is measured subjectively by the instructor as acceptable or unacceptable (if the latter, specific deficiencies would be noted).

2. Head down and eyes on ball until after the ball lands on the green; keeping the head still is important for a precise ball strike. The process is measured subjectively by the instructor as acceptable or unacceptable.

Reference:

Owens, D., & Bunker, L.K. (1995). *Golf: Steps to success.* Champaign, IL: Human Kinetics.

   b. Hitting a defensive lob shot in tennis.

Outcome measures:

1.
2.

Process measures:

1.
2.

   c. Hitting a "z" serve in racquetball.

Outcome measures:

1.
2.

Process measures:

1.
2.

   d. Driving a car on an icy road.

Outcome measures:

1.
2.

Process measures:

1.
2.

Problem-Solving Exercises

The following exercises challenge you to demonstrate your comprehension of several important concepts presented in chapter 7 of the textbook. In Exercise 7.1 you discuss the goal-setting process and suggest examples of a process goal, a performance goal, and an outcome goal. In Exercise 7.2 you describe target behaviors that might be associated with skill improvements and suggest ways these behaviors might be measured. In Exercise 7.3 you explain ways of identifying and measuring target behaviors that might indicate positive near transfer.

Exercise 7.1

Determining Goals and Measuring Goal Achievement

Goal setting is an important part of the instructional process. Practitioners must know what the learner wants to accomplish and where the learner wants to be able to perform the skill (i.e., the target context). You are to select a skill you are familiar with here, and suggest examples of a process goal, a performance goal, and an outcome goal that might be appropriate for a learner. Your solution should do the following:

- Describe the skill, emphasizing the goal of the movement and the basic actions required of the performer.

- Describe the learner (you may invent an individual or describe someone you know), including abilities and movement experiences that might be advantageous to skill performance.

- Describe one process goal, one performance goal, and one outcome goal that might be appropriate for this individual.

- Discuss how the three goals satisfy the CARS criteria of effective goal setting.

Carrie's Solution

The behind-the-back pass in basketball (see the figure on the following page) has as its goal to pass the ball to a teammate when a defender is preventing the execution of a more conventional, front-of-body pass. According to Wissel (1994), executing the behind-the-back pass involves (1) pivoting on the ball of the back foot, (2) turning the body to the passing-arm side, (3) moving the ball with both hands to a position behind the hip, (4) shifting the weight from back foot to front foot, and (5) passing the ball by extending the passing arm and flexing the wrist and fingers.

The learner is a 15-year-old female who has played organized basketball for 5 years. She is highly skilled in most aspects of basketball and wishes to add the behind-the-back pass to her other skills. In addition to extensive experience with the sport, the player has several abilities identified by Fleishman (1964) that may help her perform the behind-the-back pass (i.e., multilimb coordination, control precision, manual dexterity, aiming, and extent flexibility).

Schmidt and Wrisberg (2000) discuss three types of goals that individuals might set when they are learning skills. Process goals concern some aspect of the intended action. In this example, a process goal might be to extend the passing arm when releasing the ball. Performance goals represent personal improvements in some aspect of performance. An example of a performance goal in this case might be seeing the target without turning the head to look. Outcome goals are those that concern the achievement of some external standard. For this basketball player an outcome goal might be 8 successful passes out of 10 to teammates during the season's games.

Reprinted, by permission, from N. Lieberman-Cline and R. Roberts, 1996, *Basketball for women* (Champaign, IL: Human Kinetics), 193.

The coach could measure achievement of the process and performance goals and rate the athlete on whether arm extension and "no-look" passing form were "acceptable" or "unacceptable."

The goals meet all four of the CARS criteria. They are challenging because they represent aspects of an advanced skill that is being attempted by an advanced performer. They are attainable because they are variations of other basketball movements the player has already mastered (e.g., passing). They are realistic because they are within the capabilities of this player. And, they are specific because they include a method for measuring each behavior (i.e., coach's rating or game statistics).

References:

Fleishman, E.A. (1964). *The structure and measurement of physical fitness.* Englewood Cliffs, NJ: Prentice-Hall.

Schmidt, R.A., & Wrisberg, C.A. (2000). *Motor learning and performance* (2nd ed.). Champaign, IL: Human Kinetics.

Wissel, H. (1994). *Basketball: Steps to success.* Champaign, IL: Human Kinetics.

Evaluation of Carrie's Solution

Some positives in Carrie's solution are her description of the goal, visual illustration of the basic actions involved, documentation for the discussion, and description of the learner. She could expand the solution by describing each ability more clearly and discussing how each ability relates to performing the behind-the-back pass.

Carrie's answer is strong in explaining how the target behaviors associated with each of the three types of goals might be measured. Here she might have also mentioned how and when the coach would assess the learner's performance. Carrie could have suggested one or two of the criteria the coach might use in rating the learner's form, although her explanation of how the goals she selects meet each of the CARS criteria is sufficient.

Brett's Solution

The skill I am selecting for this exercise is splitting wood with an axe. The goal of this skill is to strike a log (2–3 feet in length and situated on the ground in an upright position) as near the center of the cross section as possible. Correctly executed, the log can be split completely in half with a single blow. The basic actions of log splitting are performed by first gripping the axe handle with both hands, with the nonpreferred hand at the base of the handle and the preferred hand aligned next to it. The two hands are aligned with each other at the base of the fingers. The splitting action begins by extending the arms and hands and resting the point of the axe blade on the anticipated target point. From this position, the eyes remain fixed on the target while the wrists and elbows are flexed so that the axe head is drawn up and over the shoulder of the preferred hand. From this position the striking action occurs by forcefully extending the arms and wrists downward in the direction of the target.

The learner is a 13-year-old male who wants to learn to split wood to improve his upper body strength and power (and because his father has decided that the boy should begin performing this service for his family). The boy has had experience with striking activities in sports like baseball and racquetball. Both of these sports require flexion and extension of the arms and hands. In addition to his sport experiences, the boy seems to have better-than-average levels of two abilities, aiming and explosive strength, that should be assets in learning the skill of wood splitting.

A process goal for this individual might be to make the hands and arms move fast during the downswing. A performance goal might be to increase the percentage of logs split in half with a single blow from 2 out of 10 to 5 out of 10. An outcome goal might be to split the allotted amount of wood required by the family each day in a time of less than 30 minutes. These goals appear to satisfy the CARS criteria because they are within the boy's capabilities (attainable and realistic), yet they are challenging because the boy has not attempted the wood-splitting activity before. The goals are specific because each one deals with a particular behavior that can be assessed periodically by either the boy or by someone watching him.

Evaluation of Brett's Solution

Brett's explanations of the goal and basic actions involved are good, but he does not mention where he obtained his information. Brett's description of the learner is more than adequate (and includes some nice humor) but he needs to add a description of the abilities he mentions and indicate how each of them might help the learner split wood.

Although Brett suggests examples of the three goals, he omits background discussion (or documentation) of the differences between the various types of goals. The examples seem appropriate and his discussion of how the goals meet the CARS criteria is quite good. Regrettably, Brett's solution is a graphic example of plagiarism, a person's failure to provide appropriate supporting documentation for borrowed material.

Your Solution to Exercise 7.1

Determining Goals and Measuring Goal Achievement

NAME_____ DATE_____

1. Definition of problem:
2. Type of instructional situation (circle one):

   Teaching   Coaching   Rehabilitation   Human factors
3. Description of the skill

   Goal of the movement:

   Basic actions required:
4. Description of the learner

   Previous experiences:

   Relevant underlying abilities:
5. Discussion of goals

   Process goal:

   Performance goal:

   Outcome goal:
6. How goals satisfy CARS criteria:

Exercise 7.2

Identifying and Measuring Target Behaviors Associated With Skill Improvements

Once learners have identified their goals, it is important for them to identify the target behaviors they need to focus on during the learning experience. In this exercise you select three target behaviors that might be associated with improvements in a person's skill performance. These behaviors could reflect conceptual, perceptual, or movement elements (or all three) of the target skill. Your solution to this exercise should do the following:

- Describe the skill, emphasizing the goal of the movement and basic actions required of the performer.
- Describe the learner (a hypothetical individual or someone you know), including abilities and experiences that might be advantageous to skill performance.
- Discuss three target behaviors that might be expected to accompany performance improvements (*note*—consider conceptual, perceptual, and movement elements of the task before making your decisions).
- Describe a performance measure you could use to assess improvements in each behavior (*note*—consider both process and outcome measures before making your decisions).

Michael's Solution

The skill I have chosen is fielding a ground ball in the sport of softball. The goal of this skill is to intercept and secure the ball in the glove without fumbling or dropping it. The sequence of basic actions in fielding a ground ball includes bending forward at the hips and only slightly at the knees, extending the arms toward the ground so that the fingers are spread and pointed down, resting the back of the glove lightly on the ground, watching the ball all the way into the glove, and, upon contact with the glove, drawing the ball toward the body with both hands (Gangstead, Rebenar, & Lamport, 1986).

The learner is a 12-year-old female who would like to play an infield position on her community softball team. The girl has had two years of softball experience but has always played in the outfield where there are fewer opportunities to field ground balls. She is physically fit, and she has good levels of several abilities that are important to successful fielding: eye-hand coordination, determination, and courage.

If I were assisting this individual in learning to field ground balls, I would look for improvements in the following three target behaviors. The fielder's glove should rest lightly on the ground until just before the ball arrives. The fielder should move to a position that places her body in front of the approaching ball. The fielder's eyes and head should be directed downward in the area of the glove at the moment that the ball is being fielded.

I would measure each of these target behaviors subjectively by watching the position of the glove, the position of the fielder's body, and the direction of the fielder's eyes and head at the moment the ball is fielded. I would award one point for each behavior that is executed correctly, with the maximum possible score for each fielding attempt being three points.

Reference:

Gangstead, S.K., Rebenar, M., & Lamport, L. (1986). Softball. In B.M. Edgley & G.H. Oberle (Eds.), *Physical education activities handbook* (pp. 191–226). Winston-Salem, NC: Hunter Textbooks.

Evaluation of Michael's Solution

Michael's description of the goals and basic actions is thorough and he provides a supporting reference for his discussion. An illustration of the action sequence would help some readers. Michael's description of the learner is not as clear. He doesn't say *what kind of experience* the individual has had (except for playing an outfield position), and he doesn't indicate why he selected the abilities he chose or cite any supporting literature on individual differences.

Although the target behaviors Michael mentions appear to be relevant to the task of fielding a ground ball, he offers no theoretical discussion or pertinent literature concerning the concept of target behaviors. In suggesting measures of each target behavior, he basically restates the behaviors themselves. Michael needs to provide more specific criteria and measures a practitioner might use to assess the fielder's body position (i.e., what constitutes proper body position?).

Melissa's Solution

The skill of pitching horseshoes has as its goal propelling the horseshoe a distance of some 40 feet so that it lands around or near a metal stake (23 inches high and about 1 inch in diameter) inserted in the ground. The horseshoe weighs approximately 2 pounds and is about 8 inches long and 7 inches wide. The basic action of the movement includes swinging the pitching arm to the rear, bending at the waist and knees while stepping forward with the opposite foot, planting the foot and extending at the waist and knees, swinging the arm forward, and releasing the horseshoe at about shoulder height.

The learner in this scenario is my grandmother. She is 62 years old and has long wanted to learn to pitch horseshoes so that she can play the game with my grandfather. My grandmother is physically fit and, when she was young, played competitive softball and basketball. In addition, my grandmother has good manual dexterity that could be beneficial in learning this skill. According to Fleishman (1964), manual dexterity involves the manipulation of relatively large objects with the hands and arms. While the horseshoe is not unusually large, it is somewhat heavy and, to be effective, the pitcher must be able to release it in such a way that the horseshoe comes out of the hand and gently rotates one revolution before landing near the stake.

Schmidt and Wrisberg (2000) discuss the concept of target behaviors. For the task of pitching horseshoes, there are three target behaviors that are important for skilled performance. The first is balance during the throw. This behavior can be measured by observing the pitcher's form to see whether she maintains her balance after she releases the horseshoe. The other two target behaviors are the location of the hand at the moment the horseshoe is released and the consistency of the release point for a series of throws. These two behaviors can be measured by observing how close to shoulder height the player releases the horseshoe and by recording how consistently she does this during a sequence of throws.

References:

Fleishman, E.A. (1964). *The structure and measurement of physical fitness.* Englewood Cliffs, NJ: Prentice-Hall.

Schmidt, R.A., & Wrisberg, C.A. (2000). *Motor learning and performance* (2nd ed.). Champaign, IL: Human Kinetics.

Evaluation of Melissa's Solution

Melissa provides a detailed description of the task and specifications and dimensions of the necessary equipment for pitching horseshoes (but she does not indicate the source of this technical information). Similarly, she describes the basic actions of the task without citing any supporting references. She should credit the source, even if it was her grandfather.

Melissa's description of the learner is sufficiently detailed, and she does document her discussion of the ability of manual dexterity. Although she indicates that the concept of target behaviors is discussed by Schmidt and Wrisberg (2000), she doesn't say anything about the nature of that discussion. The significance of the concept is worth explaining.

Melissa provides adequate examples of three target behaviors for horseshoe pitching along with suggested measures of each. Here, her answer is weak in not indicating how an observer would determine the cutoff for distinguishing correct and incorrect release point and balance during the throw.

Your Solution to Exercise 7.2

Identifying and Measuring Target Behaviors Associated With Skill Improvements

NAME_____ DATE_____

1. Definition of problem:
2. Instructional situation (circle one):
   Teaching   Coaching   Rehabilitation   Human factors
3. Description of the skill
   Goal of the movement:
   Basic actions required:
4. Description of the learner
   Previous experiences:
   Relevant underlying abilities:
5. Discussion of target behaviors:
   1.
   2.
   3.
6. Description of performance measures:
   1.
   2.
   3.

Exercise 7.3

Identifying and Measuring Target Behaviors Indicative of Positive Near Transfer

A common goal of motor learning is the transfer of skills from the practice context to the target context. Not only do individuals want to acquire particular skills, they also want to be able to perform those skills in particular contexts (i.e., target contexts). Chapter 7 of the textbook explains the concepts of *positive transfer* and *near transfer*. A combination of these two types of transfer is assumed to occur whenever individuals are able to perform the movements they have learned in the desired target contexts.

Here you are to consider a learning situation for which positive and near transfer is an anticipated outcome. Your solution to this exercise should do the following:

- Describe a skill, emphasizing its movement goal and the basic actions required of the skill's performer.
- Describe the learner (either a hypothetical individual or someone you know), including the person's abilities and experiences that might be advantageous to skill performance.
- Discuss the target context.

- Give two target behaviors that might indicate positive near transfer and one performance measure for each behavior (*notes*—consider conceptual, perceptual, and movement elements of the task and both process measures and outcome measures before deciding on the target behaviors and their respective measures; describe the target behaviors amply).

Nathan's Solution

The skill I am describing is table tennis, and the goal in table tennis is to win points by making shots that an opponent is unable to return. The basic shots of table tennis are the serve and the forehand or backhand returns. The basic action of the serve begins with the server holding the ball in the open palm of the free hand in full view of the opponent. The server then tosses the ball vertically into the air and strikes it with the paddle, using a rapid extension or rotation of the elbow and wrist. The basic action of the forehand and backhand returns is performed with the elbow positioned at a 90-degree angle. Both returns begin with a slight backward rotation of the shoulders toward the side of the body on which the ball will be contacted (i.e., forehand or backhand). For the forehand return, the player extends the wrist to the rear. For the backhand return, the player reaches across the front of the body and flexes the wrist to the rear. Contact with the ball is made by rotating the shoulder forward and rapidly flexing (for the forehand) or extending (for the backhand) the wrist in the direction of the intended shot.

The learner is a 14-year-old female who has played table tennis recreationally with her family for two years but wants to improve her skills so that she can play competitively with members of the table tennis club at her school. The girl seems to have good levels of both perceptual timing and motor timing. She can hit her returns accurately and consistently. However, she wants to be able to hit the ball with more force.

The target context for this learner is the auxiliary gymnasium at her school. Whenever the table tennis club meets for competition, six tables are arranged in two rows of three tables each in the center of the gym. While there is considerable room between the two rows, players situated in the space between the two rows must play with their backs to each other. Members of the club who are not playing may watch the games, and they sometimes talk with each other or walk around the perimeter of the gym.

Two target behaviors for this individual could be the force with which she hits her shots and the depth of her shots (i.e., how close to the end of the opponent's side of the table the ball lands each time). Force could be measured indirectly by observing the position of the opponent during a rally. Usually when a player is hitting the ball with more force, her opponent must move farther away from the end of the table to hit her returns. The depth of the learner's shots could be measured by observing the percentage of her returns that land less than one foot from the opponent's side of the table. To determine how well the learner is performing in the target context, force and depth measures could be obtained under different types of environmental conditions (e.g., when others are watching, when the learner must play with her back to another player).

Evaluation of Nathan's Solution

Nathan's description fails to address the actions themselves (e.g., the goal in the returns might be to visually track the approaching ball and redirect it over the net using a rapid arm and hand movement). Instead, he discusses the goal of the movement in terms of the desired *outcome* of a rally (i.e., winning the point). Nathan also gives the reader the impression that he will address all three of the fundamental shots of the game of table tennis (i.e., serve, both kinds of return) by describing the basic actions of each. However, he omits discussion of the serve, so there is no need to have mentioned it in his introduction. And Nathan offers no documentation for his discussion of the goal of the movements or the basic actions of each shot.

Nathan's description of the learner needs sharper focus. He could describe her present skill level and define motor and perceptual timing ability. On the positive side, Nathan specifies that the learner wants to improve the force with which she hits her shots.

Nathan should add some theoretical discussion of the concept of the target context. After indicating that the target context in this scenario consists of both spectators and other players performing at adjacent tables, he might discuss the implications of these individuals and objects on the learner's performance (e.g., possible distractions).

The measures of the two target behaviors that Nathan suggests seem appropriate, and he correctly recommends that each be obtained during the individual's performance in the target context. Here, too, some theoretical discussion (with supporting documentation) of the concepts of target behaviors and valid measures of performance would improve his solution.

Monique's Solution

The skill I have chosen for this exercise is the front kick, which is a basic kick used in self-defense with the goal of defending against a frontal attack by another person. Properly executed, the front kick is fast and short; it is an effective surprise action against an attacker. The front kick sequence is performed from the basic defensive position (see figure *a* below).

From this position, the body weight is slowly shifted to the back foot. Then the hip is flexed and the knee is raised and pointed in the direction of the target. The knee is then extended and the toe of the shoe or ball of the foot is thrust at the target (see figure *b* below). The entire kicking action is performed with lightning-like speed followed by a quick return of the leg to the starting position (Peterson, 1989).

a   b

Reprinted, by permission, from J.M. Nelson, 1991, *Self-defense: Steps to success* (Champaign, IL: Human Kinetics), 70.

The learner in this scenario is a 35-year-old female who is single and employed as an accountant at a law firm in the city. The woman enjoys dinner and other social activities with her friends, and often travels alone and is concerned about the possibility of an attack at night while she is walking to her car. The woman jogs and lifts weights regularly; she is physically fit. However, she has never participated in competitive or combative sports and appears to possess only average levels of several of the abilities (multilimb coordination, aiming, and speed of limb movement) identified by Fleishman (1964) that might be important for performing the front kick. On the other hand, she seems to have above-average reaction time, which should help her initiate her kicking action more quickly.

The target context for this skill is a dimly lit city sidewalk or parking garage at night. After all other precautions have been taken (e.g., crossing the street, moving in the direction of a more public place, screaming, blowing a whistle for help, etc.) and it is clear that an attack is imminent, the woman stops and faces the assailant while assuming a good defensive stance. The woman then asks, "What do you want?" or "Are you following me?" Sometimes this is all that is needed to discourage an attack. If not, the woman must be prepared to fight (Peterson, 1989).

Target behaviors that are important for successful performance of the front kick are accuracy of the kick and the speed of execution. Accuracy could be measured by observing whether the kicks successfully contact the most vulnerable spots on the attacker's body (i.e., shin, knee, or groin). The speed of execution might be measured by observing the frequency of contacts with the target. If kicks are performed at an effective speed, some type of contact with the assailant should be made on most kicks. While there are obvious difficulties associated with simulating the target context, it is possible to create somewhat similar conditions in the private setting of a person's driveway or basement. A simulated "attacker" should probably wear protective padding to prevent injury.

References:

Fleishman, E.A. (1964). *The structure and measurement of physical fitness.* Englewood Cliffs, NJ: Prentice-Hall.

Peterson, S. (1989). *Self-defense.* Englewood, CO: Morton Publishing.

Evaluation of Monique's Solution

Monique selects an interesting skill for this exercise, but she could have described the movement goal more specifically. For example, she might have indicated that the goal is to rapidly move the foot and leg in order to strike an attacker in a vulnerable spot on the body. Her description of the basic action of the front kick (along with an illustration of the action sequence and supporting documentation) is successful, although she might have tried to locate a higher-quality illustration to use.

The descriptions of the learner and the learner's goal are also strong. She could still do better by defining the abilities she lists and discussing their relative importance to the performance of the front kick. To her credit, Monique states that the learner's rapid reaction time might offset modest levels of her other abilities by allowing her to initiate a response to an attack in a shorter time. She gives good detail in describing the target and discusses some of the basic self-defense procedures a person should observe in threatening situations (with a supporting reference).

Monique proposes two target behaviors that appear to be relevant to the learner's goal. However, she could add more about the performance measures (such as the approximate size of the target areas of the shin, knee, and groin that an observer would consider when scoring the accuracy of "hits"). Monique might want to rethink her rationale for using the frequency of successful contacts as a performance measure. There is probably no *a priori* frequency or number of successful contacts that would constitute effective performance during an attack. In fact, it might be reasoned that a person who is defending herself is primarily concerned about landing the highest proportion or percentage of kicks, regardless of how many kicks she attempts in a given situation.

Although Monique does not provide any theoretical discussion of the concepts of target behaviors, target context, or performance measures, she does emphasize the importance of assessing performance in situations that might resemble those of the target context. She mentions her awareness that simulating an attack is difficult and offers several possible suggestions for doing so.

Your Solution to Exercise 7.3

Identifying and Measuring Target Behaviors
Indicative of Positive Near Transfer

NAME_____ DATE_____

1. Definition of problem:
2. Instructional situation (circle one):
   Teaching   Coaching   Rehabilitation   Human factors
3. Description of the skill
   Goal of the movement:
   Basic actions required:
4. Description of the learner
   Previous experiences:
   Relevant underlying abilities:
5. Discussion of the target context:
6. Description of target behaviors and performance measures
   First behavior:
   Measure:
   Second behavior:
   Measure:

CHAPTER 8

Supplementing the Learning Experience

Instructors may break practice into parts to help people learn complex skills such as pole vaulting.

© Victah Sailer

◀◀◆ Key Concepts

Effective movement practitioners know how and when to provide instructional assistance for learners. Chapter 8 of the textbook introduces a variety of techniques practitioners can use in supplementing people's motor learning experiences. They can first increase the receptivity of learners to instruction by establishing open, two-way communication. When they do this, practitioners are more likely to obtain input from learners about their needs and the effectiveness of various forms of instructional assistance. Practitioners can also prepare individuals for the learning experience by familiarizing them with the learning environment. When learners know what to expect from the practitioner and what they can anticipate from the learning environment, they approach the learning experience with greater enthusiasm and less apprehension.

Once practitioners establish open communication with learners and familiarize them with the learning environment, they must decide what types of assistance to provide. Some learners benefit from assistance that helps them manage their focus. You learned in chapter 3 that the attentional capacity of humans is limited. As a result, learners must learn to *manage their attention effectively*. Practitioners can assist individuals in this by helping them identify the most relevant focus for performing the target skill. For closed skills, the focus might involve attending to an important component of the movement (e.g., the feel of the follow-through in the golf swing). For open skills, the focus might be on some aspect of the environment (e.g., the speed and spin of an approaching ball in tennis). During the early stages of learning, individuals can be encouraged to shift their focus back and forth between external cues and internal cues (e.g., seeing the anticipated target of a volleyball serve, anticipating the feel of the movement, seeing the ball once it is tossed).

Anxiety is one factor that influences the attentional focus of learners. When people are anxious, they are less effective in controlling their attention. One way practitioners can reduce a learner's anxiety is by assisting the person in setting realistic performance goals. In chapter 7 you learned that goals are more effective when they are attainable and realistic. When learners feel capable of achieving their goals, they also feel less anxious. Having a *process* goal usually increases learners' feelings of capability. From chapter 7 you know that process goals concern components of the action that are under the performer's control (e.g., keeping the head still during the golf swing, arching the back during the back dive, keeping the eyes on the ball when batting). By encouraging learners to set process goals, practitioners increase individuals' feelings of capability and control and diminish feelings of anxiety. The fringe benefit of decreased anxiety is more effective attentional control.

Another factor to consider in giving instructional assistance is the possibility of physical or mental fatigue. Depending on the physical fitness level of the learner, the energy requirements of the movement, the risk of injury, and the information-processing demands of the skill, practitioners may decide to schedule practice sessions that are shorter and more spread out, rather than longer and bunched together. As the skill proficiency and fitness levels of learners increase, they can usually practice for longer periods of time.

When introducing the target skill, practitioners usually need to decide on some combination of instructions and demonstrations that best conveys the general idea of the movement. The most effective instructions are brief and simple. They emphasize concepts that learners are familiar with or that remind them of past experiences to draw on to perform the target skill. Demonstrations tend to be more effective when they convey essential features of the movement. Sometimes learners need to have features pointed out by the practitioner, at least until individuals are able to recognize the features on their own.

Initially, practitioners may need to physically assist learners with their movements. However, they should cease using physical guidance as soon as learners achieve the basic idea of the skill or can practice it without the risk of injury. Other modifications of physical rehearsal include the use of simulators, part practice of skills, slow-motion practice, and error-detection practice. In addition, practitioners might encourage learners to mentally rehearse cognitive strategies or procedures of the target skill as well as to use mental images containing key features of the desired movements.

 Key Terms

In order to respond to the questions and complete the exercises in this chapter you need to have a basic understanding of the following terms or concepts:

attentional focus
broad focus
narrow focus
external focus
internal focus
limited attentional capacity
demonstrations
modeling
observational learning
generalized motor program
invariant features
relative timing pattern
two-way communication
target skill
relevant cues
part practice
fractionization
segmentation
simplification

Review Questions

Answer each of the following questions and *provide rationale for your answers*. If you are not familiar with the skill or activity presented in a particular scenario you might want to discuss it with an expert or consult a book or training manual that contains more detailed information.

1. One thing practitioners can do to prepare individuals for learning is to direct the learner's attention to relevant task or environmental cues. Each of the following four scenarios includes a description of a hypothetical learner and learning task. In the first scenario, three examples are provided (along with supporting rationale) of relevant task or environmental information that a practitioner might direct the learner's attention to. You are to provide three examples of relevant information (with supporting rationale) for each of the remaining scenarios.

   a. *Scenario:* A 26-year-old female tennis player wants to improve her performance of the service return. The player says that she often finds herself "not ready" for her opponents' serves and feels fortunate to just get them back over the net. Her goal is to be able to successfully return 75 percent of her opponents' first serves and hit the returns to various targets with various degrees of pace and depth.

Learning task:

The service return will always be either a forehand or backhand ground stroke. According to Brown (1995), three keys to successful service returns are to watch the opponent's racket face, to play the ball and not the opponent, and to adjust the length of the backswing according to the speed of the serve. All three of these "keys" represent relevant information that the player's coach might direct her attention to.

Relevant information the learner might attend to:

1. The opponent's racket face—by visually attending to the racket face of the opponent, the player will be able to see the ball the moment it comes off of the opponent's racket. This allows the player more time to anticipate the direction and speed of the approaching ball.

2. The ball and not the opponent—beginning players often think too much about who is hitting the serve, rather than playing it just like any other ground stroke. By "seeing" the seams of the approaching ball, the player can prepare for and produce the most effective return.

3. The length of the backswing relative to the speed of the serve—the harder the server hits the ball, the more rapidly it approaches the person returning the serve and the less time the person has to produce the swing. By attending to how the length of the backswing feels and watching how fast the ball is traveling, the player should become more adept at shortening the backswing for faster-paced serves or lengthening it for slower-paced serves.

Reference:

Brown, J. (1995). *Tennis: Steps to success* (2nd ed.). Champaign, IL: Human Kinetics.

   b. *Scenario:* A 10-year-old female is interested in modern dance but must first learn the basic body alignment. According to Penrod and Plastino (1970, p. 19), "Modern dance is an art form that came about by breaking the 'rules' of what dance was 'supposed' to be." Thus, any line, any shape, and any form that the body can assume in space is valid to the modern dancer. However, all movements are performed within the framework of the body's basic alignment.

Learning task:

Simply put, the basic body alignment of modern dance is "good posture." According to Penrod and Plastino (1970), modern dancers should think of their body as being stretched upward from the foot support through the top of the head. The stretch should feel as if the person is holding onto a bar above the head and hanging down from it. Dancers should think of a straight line running from the top of the head down through the neck, torso, pelvis, and legs. This line represents the central axis of the body and, regardless of whether the dancer is standing, jumping, kneeling, or sitting, the head, chest, and pelvic area should remain in a straight line.

Relevant information the learner might attend to:

1.

2.

3.

Reference:

Penrod, J., & Plastino, J.G. (1970). *The dancer prepares: Modern dance for beginners.* Palo Alto, CA: Mayfield.

    c. *Scenario:* A 32-year-old male golfer wants to improve the distance and control of his drives off the tee. The man has played golf for 10 years and is usually consistent with his approach shots and putting, but he is inconsistent in both the distance and direction of his drives.

Learning task:

Among the numerous components of the successful golf swing, according to Owens and Bunker (1995), three of the more important aspects are cocking the wrists at hip level during the backswing, rotating the hips toward the target during the downswing, and achieving a balanced finish with hands above the head and the rear shoulder closer to the target than the front shoulder.

Relevant information the learner might attend to:

    1.

    2.

    3.

Reference:

Owens, D., & Bunker, L.K. (1995). *Golf: Steps to success* (2nd ed.). Champaign, IL: Human Kinetics.

    d. *Scenario:* A 19-year-old college soccer player is recovering from surgery to the anterior cruciate ligament of his left knee and must learn how to walk with crutches. He is particularly concerned about descending stairs.

Learning task:

When descending stairs on crutches, the individual should place his healthy leg close to the edge of the step, place both crutches and the injured leg on the next step, bend the knee of the healthy leg for balance, and bring the healthy leg down to the next step (Adams & McCubbin, 1991).

Relevant information the learner might attend to:

    1.

    2.

    3.

Reference:

Adams, R.C., & McCubbin, J.A. (1991). *Games, sports, and exercises for the physically disabled* (4th ed.). Philadelphia: Lea & Febiger.

  2. Nideffer (1995) has proposed that the most appropriate attentional focus required of movement performers sometimes changes from moment to moment. Therefore, individuals must be able to shift their focus when necessary from one information source to another. The following scenarios each describe a hypothetical learner and learning task. You are to propose an appropriate focus with supporting rationale (the first scenario has been done as an example) for each of three moments of performance.

Reference:

Nideffer, R.M. (1995). *Focus for success.* San Diego: Enhanced Performance Services.

    a. *Scenario:* A 30-year-old male wants to learn the Virginia reel so that he can enjoy the dance when he attends a family reunion.

Learning task:

The dance is performed with four to eight couples in a formation of the partners in two lines facing each other. The first few components of the Virginia reel are as follows (Harris, Pittman, & Waller, 1994, p. 69):

- Forward and bow (8 counts); lines walk forward, curtsey and bow to partners, and walk backward to place.
- Forward and right hand 'round (8 counts); lines walk forward, partners join right hands, turn clockwise once around, and move backward to place.
- Forward and left hand 'round (8 counts); lines walk forward, partners join left hands, turn counterclockwise once around, and move backward to place.
- Forward and two hands 'round (8 counts); lines walk forward, partners join two hands, turn clockwise once around, and move backward to place.
- Forward and do-si-do (8 counts); lines walk forward, partners do-si-do (i.e., partners pass each other, right shoulder to right shoulder; move around each other, back to back; and return to original position), and move backward to place.

Possible shifts of attentional focus:

1. Rhythm of counts (4 each) during forward and backward movements. The dancer must focus externally on the tempo of the music to time his movements accurately and return to the original position at the proper time.

2. Hand(s) of partner and direction of turn for the right hand 'round, left hand 'round, and both hands 'round. The dancer must focus externally on the appropriate hand(s) of the partner for each type of turn and focus internally to recall the appropriate direction of each turn.

3. Shoulder of partner and direction of turn for do-si-do. The dancer must focus externally on the right shoulder of the partner and internally on the feel of the clockwise, back-to-back circling motion.

Reference:

Harris, J.A., Pittman, A.M., & Waller, M.S. (1994). *Dance a while: Handbook of folk, square, contra, & social dance* (7th ed.). New York: Macmillan.

   b. *Scenario:* A 10-year-old male wants to learn how to head a soccer ball. The boy is physically fit and has good mastery of most of the essential kicking skills. He appears to possess good levels of several abilities that are important to successful heading performance: gross body coordination (Fleishman, 1964) and perceptual and motor timing (Keele & Ivry, 1987).

Learning task:

The correct attitude for heading a soccer ball is "You hit the ball; don't let the ball hit you" (Pronk & Gorman, 1991, p. 51). Timing is a crucial component of successful heading. The ball should be contacted with the forehead at the maximum height of the jump and while the player is "hanging" in the air. The arms are used to achieve a good takeoff and maintain balance. The player arches the back and stiffens the neck muscles prior to the heading movement. The ball is contacted by hitting through it with the forehead. To head the ball low, the player should aim for the top half of the ball. To head the ball high, the player should aim for the bottom half.

Possible shifts of attentional focus:

   1.

   2.

   3.

References:

Fleishman, E.A. (1964). *The structure and measurement of physical fitness.* Englewood Cliffs, NJ: Prentice-Hall.

Keele, S.W., & Ivry, R. (1987). Modular analysis of timing in motor skill. In G.H. Bower (Ed.), *The psychology of learning and motivation,* vol. 21 (pp. 183–228). San Diego: Academic Press.

Pronk, N., & Gorman, G. (1991). *Soccer everyone.* Winston-Salem, NC: Hunter Textbooks.

c. *Scenario:* A 15-year-old female is learning the basketball technique of defensive rebounding. The defender performs the defensive rebounding skill whenever a member of the opposing team takes a shot. The key to defensive rebounding is getting between an opponent and the basket and then going for the ball as it rebounds off the rim or backboard (Wissel, 1994).

Learning task:

Defensive rebounding includes these components: watching the opponent, blocking out the opponent after the shot is taken (by putting one's back to the opponent's chest), maintaining balance, watching the bounce of the ball in order to time the jump, catching the ball with two hands at the maximum height of the jump, and spreading the legs and elbows to protect the ball when returning to the floor.

Possible shifts of attentional focus:

1.
2.
3.

Reference:

Wissel, H. (1994). *Basketball: Steps to success.* Champaign, IL: Human Kinetics.

d. *Scenario:* A 50-year-old female is learning to bowl using the four-step approach. The woman is right-handed, physically fit, and experienced in several sports (e.g., field hockey, basketball, softball).

Learning task:

The four-step approach in bowling begins with the bowler facing the pins and holding the ball in front of the body with elbows flexed at about 90 degrees. The first step for a right-handed bowler is with the right foot, accompanied by a forward push of the hands. The second step is accompanied by the pendulum-like swing of the right arm to the rear. On the third step the ball reaches peak height, and on the fourth step the arm swings forward so that the ball and foot reach the foul line at about the same time. As the left foot contacts the floor, the ball is released and the hand continues forward and upward to a finishing position above the head. Key components to successful four-step bowling include the timing of the arm swing, a visual focus on the target, proper balance and position during ball release, and an exaggerated follow-through and pause after ball release (Agne-Traub, Martin, & Tandy, 1998).

Possible shifts of attentional focus:

1.
2.
3.

Reference:

Agne-Traub, C., Martin, J.L., & Tandy, R.E. (1998). *Bowling* (8th ed.). Dubuque, IA: WCB/McGraw-Hill.

3. The first challenge facing many individuals who are attempting to learn a motor skill is getting a general idea of the movement. One way practitioners can assist learners in meeting this challenge is by providing verbal instructions. The best instructions are brief and simple and give learners a clear idea of what they should attempt to do. For each of the following four skills, a brief description of a skill along with a list of possible instructions are given. Following the first example, you are to offer your own critique of the instructions for the other skills.

> **a.** The chip pass in soccer is used when a player wants to pass the ball over the head of an opponent to a teammate a short distance away. The player kicks the ball so that it rises quickly and has an underspin that causes it to "bite" or hold position when it hits the ground (Pronk & Gorman, 1991).

Instructions:

1. Approach the ball in the direction that you want it to go.
2. Place the nonkicking foot alongside and slightly in front of the ball.
3. Keep your eyes on the ball and place your head directly over the ball.
4. Use a stabbing action of your kicking foot to contact the underside of the ball.

Critique:

These instructions for the chip pass are brief and relatively simple. They lack clarity in several places, however, such as the desired position of the nonkicking foot "alongside and slightly in front of the ball." For clarity and precision, add that the instep of the nonkicking foot should be placed a distance of 4 to 6 inches from the side surface of the ball or that the toe of the nonkicking foot should be extended 4 to 6 centimeters beyond the forward surface of the ball. Research by Beek and van Santvoord (1992) revealed that individuals who are learning how to juggle, for example, benefited from verbal instructions that emphasized the spatial position of the hands and balls.

The practitioner may also need to offer further description of the "stabbing action" required in the kicking motion. In fact, a demonstration could probably convey the image or motion better than verbal instructions could. Schoenfelder-Zohdi (1992) found that modeling the action of a slalom-skiing task facilitated learning the skill to a greater extent than did providing only verbal instructions.

References:

Beek, P.J., & van Santvoord, A.A.M. (1992). Learning the cascade juggle: A dynamical systems analysis. *Journal of Motor Behavior, 24,* 85–94.
Pronk, N., & Gorman, B. (1991). *Soccer everyone.* Winston-Salem, NC: Hunter Textbooks.
Schoenfelder-Zohdi, B.G. (1992). *Investigating the informational nature of a modeled visual demonstration.* Unpublished doctoral dissertation, Louisiana State University, Baton Rouge.

> **b.** The racquetball ceiling shot is the primary defensive shot used by racquetball players. The purpose of the shot is to move an opponent out of the center court position to a position near the back wall. Because the ceiling shot usually travels a longer distance than the drive shot or kill shot, the player hitting the ceiling shot has additional time to move to a position in the center of the court (Edgley & Oberle, 1986).

Instructions:

1. Always hit the ball from a set position.
2. Use a sidearm or overhand throwing motion.
3. Follow through in the direction of the intersection of the ceiling and the front wall.
4. Swing the racquet more slowly when hitting the ceiling shot than you do when hitting a drive shot or a kill shot.
5. Try to hit the ball so that it strikes the ceiling at a distance of 2 to 5 feet from the front wall.

Critique:

Reference:

Edgley, B.M., & Oberle, G.H. (1986). *Physical education activities handbook* (2nd ed.). Winston-Salem, NC: Hunter Textbooks.

    c. The breaststroke is the oldest known swimming stroke. It is a popular stroke for leisure swimming because the individual can keep the head up for better vision and breathing and can rest momentarily between strokes (American Red Cross, 1992).

Instructions:

1. In the glide position (body fully extended and arms outstretched in front), angle the hands slightly downward and rotate the palms outward at a 45-degree angle.
2. Press the palms directly out until the hands are wider than the shoulders (known as the catch position).
3. Bend the hips and knees and bring the heels up toward the buttocks.
4. Bend the elbows and sweep the hands downward and outward until they pass under the elbows with forearms vertical.
5. Flex and rotate the ankles outward and then press the feet outward and backward until they touch.
6. Rotate the wrists and sweep the hands inward, upward, and back slightly toward the feet until your palms are below the chin, facing each other and almost touching.
7. Recover the arms immediately after the power phase by sweeping the hands in together, squeezing the elbows toward each other, and extending the arms forward to the glide position.

Critique:

Reference:

American Red Cross. (1992). *Swimming and diving.* St. Louis: Mosby-Year Book.

    d. The forearm pass is perhaps the most widely used skill in the game of volleyball, particularly as a serve-receive action. The goal of the forearm pass is usually to direct the ball to a setter who can effectively set the ball for a hitter (Neville, 1994).

Instructions:

1. Assume a ready position in which the feet are comfortably spread about shoulder-width apart (one foot slightly in front of the other), the waist and knees are flexed, and the head is up, with the eyes looking in the direction of the approaching ball.
2. Let the arms dangle down between and slightly in front of the knees.
3. Watch the ball and anticipate the point of contact.
4. Facing the approaching ball, get low enough so that the ball can be played on the extended forearms.
5. Create a contact surface by putting the wrists and thumbs together (with thumbs pointed down).
6. Extend the shoulders and arms forward to contact the ball in front of the body.
7. Modify the rebound angle by raising or lowering the forearms or by dropping one of the shoulders.

8. Estimate the speed of the ball to determine how much impetus or cushion to use during contact (e.g., a ball that is approaching at a faster speed should be contacted by slightly retracting the forearms at impact).

Critique:

Reference:

Neville, W. (1994). *Serve it up: Volleyball for life.* Mountain View, CA: Mayfield.

4. Skill practitioners often provide learners with visual demonstrations of an activity to give them an image they should try to produce. The best demonstrations convey a movement's essential features, ones that the learner can visually detect and reproduce with some degree of success. Three movement activities are described next, the first filled in as an example. You are to suggest two features of a demonstration (pick the viewing perspective of the observer and provide supporting rationale for your choices) that learners might be able to detect and reproduce in their own movements.

a. The backhand swing in racquetball: The backhand swing begins with the player's body turned 90 degrees so that the hitting shoulder is pointed toward the front wall. The knees are bent and the feet are about shoulder-width apart. The player begins the movement by bringing the racquet back and across the front of the body, ending with the wrist flexed and the racquet's head near the opposite ear. The elbow of the hitting arm is bent and pointed toward the floor. From this position, the player swings the racquet forward by extending at both the elbow and wrist in a single, whip-like action. The racquet should travel in a plane parallel to the floor with the head of the racquet being in the same plane as the wrist. Contact with the ball is made near the front foot (i.e., the foot closest to the front wall) (Kozar & Catignani, 1997).

Observable features (viewed from the side that the player would be facing after she turns her body 90 degrees to the front wall):

1. The positioning of the racquet head near the opposite ear at the end of the backswing. Viewing the performer from the side reveals a clear spatial relationship between the racquet head and the opposite ear and also the racquet head and the hand gripping the racquet. The shape formed by these three components (i.e., a triangle) is familiar to learners and one that they should be able to reproduce easily.

2. The pattern of relative motion of the upper arm, lower arm, and racquet during the forward swing. According to Schmidt and Wrisberg (2000), an important invariant feature of the generalized motor program for a movement is the relative timing pattern. Observing the forward swing of the backhand shot, one sees the pattern of progressively increasing velocity between the upper arm and the racquet—created by the rapid extension of the shoulder, elbow, and wrist. This whip-like, slinging motion is one learners should be able to reproduce.

References:

Kozar, A., & Catignani, E. (1997). *Beginning racquetball.* Winston-Salem, NC: Hunter Textbooks.
Schmidt, R.A., & Wrisberg, C.A. (2000). *Motor learning and performance* (2nd ed.). Champaign, IL: Human Kinetics.

b. Throwing the javelin consists of two fundamental movements: running and throwing. The generally accepted method of carrying the javelin is to hold it in the palm of the hand with the second finger hooked slightly over the back of the grip and the elbow bent above the shoulder at eye level. The front point of the javelin is positioned slightly higher than the rear end, and the thrower's arm is relaxed. The length of the run is determined by the performer's ability to gain enough speed to prepare for the final throwing action. The thrower should gradually gain speed throughout the run. A check mark should be placed a sufficient distance from the foul line to allow the thrower to achieve critical momentum without stepping over the line. Normally a distance of 30 to 35 feet is needed for the last five steps (Cooper, Lavery, & Perrin, 1970).

As the thrower reaches the check mark, he moves the javelin back, straightens the arm out to the rear, and assumes a backward lean. As the right foot (for right-handed throwers) hits the check mark, the thrower points it straight ahead and then does the same with the left foot on the subsequent step. On the next two steps, the thrower places the feet at a 45-degree angle to the direction of movement. On the final two steps, the thrower places the right foot at a 90-degree angle to the direction of the run and the left foot at a 25-degree angle. The right knee is bent and the left knee is straightened to achieve sufficient backward lean and the braking of forward momentum. This enables the thrower to transfer momentum from the body to the javelin. The thrower's elbow leads the rest of the arm as the right hip is thrust forward and the elbow is pulled straight over the shoulder. The thrower releases the javelin at between a 45- and 50-degree angle in the direction of the run.

Observable features:

Indicate the perspective(s) from which the observer would be viewing the person modeling the skill or provide a figure to illustrate what the observer would be viewing:

1.

2.

Reference:

Cooper, J.M., Lavery, J., & Perrin, W. (1970). *Track and field for the coach and athlete* (2nd ed.). Englewood Cliffs, NJ: Prentice-Hall.

c. Juggling three beanbags involves two basic actions: the toss and the exchange. The juggler does the toss by standing in a relaxed position with the elbows near the body and hands at about waist height. The beanbag is cradled in the center of the hand (not on the fingers) and is tossed in an easy arc about as high as the eyes and as wide as the body. Initially, the learner should attempt to toss one bag back and forth in a natural scooping motion between the hands until some measure of control is achieved.

The two-bag exchange is performed by cradling one beanbag in each hand. The exchange begins by tossing one of the bags in the direction of the opposite hand. As the bag reaches the peak of its arc and begins to descend, the second bag is tossed (passing to the inside of the first bag) and the first is caught. If only one exchange is performed, the sequence would be as follows: toss, toss, catch, catch.

The three-bag exchange is performed the same way as the two-bag exchange except that it begins with two bags in one hand and one in the other. One of the bags in the hand with two bags is tossed and, as it reaches the peak of its arc and begins to descend, the bag in the opposite hand is tossed. The first bag is caught and, as the second bag reaches the peak of its arc and begins to descend, the other bag in the first hand is tossed. Depending on how many exchanges are performed, the sequence would be as follows: Toss, toss, catch, toss, catch, toss, catch, toss, and so forth (Cassidy & Rimbeaux, 1994).

Observable features:

Indicate the perspective(s) from which the observer would be viewing the person modeling the skill or provide a figure to illustrate what the observer would be viewing:

1.

2.

Reference:

Cassidy, J., & Rimbeaux, B.C. (1994). *Juggling for the complete klutz.* Palo Alto, CA: Klutz.

 Problem-Solving Exercises

In the following exercises you are challenged to demonstrate your comprehension of several important concepts presented in chapter 8 of the textbook. In Exercise 8.1 you are asked to discuss some ways a practitioner might open communication with a learner and familiarize the person with the learning environment. In Exercise 8.2 you are asked to provide a set of verbal instructions and a visual demonstration (using a photo or figure) that conveys the essential features of a target skill. In Exercise 8.3 you are asked to explain how the part practice of a task (i.e., fractionization, segmentation, simplification) might be used to promote whole task performance.

> ### Exercise 8.1
> ### Communicating With Learners and Familiarizing Them With the Learning Environment

It is important for practitioners to establish communication with learners and familiarize them with the learning environment before formal practice begins. Doing this, practitioners diminish learners' apprehensions about the instructional process and encourage them to communicate their feelings and needs more freely during the learning experience. Select a skill you are familiar with and explain how a practitioner might open two-way communication with a learner and familiarize the individual with the learning situation. Your solution should do the following:

- Describe the target skill, emphasizing the goal of the movement and basic actions required of the performer.

- Describe the learner, preferably someone inexperienced with the target skill (a hypothetical individual or someone you know).

- Describe how a practitioner might open two-way communication with the learner and then familiarize the individual with the learning situation.

Todd's Solution

The target skill, batting a softball, has as its goal hitting a pitched ball as forcefully as possible by timing the bat swing so that the bat head arrives in the hitting zone at the same time and in the same location as the approaching ball. The basic actions of batting are the stride and the swing (Reach & Schwartz, 1992). Before initiating the basic hitting action, however, the batter must assume a comfortable stance. The ingredients of an effective stance are stable posture, a slight knee bend, elbows bent and held away from the body, positioning the bat so that it does not contact the shoulder, head still, and eyes fixed on the ball.

The stride, which allows the batter to transfer weight from the rear foot to the front foot, begins when the pitcher releases the ball (Hubbard & Seng, 1954) and involves moving the front foot a short distance (4 to 6 inches) in the direction of the approaching ball.

The swing is initiated at about the same time the striding foot is planted. Although swing styles vary among individuals, all effective swings have these characteristics: shoulders level, bat held motionless prior to initiating the swing, hips rotated in the direction of the approaching ball, arms and hands extended at the moment of contact, and a full follow-through.

A 9-year-old female wants to learn to bat in the game of fast-pitch softball. Once she learns this task, the girl wants to try out for a local team that includes several of her friends. This learner participates in a few recreational activities (water skiing and ice skating) but has had no experience with ball skills of any kind.

Schmidt and Wrisberg (2000) discuss the importance of familiarizing learners with the learning environment and of opening communication before beginning formal practice. In this example, the practitioner is a 25-year-old female with extensive experience as a softball player and coach but with no previous knowledge of or contact with this learner.

To open communication, the practitioner might arrange an initial visit to the learner's home to learn the girl's feelings about softball and about her motivation. The home environment should be nonthreatening to the girl, and this setting would hopefully encourage her to express her interests and needs clearly. During this meeting, the practitioner could explain her approach to teaching and indicate her desire for feedback to help her assist the learner.

Based on her experience as a player, the practitioner knows that most individuals learning to bat fear being hit by the ball. Therefore, at the first formal practice session, the instructor might explain how she would try to modify instruction so that the learner not only acquires the basic batting movements but also becomes accustomed to responding to fast pitches without feeling threatened by them.

References:

Hubbard, A.W., & Seng, C.N. (1954). Visual movements of batters. *Research Quarterly*, 25, 42–57.

Reach, J., & Schwartz, B. (1992). *Softball everyone*. Winston-Salem, NC: Hunter Textbooks.

Schmidt, R.A., & Wrisberg, C.A. (2000). *Motor learning and performance* (2nd ed.). Champaign, IL: Human Kinetics.

Evaluation of Todd's Solution

Todd selects an appropriate task and adequately describes the goal of the movement and the basic actions required; he provides primary source documentation for his suggestion that the initiation of the stride should begin when the pitcher releases the ball. However, Todd might have talked about the role of vision in batting, since he later discusses the potential fear batters have of being hit by a pitched ball—a problem that is diminished by focused visual tracking of the ball.

Todd states that the learner is inexperienced with ball skills but does not indicate whether she has had experience with other types of eye-hand coordination activities (e.g., rope skipping, catching a Frisbee) that might be helpful to her in learning how to anticipate and respond to a moving object.

His answer is strong in discussing several ways the practitioner might open communication with the learner and familiarize her with one usually problematic aspect of batting (i.e., the possibility of being struck by a rapidly moving ball). Todd's suggestion that the practitioner arrange for an initial meeting at the learner's house has merit, but he *assumes* that the learner's home is a nonthreatening environment, which may or may not be the case.

What Todd doesn't mention is how the practitioner would know whether her instructional approach was appropriate for or acceptable to the learner. It is possible, for example, that the learner has no fear of being hit with the ball. For the practitioner to assume otherwise may cause her to schedule unnecessary lead-up activities that could actually delay the girl's learning. Thus, Todd should discuss some specific ways the practitioner might encourage and obtain feedback from the learner about the helpfulness of instructional assistance. Just because the practitioner requests feedback does not guarantee the learner will provide it.

Paul's Solution

The target skill is the box turn in the waltz (Harris, Pittman, & Waller, 1994). The goal of this skill is to execute an effective turn in either direction while waltzing. To achieve this goal, both partners must coordinate their dance steps effectively. I will be emphasizing the basic actions of the lead dancer when executing a box turn to the left.

The waltz is a smooth dance with an even pattern of swinging and turning movements. The dance is performed in 3/4 time to a 1-2-3 count. The first step of each 3-step sequence is made on the heel of the foot (flat); the second and third steps are made on the ball of the foot, causing the body to rise (lift). In executing a turn to the left, the lead dancer executes the following sequence:

Steps	3/4 Counts	Style Cue
Forward with L foot, toe out, 1/4 turn L	1	Flat
Sideward with R foot, gliding past L foot	2	Lift
Close L to R, taking weight on L foot	3	Lift
Backward with R foot, toe in, 1/4 turn L	1	Flat
Sideward with L foot, gliding past R foot	2	Lift
Close R to L, taking weight on R foot	3	Lift
Forward with L foot, toe out, 1/4 turn L	1	Flat
Sideward with R foot, gliding past L foot	2	Lift
Close L to R, taking weight on L foot	3	Lift
Backward with R foot, toe in, 1/4 turn L	1	Flat
Sideward with L foot, gliding past R foot	2	Lift
Close R to L, taking weight on R foot	3	Lift

As you can see, the first and third 3-step sequences are identical, as are the second and fourth 3-step sequences. Ideally, the feet should make little or no sound but should seem to float in a silent pattern. In the start position, the partners stand directly in front of each other with their shoulders parallel. As the lead dancer executes the sequence, the partner executes the reverse pattern, except that when the partner steps forward with the left foot, instead of toeing out, she steps between the lead dancer's feet so that her left foot is next to the lead dancer's left instep.

The learner in this example is a 75-year-old male who wants to waltz at the Friday night social gatherings in a local community center. As a young man, he was a gifted athlete, and he is still physically fit for his age. However, the man becomes impatient when he is unable to perform any activity at a high level. He is also quite proud and does not take criticism well. The man wishes he could learn the box turn without instructional assistance but realizes that that is not going to happen.

The dance instructor is a 35-year-old female who teaches aerobics and social dance at the community center. She knows the man by name and reputation but until now has had no direct contact with him. The man telephones her to schedule a lesson and they meet at the community center. When the man arrives, the instructor asks him about his learning goals. He replies that he knows the basic waltz steps but wants to learn the turns so he won't embarrass himself at the Friday night socials. Because the man is a prominent figure at the community center, the instructor assumes that he doesn't need to be familiarized with the facility. To determine his current dancing skill, the instructor asks him to dance a simple waltz step with her. He consents and so the two of them dance a slow waltz together.

Now the instructor feels that the man is ready to begin the formal learning process. The instructor starts him out slowly, introducing only a small amount of information at a time. If the man has difficulty producing a movement sequence, the instructor encourages him to keep trying until he performs it correctly. If the man starts to get frustrated, the instructor tells him to take a break. Sometimes the instructor decides to end the lesson if she thinks the learner is getting too upset with his performance. By continually paying attention to the man's reactions to her instruction, the practitioner is able to modify her approach whenever she feels it is necessary.

Reference:

Harris, J.A., Pittman, A.M., & Waller, M.S. (1994). *Dance a while* (7th ed.). New York: Macmillan.

Evaluation of Paul's Solution

Paul offers a thorough explanation of the sequence of basic steps for dancing the lead and appropriately documents this, but a figure usually helps in explaining dance-step sequences. Paul's description of the partner's movements gets tedious, and he could have omitted it since he does not address them in his solution.

The description of the learner has interesting background information that could help an instructor. Paul says less about the practitioner but does indicate that she is an experienced teacher of aerobics and social dance.

Unfortunately, Paul does not document his discussion of the instructional approach taken by the practitioner and he says too little about the way the practitioner attempts to open communication with the learner. Although he states that the practitioner asks the learner about his goals and to demonstrate his waltzing skills, Paul fails to mention the nature of the information obtained from the learner's responses or skill demonstration. So we don't know how the practitioner might use this information for instructional assistance.

Paul says the instructor proceeds based, apparently, on her observations. She assumes the learner needs no familiarization with the instructional setting but that he needs to be encouraged to keep trying when he makes a mistake. She assumes the man should be introduced to the box turn very gradually, that he should be told to take a break when he is frustrated, and that he should cease practicing altogether when he becomes too upset with his performance. At no time does the instructor attempt to solicit input from the learner about how he would prefer to be assisted. In Paul's solution, communication is essentially a one-way street (i.e., teacher to student). But given Paul's description of the learner, this individual has a high need to feel in control of things. If this is the case, the man might be expected to respond with some resistance to an authoritarian instructional approach such as Paul's practitioner seems to have taken.

Your Solution to Exercise 8.1

Communicating With Learners and Familiarizing Them With the Learning Environment

NAME_____ DATE_____

1. Definition of problem:
2. Instructional situation:
   Teaching   Coaching   Rehabilitation   Human factors
3. Description of the skill:
   Goal of the movement:
   Basic actions required:
4. Description of the learner:
5. How can the practitioner open communication and familiarize the learner with the learning environment?
6. References:

Exercise 8.2

Providing Instructions and Demonstrations That Convey the Essential Features of a Target Skill

Once learners have been familiarized with the learning environment, they want some general idea of the basic requirements of the target skill. Two techniques that practitioners can use to convey essential task information are verbal instructions and visual demonstrations. Here you are to describe a set of verbal instructions and provide a visual demonstration (using photos or figures) that contains the kinds of information a learner could use to begin practicing the target skill. Your solution to this exercise should do the following:

- Describe the target skill, emphasizing the goal of the movement and basic actions required of the performer.
- Describe the learner, preferably an individual inexperienced with the target skill (a hypothetical person or someone you know).
- Formulate a set of verbal instructions emphasizing two essential features of the target skill.
- Provide an illustration of the target skill (using photos or figures) that conveys two of its essential features.

Allen's Solution

The lofted drive is a pass that players can use to project the ball long distances over the heads of opponents. As in many other types of soccer passes, the lofted drive is accomplished by striking the ball with the instep of the foot surface.

The basic actions of the lofted drive include keeping the eyes on the ball and the head steady, approaching the ball from an angle, keeping the nonkicking or planting foot behind the ball, striking the ball as low on its surface as possible, keeping the foot extended and the ankle locked throughout the kick, and following through with the kicking leg after contacting the ball (Pronk & Gorman, 1985).

The learner is a 12-year-old male who knows the basic soccer kicks but wants to add the lofted drive to his repertoire. The boy has played organized soccer for 5 years and hopes one day to play for the varsity soccer team at his high school.

In assisting this learner, I give him these verbal instructions: "The keys to performing the lofted drive are to approach the ball from an angle; aim for a spot that is on the lower half of the ball; and keep your knee bent, your foot extended, and your ankle locked throughout the kick." These instructions emphasize several essential elements of the task: the angle of approach, the intended point of contact on the ball, and the firmness of the kicking leg.

I would demonstrate the skill, doing a sequence that looks something like the one in this series of drawings:

Reprinted, by permission, from J.A. Luxbacher, 1991, *Soccer: Steps to success* (Champaign, IL: Human Kinetics), 27–29.

By observing this demonstration, the learner should be able to notice the following essential elements of the lofted drive: the angle of approach, the location of the plant foot, the fixation of the head and eyes on the ball, the extended foot and locked ankle, and the low to high trajectory of the bent leg.

Reference:

Pronk, N., & Gorman, B. (1985). *Soccer everyone.* Winston-Salem, NC: Hunter Textbooks.

Evaluation of Allen's Solution

Allen explains the goal of the target skill and provides a rather thorough description (with appropriate documentation) of the basic actions involved. He offers plausible suggestions for instructions and a nice visual sequence to illustrate the basic actions. Allen could have described the learner in more detail but he does suggest that the boy is capable of learning the lofted drive kick.

The primary deficiency of Allen's solution is that his only source of documentation is a standard soccer text. Such a book is certainly appropriate for documenting the basic actions of the lofted drive, compiling a possible list of instructions, and obtaining a sequence of drawings to illustrate the action sequence. But Allen has not discussed and documented the principles in the motor learning literature that address factors that instructors need to consider. Allen's solution is also quite repetitive. He essentially says the same thing when describing the skill, reciting the instructions, and discussing the demonstration.

The instructions Allen provides contain several of the essential elements of the lofted drive, but he does not give any theoretical rationale for his choice of elements. Does Allen feel that these elements are the most important ones for skill learning? Does he think they are the simplest for a beginner to grasp? Does he believe these elements are the ones that should be introduced *first* when teaching this skill? If so, why?

Allen assumes that the learner in this scenario can detect the essential features with little difficulty. What if this 12-year-old boy is not able to detect the essential features? Should the practitioner present the demonstration again? Direct the learner's attention to certain elements of the demonstration? Allow the boy to discover the relevant features on his own? If Allen had consulted the motor learning literature when compiling his solution, he might have anticipated some of these questions and identified some sound principles for addressing them.

Martina's Solution

The target skill, the backhand drive shot in table tennis, is aimed at hitting the ball over the net and as deep as possible to the opponent's side of the table. Ideally, the player should be able to hit the backhand drive to a variety of locations, using top-spin or underspin. The basic actions of the backhand drive include a lateral rotation of the shoulder, a supination of the forearm, and a slight extension of the wrist. The player must watch the ball carefully to estimate its speed, spin, and trajectory. By accurately anticipating these characteristics of ball flight, the player should be better able to determine the appropriate moment of response execution (Schmidt & Wrisberg, 2000).

The learner in this scenario is a 15-year-old male who has lost functional finger flexion due to nerve damage sustained in a cycling accident. Since the individual is unable to grasp the handle of the table tennis paddle, a device must be attached to the back of the handle that allows the paddle to be secured to his hand. When securely fastened, the paddle enables the performer to strike the ball by using a backhand motion (Adams & McCubbin, 1991). The learner in this scenario is physically fit, has no other physical or mental impairments, and has had previous experience in a variety of sport skills including other racket sports (badminton and tennis).

These are possible verbal instructions for this learner: watch the ball, orient the face of the paddle in the direction you want the ball to go, try to hit the ball when it reaches its highest point after the bounce, and follow through in the direction of the target. The essential features of the backhand drive in these instructions include watching the ball to obtain information about its flight characteristics, adjusting the face of the paddle to achieve the desired direction of ball flight, identifying the optimal point of contact, and moving the paddle in the direction of the intended target. Landin (1994) suggests that instructions can sometimes be condensed into simple verbal cues that alert learners to the things they should try to do when performing the desired movement. Verbal cues that illustrate the essential features of the backhand drive might be "Ball, paddle face, peak, and finish."

An initial demonstration of the backhand drive for this learner should probably emphasize the modified stroke technique necessitated by using the strap-on paddle.

References:

Adams, R.C., & McCubbin, J.A. (1991). *Games, sports, and exercises for the physically disabled* (4th ed.). Philadelphia: Lea & Febiger.
Landin, D. (1994). The role of verbal cues in skill learning. *Quest, 46*, 299–313.
Schmidt, R.A., & Wrisberg, C.A. (2000). *Motor learning and performance* (2nd ed.). Champaign, IL: Human Kinetics.

Evaluation of Martina's Solution

Martina provides a concise, technical or biomechanical explanation of the basic actions. Some readers might appreciate a less-technical explanation or at least more discussion of the basic movements involved. Martina should add documentation for the sources she uses in compiling her description of the task, but does at least document her comment about the relationship between effective anticipation and response execution. However, a more extensive discussion of the relationship would help, and she should clarify how the supporting reference (i.e., Schmidt & Wrisberg, 2000) supports the point she is trying to make.

Martina's description of the learner and explanation (with documentation) of the strap-on device used to secure the table tennis paddle to the learner's hand are thorough and helpful. Martina offers verbal instructions but she does not indicate where they came from. She does, however, suggest several examples of verbal cues that might be condensed from the instructions, and she documents her remarks with a paper by Landin (1994). Martina correctly points out that simply worded verbal cues can serve as helpful reminders to help learners keep focused when performing their movements.

Martina emphasizes the importance of the strap-on paddle. Specifically, she notes several aspects of the performer's backhand drive that are evident when this device is being used and points out that the practitioner may need to direct the learner's attention to the less-obvious essential features to assure more immediate detection. Unfortunately, Martina provides no figure to illustrate the modified technique. A good illustration would include a parallel series of photos depicting differences in the entire actions of performers under the two types of paddle conditions. Given what we know about the importance of relative timing in the generalized motor program, it might be interesting to see how the relative timing pattern of the backhand drive differs for the two types of paddle conditions (i.e., standard grip and strap on).

Your Solution to Exercise 8.2

Providing Instructions and Demonstrations That Convey the Essential Features of a Target Skill

NAME_____ DATE_____

1. Definition of problem:
2. Instructional situation:
   Teaching   Coaching   Rehabilitation   Human factors
3. Description of the skill
   Goal of the movement:
   Basic actions required:
4. Description of the learner:
5. Verbal instructions that emphasize two essential features of the target skill
   Instructions:
   Essential features:
      1.
      2.
6. Illustration of the target skill (photos or figures) that conveys the two essential features
   Photos or figures:
   Essential features:
      1.
      2.
7. References:

Exercise 8.3

Using Part Practice to Facilitate Transfer to Whole Task Performance

Sometimes learners must initially practice a simplified version or a part of the target skill because the whole task is too complex or dangerous for them to practice in its entirety. In chapter 8 of our book, Dick and I discuss three types of part practice—fractionization, segmentation, and simplification—that have the potential to facilitate transfer to performance of the whole task.

In this exercise I want you to consider a learning situation for which part practice of a target skill might be necessary or helpful for a learner. Your solution to this exercise should include the following information:

- A brief description of the target skill, giving particular emphasis to the goal of the movement and the basic actions required of the performer that make part practice a necessary or viable option.

- A brief description of the learner (this may be a hypothetical individual or someone you actually know).

- A description of the type(s) of part practice that would be appropriate for the target skill and learner in question.

Abby's Solution

When someone drives a standard transmission automobile, the goal is to manipulate the steering wheel, gear shift, clutch pedal, accelerator, and brake pedal in a coordinated fashion. Skilled drivers are able to perform various combinations of these tasks smoothly and effectively, maintaining control of the vehicle and achieving safe operation under all types of driving conditions.

The basic actions of operating a standard transmission vehicle are not complex, but each must be performed smoothly and accurately. The driver manipulates the steering wheel and gear shift by positioning movements of the hands. He or she depresses and releases the accelerator, clutch, and brake pedals by flexing and extending the ankles and knees.

Driving a standard transmission automobile initially requires some form of part practice because of the sheer number of tasks the driver must learn. A particularly difficult task for most beginners is coordinating the clutch and accelerator movements. Therefore, these movements are particularly good candidates for part practice.

The learner is a 15-year-old female who wants to learn how to drive a standard transmission car in order to successfully pass the driving test required for an operator's license. She has no handicapping conditions, but is not physically active and has had little or no previous experience with sports and physical activities requiring coordinated movements.

The type of part practice I would suggest for this learner is a combination of fractionization and segmentation (Wightman & Lintern, 1985). *Fractionization* is a type of part practice in which two or more parts of a complex skill are practiced separately. *Segmentation* is a type of part practice in which one part is practiced until it is learned, then another part is added to the first part and the two are practiced together, and so on, until the entire skill is practiced (Schmidt & Wrisberg, 2000).

One type of fractionized practice would involve rehearsing the accelerator and clutch movements to achieve the correct balance of pressure that results in smooth acceleration. This activity should be practiced in a large, level area (e.g., a parking lot) where there are no other moving vehicles in the vicinity. The learner initially performs the task with the gear shift positioned in first or low gear. The driver depresses and holds down the clutch pedal and then turns on the engine. Once the engine is idling smoothly, the driver slowly releases the clutch pedal with the left foot and depresses the accelerator pedal with the right foot until the car begins to move forward. At this point, the driver depresses the brake pedal and the clutch until the vehicle comes to a complete stop with the engine idling. The driver repeats this sequence until she is able to coordinate clutch and accelerator movements and achieve consistently smooth acceleration.

Once the driver is able to smoothly accelerate the vehicle in first gear, she can try several types of segmented rehearsal. For example, the driver might accelerate the car until it reaches the upper boundaries of first gear, then depress the clutch, release the accelerator, and move the gear shift into second gear. At this point, the driver can depress the brake and slowly bring the car to a stop. She has added only one gear shift movement to the original fractionized exercise. After several repetitions of this task, the driver might decide to accelerate the car after she shifts into second gear. Any time she wants to return to the original condition, she simply depresses the brake and the clutch until the vehicle comes to a stop. The learner can gradually build more actions into the shifting sequence until she learns to smoothly accelerate the vehicle from one gear to another. Once the shifting process is fairly automated, the learner can operate the vehicle over longer distances and add steering movements.

References:

Schmidt, R.A., & Wrisberg, C.A. (2000). *Motor learning and performance* (2nd ed.). Champaign, IL: Human Kinetics.

Wightman, D.C., & Lintern, G. (1985). Part-task training strategies for tracking and manual control. *Human Factors, 27*, 267–283.

Evaluation of Abby's Solution

Abby explains the goal of the skill well enough, but her description of the basic actions is a bit simple and could use beefing up. The rationale for selecting the task of driving for this exercise is apparently based on the sheer number of components the learner must master, as well as on the difficulty of mastering the timing of accelerator and clutch movements. Abby should discuss some relevant *principles of motor performance* (e.g., limitations in people's capacity to attend to multiple sources of information or to hold a number of things in short-term memory at one time).

Abby mentions that the learner has had little experience with sport skills or other types of motor activity but doesn't explain the implications of this lack of experience for a person who is learning how to drive.

The best part of Abby's solution is her proposed types of part practice. Citing the work of Wightman and Lintern (1985), Abby describes two different forms of part practice that seem quite appropriate for an individual trying to learn to operate a standard transmission vehicle. Using the first type of part practice, fractionization, Abby shows how the learner repeatedly goes through the sequence of manipulating the clutch and accelerator pedals (keeping the vehicle in first gear) to achieve the necessary feel of smooth coordination between the two. The second type of part practice, segmentation, involves the gradual addition of other driving components (e.g., shifting gears, steering) once the learner achieves sufficient skill in coordinating accelerator and clutch movements.

Larry's Solution

The target skill I have chosen for this exercise is the flip turn that swimmers use to reverse the direction of movement. In particular I have decided to focus on the flip turn used in the backstroke. The goal of the flip turn in a competitive situation is to reverse the direction the performer is swimming in as short a time as possible. Because the flip turn comprises a sequence of several motions, it may be too difficult for some learners to practice in its entirety.

The sequence of motions used in the backstroke flip turn is shown in the figure on the next page. The swimmer starts the flip turn one stroke from the wall by turning the head and looking toward the pulling arm as it begins the catch (*a*). As the swimmer executes the pull, he rotates onto the stomach and drives the head downward (*b*). As the pulling hand stops at the hip, the other arm enters the water in the same position as in the front crawl and is pulled to the hips. The swimmer then drives the head downward, tucks the knees tightly into the chest, and begins the somersault. Both palms are immediately turned toward the body and swept toward the head to complete the flip (*c*). The swimmer keeps the legs tucked until the feet contact the wall with the toes pointed upward. While still on the back, the swimmer forcefully pushes straight off the wall (*d*) and assumes a streamlined position.

The learner in this situation is a 10-year-old male who has been swimming the backstroke for two years. In order to prepare for competition, the boy wants to learn the flip turn so that he can minimize his times in the 200-meter backstroke. The boy's coach tells him that, if properly done, flip turns can improve his time by as much as 1/2 second per turn.

Schmidt and Wrisberg (2000, chapter 8) discuss several types of part practice that might be used for tasks that are too complex to be practiced in their entirety, at least

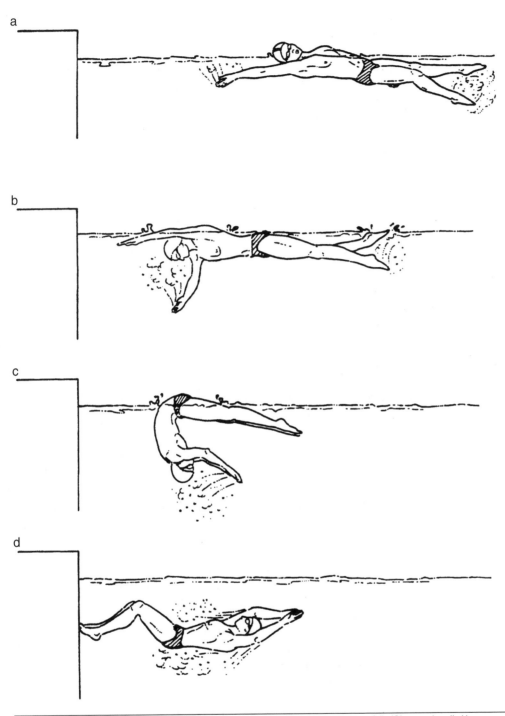

Reprinted, by permission, from D. Hannula, 1995, *Coaching swimming successfully* (Champaign, IL: Human Kinetics), 86.

initially. They point out that part practice is especially effective for serial tasks where the actions (or errors) in one part do not influence the actions involved in the next (e.g., the baton pass in relay races). In one sense, the flip turn might be viewed as one component in a serial skill that does not influence subsequent actions (i.e., the swimming stroke). Thus, the flip turn appears to be a good candidate for fractionized practice. However, it also appears that caution should be exercised if the flip turn is broken down for practice. As Schmidt and Wrisberg (2000) point out, part practice is not recommended if the dynamics of a part of an action are different when practiced in isolation than when performed in the context of the entire action.

With these principles in mind, I believe that two components of the flip turn could be fractionized for practice (Wightman & Lintern, 1985). Practice of these components should simplify the learner's task, preserve the dynamics of each part, and facilitate eventual transfer of the parts to the performance of the entire target skill. The learner could practice the flip itself by rehearsing only components *b through d*, since they appear to be dynamically related. The swimmer begins by approaching the wall using the basic freestyle stroke (*b*). As he nears the wall, the swimmer drives the head downward and tucks the knees to the chest (*c*), completing the flip with the feet against the wall (*d*). With sufficient repetition of this component, the swimmer should be able to perform the flip as one single action. Once he achieves this goal, the swimmer could fractionize practice of the other major component of the flip turn: the transition from the backstroke to the freestyle stroke in preparation for the flip (i.e., step *a* to *b* in the figure). As in the case of the flip component, the parts of this component also appear to be dynamically related. When the swimmer masters the transition component, he should be ready to combine it with the flip component and perhaps even add the push-off. Hopefully, the swimmer will notice that the dynamics of the components are basically the same under whole-task conditions as when practiced separately.

References:

Schmidt, R.A., & Wrisberg, C.A. (2000). *Motor learning and performance* (2nd ed.). Champaign, IL: Human Kinetics.

Wightman, D.C., & Lintern, G. (1985). Part-task training strategies for tracking and manual control. *Human Factors, 27,* 267–283.

Evaluation of Larry's Solution

Larry provides a clear goal statement and suggests that the flip turn consists of a sufficient number of components to make it a good candidate for part practice. However, Larry mentions nothing about the number of components that might be considered "sufficient" for part practice or about the limited capacity of humans for processing information.

Larry provides an excellent description (with appropriate documentation) of the basic actions of the backstroke and includes a sequence of figures that illustrate the serial components of the task. This combination of verbal description and visual illustration make understanding a rather complex target skill much easier.

Larry's description of the learner is rather brief. He goes on to explain (with appropriate documentation) that part practice is particularly beneficial for serial skills with several separate components. He further mentions that the components of a sequence of actions are particularly conducive to part practice when they are not highly dependent on each other (i.e., when errors in one component do not influence performance of another component). Further, he suggests that though the flip turn is a good candidate for fractionized practice, some of its actions should be kept together to preserve the dynamics of the component. While Larry documents this comment with a supporting reference, he might have said a bit more about the concept of movement dynamics and its importance to the part practice of tasks.

Larry suggests two aspects of the target skill (i.e., the flip and the transition from backstroke to freestyle stroke immediately before the flip) that might be practiced in isolation. However, he might have discussed how the two components are relatively independent of each other and how part practice preserves the dynamics of each component. A more detailed theoretical discussion of these issues, with supporting literature, would strengthen the presentation. Larry suggests that once the swimmer has automated performance of each component, he integrates them for whole-task practice. This would have been a good place for Larry to also mention (with a supporting reference) that the processing demands of movements diminish over practice, allowing performers to produce progressively longer sequences of actions.

Your Solution to Exercise 8.3

Using Part Practice to Facilitate Transfer to Whole Task Performance

NAME_____ DATE_____

1. Definition of problem:
2. Instructional situation:
   Teaching   Coaching   Rehabilitation   Human factors
3. Description of the target skill
   Goal of the movement:
   Basic actions required:
4. Aspect(s) of the skill that make part practice necessary or viable:
5. Description of the learner:
6. Type(s) of part practice appropriate for the target skill and learner in question:

Structuring the Learning Experience

The target skill involves decisions about where to hit the ball, which club to use, how to adjust the stance depending on the slope of the ground, and how far to take the backswing back.

© Greg Voight/International Stock

◀◀◆ Key Concepts

Effective practice structures facilitate a learner's capacity to perform the target skill in the target context. To help learners achieve their goals, practitioners structure practice sessions that maximize the *quality* of learning experiences; chapter 9 of the textbook explains some of the ways they can do this.

Sometimes individuals need to learn several component tasks of a particular sport or activity (e.g., tennis ground strokes, volleys, and serves). One practice structure that has proved beneficial in this type of situation is *random practice.* During random practice, learners perform several different tasks in a mixed or random order. Compared with a blocked-practice structure, involving the repeated performance of one task before moving to another, random practice promotes superior skill retention and transfer to the target context. This is particularly so when the target context calls for a random order of task performance (e.g., a tennis serve might be followed by a ground stroke and then a volley). Movement scientists believe that random practice is effective because it requires performers to generate movement solutions more frequently and increases the meaningfulness of movement representations. Learners sometimes object to random practice because performance does not improve as immediately in this context as it does in a blocked format. Therefore, an instructor may have to encourage learners to be patient and remind them that the rewards of random practice are often realized later on, when individuals are required to perform skills in the target context.

In other situations people want to learn a single motor skill that they can adapt to meet the environmental demands of different situations (e.g., the basic golf swing can be adapted for hitting tee shots, sand shots, and chip shots). For tasks like this, a practice structure that includes the performance of a number of movement variations is more effective than one that calls for the repetition of a single variation. In the motor learning literature, the former type of practice is referred to as *varied* (or *variable) practice*, while the latter type is labeled *constant practice.* The primary benefit of varied practice is the development or strengthening of the generalized motor program (discussed in chapters 5 and 6 of the text). By practicing variations of a basic movement pattern, learners develop the capability of adjusting the parameters of the generalized program (e.g., force, movement time) to achieve different outcome goals (e.g., hitting a tee shot that requires more force or a chip shot that requires less).

Random practice involves the practice of several *different* tasks, whereas *varied practice* involves the practice of several versions of the *same* task. Depending on the learner's goals and the eventual target context, practitioners may want to provide various combinations of random, varied, and constant or blocked practice when assisting learners. Say that someone is trying to learn the different shots of tennis, for example. Her instructor might structure the practice in both a random and varied format, including the rehearsal of ground strokes, volleys, and serves in a mixed order (random practice) and the production of different levels of force each time a shot is produced (varied practice).

Occasionally individuals must learn to produce rapid responses to various types of environmental stimuli. In consistent *stimulus-response mapping situations* the performer responds to a given stimulus with the same action each time, whereas in *varied-mapping situations* the individual might produce any of several different responses. For example, a cricket player typically responds to a batted ball by fielding it (consistent mapping), but a hockey goalie could respond to a shot on goal by blocking it, deflecting it to a teammate, or catching it (varied mapping). Not surprisingly, automatic processing (see chapter 3) is much easier to develop in situations that involve the consistent mapping of stimuli and responses than in those involving varied mapping.

Key Terms

To answer the questions and complete the exercises in this chapter you need a basic understanding of the following terms or concepts:

blocked practice
random practice
varied practice
constant practice
generalized motor program
schema development
invariant features
relative timing
parameters
parameterization
parameter values
target skill
target context
consistent stimulus-response mapping
varied stimulus-response mapping
automatic responding

Review Questions

Answer each of the following questions and *provide rationale for your answers*. If you are not familiar with the skill or activity in a particular scenario, you may discuss it with an expert or consult a book or training manual that contains more detailed information.

1. The results of motor learning research on practice structure generally suggest that the retention and transfer of skills is better when practice is structured in a random fashion than when it takes place in a blocked format (Schmidt & Wrisberg, 2000, chapter 9). However, there is also evidence that some types of learners (e.g., children and physically or mentally challenged individuals) and the performance of some types of tasks (e.g., complex coordination activities) may benefit more from some limited amount of practice repetition (i.e., blocked practice), at least during initial skill rehearsal. The first of the following scenarios has an example (with supporting rationale) of how random practice and blocked practice might be effectively used for a given hypothetical learner and learning task. You propose an example of an appropriate use of each type of practice structure (with supporting rationale) for the remaining scenarios.

    a. Scenario: Preparing for a biathlon competition.

Hypothetical learner:

A 28-year-old man wants to learn how to cross-country ski and shoot a rifle so that he can participate in an annual biathlon competition. He is physically fit and has competed in numerous triathlon events (i.e., swimming, cycling, running) over the past 5 years.

Learning tasks:

The biathlon is a winter sport that combines cross-country skiing and rifle shooting. Participants must ski distances of 10, 15, or 20 kilometers and fire the rifle from both prone and standing positions at targets 150 meters away. The targets are pairs of concentric circles that are smaller in diameter for the prone position (12.5 and 25 centimeters) than for the standing position (35 and 45 centimeters). Biathlon competitors follow a course that is marked by flags, stopping to shoot at designated firing points. When the participant arrives at a firing point, he loads the rifle with five rounds and then fires in his own time, with skis either on or off. The first and third shoots are from a prone position, and the second and fourth shoots are from a standing position. A person's score is the elapsed time from start to finish plus penalty minutes (e.g., 1-minute penalties for hits in the outer circle, 2-minute penalties for complete misses, assorted penalties for violations such as taking shortcuts and carrying a loaded rifle). Between firing points the biathlete must ski a distance of at least 3 kilometers (The Diagram Group, 1974).

Suggested random-practice structure:

Since the biathlon requires a combination of tasks—skiing, prone shooting, and standing shooting—a random-practice structure might combine intermittent bouts of each activity. For example, the performer might ski a short, designated distance (e.g., 100 meters), load and fire one round from the prone position, ski a short designated distance (e.g., 50 meters), load and fire one round from the standing position, and so forth. In this way, the performer would be practicing the retrieval of the appropriate program (Bjork, 1979) for each of the different tasks.

Suggested blocked-practice structure:

Since biathletes must also fire multiple rounds at each firing point, a blocked-practice structure might involve intermittent bouts of blocked firing from the prone and standing positions. For example, the performer might ski a short distance, load and fire five rounds from the prone position with the skis on, ski a short distance, load and fire five rounds from the standing position with the skis off, and so forth. Blocks of five rounds could be repeated in this manner until the performer achieves five consecutive hits within the larger target area at one of the firing points. As the performer's skill level improves, the standard of acceptable performance could be progressively increased (e.g., two consecutive rounds of five hits). In this way, the learner would be experiencing bouts of blocked practice that conform to the demands of the biathlon event (i.e., the target context) and that encourage improvements in performance.

References:

Bjork, R.A. (1979). *Retrieval practice.* Unpublished manuscript, University of California, Los Angeles.

The Diagram Group. (1974). *Rules of the game.* New York: Paddington Press Ltd.

     b. Scenario: Learning to play Australian-rules football.

Hypothetical learner:

A 22-year-old male wants to learn to play Australian-rules football so that he can participate on a team at the club level. The learner is in excellent physical condition and has had numerous experiences in a variety of sports and recreational activities.

Learning tasks:

Australian football is played on a large oval pitch by two opposing teams of 18 players each. The primary tasks include running with, passing, kicking, and receiving the ball by catching a pass or by picking the ball up after it bounces on the ground. When a player runs with the ball, he must bounce it on the ground or touch it to the ground at least once every 10 meters. He must pass the ball with a punching action that involves holding the ball in one hand and striking it with the other in order to propel it toward a teammate. To perform a kick, he drops the ball and contacts it with the foot before it strikes the ground (The Diagram Group, 1974).

Suggested random-practice structure:

Suggested blocked-practice structure:

Reference:

The Diagram Group (1974). *Rules of the game.* New York: Paddington Press Ltd.

c. Scenario: The recovery of feeding skills by a stroke patient.

Hypothetical learner:

The learner is a 51-year-old female who suffers from left hemiparesis (i.e., partial paralysis of the left side of the body) as a result of a stroke that affects the right side of her brain (Adams & McCubbin, 1991). She tends to have difficulty performing spatial-perceptual tasks and using visual cues to plan and control her movements. The learner has recovered the basic function of her legs and can perform most types of gross motor skills (e.g., walking, jumping). She is now ready to practice fine motor skills and is particularly motivated to recover the control of feeding movements.

Learning tasks:

The skills of feeding include using a spoon to transfer soup from a bowl to the open mouth, a knife and fork to cut food and transport it to the mouth, and the left hand to drink from a cup.

Suggested random-practice structure:

Suggested blocked-practice structure:

Reference:

Adams, R.C., & McCubbin, J.A. (1991). *Games, sports, and exercises for the physically disabled* (4th ed.). Philadelphia: Lea & Febiger.

d. Scenario: Learning to play tennis.

Hypothetical learner:

A 21-year-old female wants to learn tennis so that she can join a beginner's league with several friends. The woman has had previous experience with recreational and sport activities, some of which involves the anticipation and timing of moving objects (e.g., volleyball and softball). She appears to possess adequate physical fitness and is highly motivated.

Learning tasks:

The essential skills for a beginning tennis player are forehand and backhand ground strokes and the flat serve. Players perform ground strokes to return an opponent's shots. For both forehand and backhand shots, the player draws the racket back early, turns the body to point the front hip and shoulder toward the net, steps toward the target, shifts the weight forward, keeps the wrist firm, swings through the ball, and finishes with the racket pointing toward the target. To perform the flat serve she tosses the ball with one hand and hits it with the other. To hit an effective serve, the player extends the tossing arm upward and forward, releases the ball gently by opening the hand and letting the ball out, keeps the eyes on the ball, reaches high to hit the ball at the top of its arc, and follows through by swinging the racket out, down, and across the body (Brown, 1995).

Suggested random-practice structure:

Suggested blocked-practice structure:

Reference:

Brown, J. (1995). *Tennis: Steps to success* (2nd ed.). Champaign, IL: Human Kinetics.

2. Humans likely control many of their skilled movements with generalized motor programs that they can adapt to meet the demands of different situations. For example, a golfer might use the same generalized motor program to produce a variety of shots. The golfer does this by adjusting several parameter values (e.g., force, swing trajectory, swing plane) that allow her to produce variations of the swing and cause the ball to travel different distances with different trajectories and spins. As chapter 9 discusses, varied practice of a skill enhances the development of the generalized motor program and improves the performer's capacity to produce variations of the program. Look again at the sets of learning activities in the previous question and see if you can identify one example from each set of skills that a learner might practice in a varied format. An example (from the first scenario in the previous question) starts you off by giving varied practice of the task of shooting from the prone position. You are to suggest a possible use of varied practice for one of the activities in each of the other scenarios.

a. The skills of the biathlon.

Suggested varied-practice structure for shooting from the prone position:

The requirements of prone-position shooting are tailor-made for varied practice. Each time the biathlete arrives at a shooting point, he is required to fire one round at each of five different targets.

This requirement presents a form of inherent varied practice. However, more extensive varied practice of prone shooting might be structured by displaying additional target locations for the learner to shoot at.

According to Schmidt and Wrisberg (2000, chapter 9), schema development is enhanced when individuals practice a wider variety of movements from the same movement class (in this case, prone shooting). Therefore, by the learner's shooting at a wider variety of targets in practice than is required for the biathlon event, he should develop a stronger set of rules (i.e., schema) for relating any specific desired outcome to the parameter values. That is, if the desired outcome is hitting one of the targets biathletes are required to shoot at, he can relate it to the parameter value of pointing or aiming needed to produce that outcome.

Reference:

Schmidt, R.A., & Wrisberg, C.A. (2000). *Motor learning and performance* (2nd ed.). Champaign, IL: Human Kinetics.

b. The skills of Australian rules football.

Suggested varied-practice structure for [give skill] _____:

References:

c. Feeding skills.

Suggested varied-practice structure for _____:

References:

d. The skills of beginning tennis.

Suggested varied-practice structure for _____:

References:

3. Performing some skills requires individuals to produce rapid responses to various types of environmental cues or stimuli. In some cases a specific stimulus calls for a particular response (i.e., consistent stimulus-response mapping); in others, a given stimulus might be responded to in one of several different ways (i.e., varied stimulus-response mapping). Practitioners can assist people in learning these types of skills by helping them identify stimulus-response situations that are characterized by consistent mapping and then creating practice opportunities for them to quickly recognize the stimulus and produce the most appropriate response. With sufficient practice of consistent stimulus-response mapping, the learner-performer begins to respond more automatically to the stimulus, a phenomenon that has been called "automatic processing" (Shiffrin & Schneider, 1977). For the first activity in this exercise, the movement activity is first described and possible examples of consistent stimulus-response mapping situations are provided (along with supporting rationale), followed by a suggested practice structure that might allow learners to develop automatic responding to stimuli. For the remaining activities, one or more consistent stimulus-response mapping situations are provided that practitioners might alert learners to. Your task is to select one situation and suggest a practice structure of consistent mapping that might help the learner recognize the stimulus and produce the most appropriate response.

Reference:

Shiffrin, R.M., & Schneider, W. (1977). Controlled and automatic human information processing: II. Perceptual learning, automatic attending, and a general theory. *Psychological Review*, 84, 127–190.

a. Playing infield defense in baseball.

Possible consistent-mapping situation(s):

An infielder in baseball must respond quickly to a variety of stimuli coming from a batter's movements. Often the infielder must wait until the ball is contacted and then merely react to it. Sometimes, however, the infielder can watch for a batter's preparatory movements and quicken his responses to the batted ball. A coach can encourage infielders to watch for two cues that occur immediately after the pitcher releases the ball. One is the preparatory movement of the batter's shifting feet to position the body to propel the ball in a particular direction. The other movement cue is the batter's sliding of the top hand up the bat to prepare to bunt (Delmonico, 1992).

Introducing consistent stimulus-response mapping practice:

During batting practice each player is instructed to bunt two or three pitches and then is given the opportunity to hit a designated number (e.g., 15 to 20) of pitches using a full swing. A coach could encourage the development of the infielders' automatic responding to bunts by instructing batters to bunt any three pitches during their time at bat (rather than always bunting the first three pitches). Infielders would then be instructed to watch and move as rapidly as possible in the appropriate direction when they see the batter's top hand begin to move up the bat. For example, the appropriate direction of movement for the first baseman and third baseman would be toward the batter, whereas the second baseman would move toward first base. With this type of consistent-mapping practice, infielders can speed up their responses to the bunt at the same time that batters improve their bunting skills.

Reference:

Delmonico, R. (1992). *Hit and run baseball.* Champaign, IL: Human Kinetics.

b. Driving on icy roads.

Possible consistent-mapping situation(s):

A common problem drivers face is maintaining control of a car that begins to skid on an icy road. Problems develop particularly when drivers confront a stimulus that normally calls for a braking response. When a car (with rear-wheel drive) begins to skid, the appropriate response is not to brake but instead to steer in the direction that the rear end of the car is moving (i.e., steer to the right if the rear end is sliding to the right). If drivers do not practice responding to the feel of a skidding vehicle, they are more likely to produce an inappropriate (braking) response whenever they encounter a skid.

Introducing consistent stimulus-response mapping practice:

    c. Playing American football.

Possible consistent-mapping situation(s):

A classical example of a consistent stimulus-response mapping situation in American football involves the reaction of defensive players to the snap of the ball by the offensive team. The stimulus is the ball's movement by the opposing center as he transfers it to the quarterback. Many defensive players (primarily linemen) attempt to anticipate the snap of the ball by listening to the voice of the opposing quarterback rather than by watching the movement of the center's hands. Unfortunately, this strategy can backfire if the quarterback varies the loudness of his voice or the cadence of his signals. The challenge for coaches is to structure consistent-mapping practice situations that encourage defensive linemen to appropriately respond as quickly as possible to the movement of the center's hands and to ignore other types of cues (e.g., the quarterback's voice).

Introducing consistent stimulus-response mapping practice:

    d. Playing team sports.

Possible consistent-mapping situation(s):

Good defenders in many team sports (e.g., volleyball, basketball, American football) are adept at reacting rapidly and appropriately to the movements of their opponents. Many develop this capability by viewing video replays of their opponent to detect possible regularities in their mannerisms and movements. Once defenders detect such regularities, they can practice responding to them during additional viewing of the videos. They might also ask teammates to simulate the opponent's mannerisms and movements during practices to help them develop more automatic responses.

Introducing consistent stimulus-response mapping practice:

    e. Pick a sport you are familiar with that might lend itself to the detection of regularities in an opponent's mannerisms and movements.

Possible consistent mapping situation(s):

  4. An important concept for practitioners when they're structuring the practice of skills is specificity of learning (see chapter 7 of the textbook). According to this notion, the best type of practice most closely resembles the performance demands of the target skill in the target context. In the first scenario with a hypothetical learner and target skill, a practice structure is suggested (with supporting rationale) that conforms to the specificity of learning principle. Propose a practice structure (with supporting rationale) that satisfies this principle for each of the other scenarios.

    a. Scenario: Learning to play pool.

Hypothetical learner:

A 19-year-old male college student wants to learn pool. The student's goal is to achieve sufficient control of the cue stick to produce the wide variation of shots necessary for playing pool recreationally. He is experienced in a variety of sports and recreational activities and has no handicapping conditions.

Learning task:

The game of pool is played on a pocket billiards table. The player uses the preferred hand to hold the cue stick near its base and the nonpreferred hand to stabilize the opposite end of the stick. He uses the cue stick to strike a cue ball so that it rolls toward and contacts a target ball, causing the target ball to roll toward a pocket situated in one of six locations on the table. Depending on the relationship of the cue ball to the target ball and the target ball to the desired pocket, the player selects the appropriate angle of target ball direction and then hits the cue ball so that it strikes the target ball and propels it in that direction. Sometimes the player aims the cue ball directly at the target ball; sometimes the player aims the cue ball at another ball instead, causing it instead to strike the target ball. For some shots the player aims the cue ball at a point along one of the four side cushions of the table so that it caroms off the cushion toward the target ball. The player may strike the cue ball with various levels of force and at various points on the ball to make it either stop, back up, or travel forward once it strikes the target ball (The Diagram Group, 1974).

Suggested practice structure:

Since the game of pool requires players to produce variations of the same generalized motor program, a varied practice structure might be used (Schmidt & Wrisberg, 2000, chapters 5 and 6). This structure should promote both the development of the appropriate invariant relative timing pattern of the cue-stick movement and the performer's capability of adjusting parameter values to achieve different outcomes (e.g., various levels of force, various cue-stick alignments, various points of contact on the cue ball). Such practice might also include variations in the angle of desired target-ball direction so that the individual learns to perceive the appropriate angle and produce a cue-stick action that propels the target ball in the desired direction.

References:

Schmidt, R.A., & Wrisberg, C.A. (2000). *Motor Learning and Performance* (2nd ed.). Champaign, IL: Human Kinetics.
The Diagram Group (1974). *Rules of the game.* New York: Paddington Press Ltd.

b. Scenario: Learning to play badminton.

Hypothetical learner:

A 26-year-old female wants to learn badminton to enjoy the game with family and friends at a local park. The woman has had previous experience with several sport and recreational activities, but none of the activities involved anticipating and timing a moving object.

Learning task:

In badminton individuals stand on opposite sides of a net 5 feet high in the center and 5 feet 1 inch high on either end. The game is like tennis except that the court is smaller, the racket is lighter, and the object being projected is a light, cone-shaped shuttlecock rather than a ball. The game's object is to hit the shuttle over the net and inside the opponent' s court boundaries. Points are usually won when the shuttle hits the ground or floor surface on the opponent's side of the net (Chafin & Turner, 1988). The variety of shots in badminton include the serve, drive, clear, smash, and drop. Most of these shots may be hit with either a forehand or backhand arm swing. Some involve different relative timing patterns (e.g., drive shot and clear shot), while others are performed with essentially the same pattern (e.g., overhead smash and overhead drop). The serve is a closed skill (see chapter 1 of the textbook), but the rest of the shots are open skills that must be executed in response to shots by the opponent. Better players can execute a wide variety of shots, changing the direction and speed of the shuttle and using a level of deception that diminishes the opponent's anticipation of the shot.

Suggested practice structure:

Reference:

Chafin, M.B., & Turner, M.M. (1988). *Badminton everyone.* Winston-Salem, NC: Hunter Text-
     books.

c. Scenario: Learning to play the piano.

Hypothetical learner:

A 70-year-old man wants to learn to play the piano so that he can accompany his
friends in singing their favorite songs. The man has a little arthritis in his hands,
but the discomfort usually subsides after a brief period of massage and therapeutic
exercise. The man has a good ear for music but has never played any musical instrument.

Learning task:

Playing the piano is a fine motor skill that requires a particular sequencing of finger
movements. Different pieces of music present different combinations of finger sequences, rhythm, loudness, touch, and tempo. To accompany singers well, a pianist
must sense the timing of the singers' voices and complement their sounds with the
sounds of the instrument (Gilbert & Lockhart, 1961).

Suggested practice structure:

Reference:

Gilbert, P., & Lockhart, A. (1961). *Music for the modern dance.* Dubuque, IA: Wm. C. Brown.

d. Scenario: Learning lifeguard rescue skills.

Hypothetical learner:

The learner is a 15-year-old female who wants to learn the necessary rescue skills to
obtain American Red Cross certification as a lifeguard. The individual is an accomplished swimmer who appears to have the strength and endurance for executing the
various rescue maneuvers.

Learning task:

Rescue skills include understanding the procedures, the appropriate use of the rescue tube, and the proper execution of the techniques of safe entry into the water;
approach to the victim; and recovery of passive, submerged, solitary, and multiple
victims (American Red Cross, 1994). The learner must also master the kicks used in
lifeguarding (i.e., scissors, inverted scissors, elementary backstroke, and rotary). Since
no two rescue situations are the same, the accomplished lifeguard must be able to
quickly recognize the demands of each situation and perform the appropriate sequence of tasks to assure safe recovery of the victim with minimal trauma to all
parties involved.

Suggested practice structure:

Reference:

American Red Cross. (1994). *Lifeguarding today.* St. Louis: C.V. Mosby.

 Problem-Solving Exercises

The following exercises challenge you to demonstrate comprehension of several
important concepts presented in chapter 9 of the textbook. In Exercise 9.1 you discuss how a practitioner might structure the blocked and random practice of skills. In
Exercise 9.2 you describe how a practitioner might design the varied practice of a
target skill to enhance learners' development of a generalized motor program and
their capability of adjusting parameter values. In Exercise 9.3 you explain how the
practitioner might use a random-practice structure to help learners automate their
responses in consistent-mapping situations.

Exercise 9.1

Blocked and Random Practice During Skill Rehearsal

It is possible to structure the practice of target skills to facilitate learning and transfer to the target context. For activities that encompass several target skills, practitioners might structure sessions that are either blocked or random in format. In this exercise you select a movement activity that includes several target skills and discuss situations for which blocked practice and random practice of the skills might be appropriate. Your solution should do the following:

- Describe the target skills, emphasizing the goal of the movement and basic actions required of the performer.
- Describe the learner (a hypothetical individual or someone you know).
- Explain how to structure a blocked-practice experience and a random-practice experience for the learner.

Gary's Solution

I have chosen volleyball for this exercise. To play effectively, the volleyball player must perform the target skills of serving, forearm passing, overhead passing, blocking, and hitting. Serving is a closed skill performed when initiating a rally. This skill is performed by tossing the ball vertically with the nonpreferred hand and contacting it with the meaty part of the preferred hand using an overarm throwing motion. Passing, blocking, and hitting are open skills that are performed in response to the actions of opposing players or teammates. Forearm passing involves contacting an approaching ball on the forearms and directing it toward a teammate. Overhead passing is performed by spreading the fingers in a ball-shaped form and gently extending the arms to contact the ball and send it in a vertical trajectory. Blocking is performed by jumping vertically and fully extending the arms above the head to redirect an opponent's hit back over the net or to force the opponent to hit over the block to a backcourt position. Hitting (or spiking) involves jumping vertically and forcefully striking the ball with the preferred hand using a whip-like arm motion (Neville, 1994).

The learner is a 13-year-old girl who wants to learn to play volleyball so she can enjoy a weekly game with friends. She has participated in a few other sport activities requiring both open and closed skills (e.g., softball and tennis) and appears to have good levels of several abilities that should help her learn the target skills of volleyball. These abilities include multilimb coordination, response orientation, and explosive strength (Fleishman, 1964).

Perhaps the best skill to practice in a blocked fashion, at least initially, is the serve. The player must first learn to coordinate movements of the tossing and the hitting arms (Schmidt & Wrisberg, 2000). Initially, the girl could be instructed to focus on a coordinated toss and hit, without worrying about how she places the ball. Once she is able to produce that action consistently, the learner could be challenged to hit a block of serves over the net and inside the boundaries of the opponent's court. After she can do this, the learner could be challenged to hit a block of serves to a variety of different targets at different speeds. In this way, blocked practice gives the learner a chance to practice parameterizing the generalized motor program to achieve different outcomes.

Once the ball is served, players usually pass, hit, and block in various sequences. To promote the learning of each skill and provide the learner with opportunities to practice retrieving and executing different programs, the practitioner could introduce a four-player game situation like that in professional beach volleyball. The court's boundaries could be reduced to facilitate court coverage by both teams. The object of the game is for each team to use three hits whenever the ball reaches their side of the court. This game would allow the learner to randomly experience all the basic skills of volleyball. For example, in one rally, she might get to serve the ball, execute a forearm pass to her teammate, hit the ball back over the net in response to an overhead pass from her teammate, and block the other team's return hit.

References:

Fleishman, E.A. (1964). *The structure and measurement of physical fitness.* Englewood Cliffs, NJ: Prentice-Hall.

Neville, W. (1994). *Serve it up: Volleyball for life.* Mountain View, CA: Mayfield.

Schmidt, R.A., & Wrisberg, C.A. (2000). *Motor learning and performance* (2nd ed.). Champaign, IL: Human Kinetics.

Evaluation of Gary's Solution

Gary selects an appropriate activity and describes the basic actions of each skill adequately. Although he does not discuss the goals of all the skills (e.g., hitting and overhead passing), Gary does document his description of them. He points out that the learner is motivated to learn the sport for recreation, not competition, as part of his fairly good description. Gary further indicates that the learner has several abilities that might help her in the skills of volleyball, but he could go on to connect those abilities and the skills of volleyball more specifically.

Gary suggests an interesting progression of blocked practice to help a beginner learn the serving action. His rationale for providing blocked practice is that two-hand coordination is difficult to master without considerable repetition. Gary offers a supporting reference but does not specify what discussion from the textbook he is referring to. It would also be better to explain some of the particular issues of managing two-hand coordination (e.g., competing relative timing patterns) and to provide primary-source evidence (e.g., Konzem, 1987). Gary might also elaborate on (and document) why he decided to gradually increase the demands of blocked serving practice (e.g., limited attentional capacity). When Gary mentions the concept of program parameterization, he neglects to cite a reference or give an example of how the parameterization process might occur when the learner is attempting to serve to different targets.

Gary offers a challenging activity for his example of random practice, rationalizing that the target context for volleyball requires performers to produce a random arrangement of several skills. However, in light of Gary's description of the learner, the demands of this activity may be greater than the individual is able to handle. A drill that combines serving, overhead passing, forearm passing, blocking, *and* hitting is probably too advanced for a beginner. Some blocked practice (particularly of the more difficult skills of hitting and passing) or some less-complex random practice (a random arrangement of two or three skills such as forearm passing and overhead passing) might represent a better start. Gary mentions a possible theoretical basis for the benefits of random practice (i.e., program retrieval) but should explain and document this notion further and suggest how program retrieval might occur when a learner is participating in the four-person drill.

Reference:

Konzem, P.B. (1987). *Extended practice and patterns of bimanual interference.* Unpublished doctoral dissertation, University of Southern California, Los Angeles.

Maria's Solution

The activity I have chosen for this exercise is social dance and, more specifically, three dances called the swing, the salsa, and the Charleston. Schmidt and Wrisberg

(2000) point out that random practice produces higher retention and transfer when individuals must learn different classes of movements (rather than when they learn variations of the same movement class). Some people might think that social dance represents a single movement class. However, closer inspection of the timing structure of the different dances suggests that they may actually come from different classes. The goal of social dance is to enjoy rhythmic movement with some sort of social group. It fulfills people's need for recreation and is one of the more popular leisure-time pursuits.

The swing is danced to a wide variety of music written in 4/4 time; the rhythm is slow, slow, quick, quick. Swing steps usually cover a circular space in one area of the floor. Footwork is characterized by close, small steps with frequent rolling and turning on the ball of the foot. The salsa is a Latin dance written in 4/4 time. The rhythm is quick, quick, slow, and the music is fast and lighthearted. The dance is performed with small, flat footsteps and a pronounced hip action that follows the action of the feet. The Charleston is also in 4/4 time and has a bouncy quality. The rhythm is jerky, and the movements include twisting of the feet, bending and straightening of the knees before each step, and arms moving in opposite direction to the feet. A more detailed explanation of each dance may be found in Harris, Pittman, and Waller (1988), but the foregoing descriptions illustrate the distinct patterns of the three dances.

The learner is a 16-year-old female who wants to prepare for a dance competition at her high school. She plays the piano and participates in a number of individual sports, including tennis and golf. The individual appears to have a better than average level of what Keele and Ivry (1987) refer to as perceptual timing, which is the ability to judge the time course of external events (such as the timing of a musical score).

Perhaps the best candidate for blocked practice is the Charleston because of the initial difficulty most learners have combining the balance and timing of the movements. Shea, Kohl, and Indermill (1990) demonstrate that beginners sometimes need to experience blocked practice until they achieve a rough approximation of the movement. One form of blocked practice that might enable the learner to forge a connection between the balance and timing of the Charleston step involves standing behind a chair and holding onto the back of it for support. From this position, the learner practices bending and straightening the legs in time to the music while at the same time pivoting on the balls of the feet in order to move the heels in and out. Once the individual achieves the basic action, she can engage in blocked practice of the step without the support of the chair.

Compared to blocked practice, random practice has been shown to produce superior retention and transfer of skills (Schmidt & Wrisberg, 2000). However, due to the limited attention capacity of individuals (Kahneman, 1973), practitioners must be careful not to overload the learner with too much information at one time. Random practice that could help a beginner might involve the intermingling of distinctive features of the three dances. For example, relative timing has been shown to be a distinguishing characteristic of generalized motor programs for movements (Shapiro, Zernicke, Gregor, & Diestel, 1981). Therefore, the learner might practice switching between the basic relative timing patterns of the three dances by dancing several bars of the Charleston followed by several bars of the swing, then several bars of the salsa, and so on. In this way the learner quickly shifts between the different relative timing patterns and practices the retrieval of different generalized programs.

References:

Harris, J.A., Pittman, A.M., & Waller, M.S. (1988). *Dance a while* (7th ed.). New York: Macmillan.
Kahneman, D. (1973). *Attention and effort.* Englewood Cliffs, NJ: Prentice-Hall.
Keele, S.W., & Ivry, R. (1987). Modular analysis of timing in motor skill. In G.H. Bower (Ed.), *The psychology of learning and motivation*, vol. 21 (pp. 183–228). San Diego: Academic Press.

Schmidt, R.A., & Wrisberg, C.A. (2000). *Motor learning and performance* (2nd ed.). Champaign, IL: Human Kinetics.

Shapiro, D.C., Zernicke, R.F., Gregor, R.J., & Diestel, J.D. (1981). Evidence for generalized motor programs using gait-pattern analysis. *Journal of Motor Behavior, 13,* 33–47.

Shea, C.H., Kohl, R., & Indermill, C. (1990). Contextual interference: Contributions of practice. *Acta Psychologica, 73,* 145–157.

Evaluation of Maria's Solution

Maria's description of each dance is generally good, focusing mainly on the style characteristics and tempo of each activity. She adds a reference for readers to find more detailed information about the dances. She concludes her task description by arguing (with supporting documentation) that the three dances are sufficiently different to be considered separate skills, making them good candidates for random practice.

Maria's learner description is sufficient and her suggestions for blocked and random practice are well conceived. She points out (and documents) that blocked practice might help the learner combine the balance and timing needed for the performance of the Charleston. Her progression of blocked practice, enabling the learner to initially use a chair to diminish task demands, is a nice illustration of the simplification method of part practice (Wightman & Lintern, 1985). Maria considers (and again documents) the limited attentional capacity of individuals as a concern in suggesting a random practice activity. By limiting random practice bouts of the three dances to a few bars of music at a time, Maria gives the learner an opportunity to practice more frequent retrieval of the different generalized programs without overloading the individual. Because the learner is shifting continually from the performance of one dance to the next, she might also be able to detect differences in the relative timing patterns of the three dances more quickly.

Reference:

Wightman, D.C., & Lintern, G. (1985). Part-task training strategies for tracking and manual control. *Human Factors, 27,* 267–283.

Your Solution to Exercise 9.1

Blocked and Random Practice During Skill Rehearsal

NAME_____ DATE_____

1. Definition of problem:
2. Type of instructional situation:
   Teaching   Coaching   Rehabilitation   Human factors
3. Description of the skill
   Goal of the movement:
   Basic actions required:
4. Description of the learner:
5. Appropriate blocked-practice experience:
6. Appropriate random-practice experience:
7. References:

Exercise 9.2

Designing the Varied Practice of a Target Skill

Many situations lend themselves to a type of varied-practice structure that enables learners to develop the correct relative timing pattern for the target skill—as well as rules (or schema) for adjusting parameter values of the generalized program to meet the demands of different situations (Schmidt & Wrisberg, 2000, chapter 9). For this exercise, first pick a class of tasks that a performer might produce with a single generalized motor program. Then describe one parameter of the program and explain how a practitioner might create a varied-practice experience to challenge the learner to adjust the value of the parameter to achieve different environmental outcomes. Your solution should do the following:

- Describe the target skill, emphasizing the goal of the movement and the basic actions required of the performer.
- Describe the learner (a hypothetical individual or someone you know).
- Identify and explain one parameter that performers might adjust to produce different environmental outcomes.
- Discuss one type of varied-practice experience that could help develop the learner's capacity to adjust the parameter.

Jane's Solution

The target skill I have chosen is shuffleboard. The goal of this game is to slide round wooden discs down a smooth and level surface a distance of 20 to 25 feet into target zones of various point values. Two opponents attempt shots alternately (4 shots per player per round). The player who tallies the highest score over 50 points at the end of a complete round wins the game. In some cases, players attempt to bump their opponent's disc out of a point zone or to protect one of their own by sliding another between the disc and their opponent. The skill requires performers to produce the same basic action on each shot but, depending on the goal of the movement, to also alter the direction and force of the movement to deliver the disc to different targets at different rates of speed.

The basic action of the shuffleboard shot begins with the player assuming a comfortable standing posture. The player holds one end of a long stick (approximately 4 feet in length) in the preferred hand. At the opposite end of the stick is a V-shaped prong the player uses to push the disc in a forward direction. Prior to initiating the movement, the player places the prong against a disc. Shortly after that the player focuses on the target, bends at the waist, takes one step forward with the nonpreferred foot, and moves the preferred arm forward. This action causes the prong to slide along the smooth ground surface and push the disc toward the target.

The learner is an 8-year-old girl who wants to learn shuffleboard so she can play it with her grandfather. The girl has been diagnosed as mildly retarded (Eichstaedt & Lavay, 1992), but she has good communication skills. She appears to have no serious physical deficiencies but usually avoids situations where her physical skills are being observed by others. As a result, the girl is sedentary and has a low level of physical fitness.

The parameter that a player adjusts the most during a shuffleboard game is overall force. Depending on the location of targets and other discs on the court surface, the player adjusts the force of arm movement to propel the disc at different speeds. On any single attempt, the player's goal might be to direct the disc into a target zone, to an area in front of another disc, or at the opponent's disc in order to dislodge it from a target zone.

A varied-practice experience that would afford the learner an opportunity to develop her ability to adjust force might be one in which the girl projects the disc different distances on each of her four attempts. For example, the learner might be asked to project the first disc any distance she wishes. Regardless of where the disc comes to a rest, the learner would then be asked to try to slide the next disc a shorter distance than the first one (i.e., requiring less force). Regardless of where the second disc comes to a stop, the learner would be instructed to push the third disc a distance that is between those of the first two discs. For her fourth disc, the learner could be encouraged to again pick her own distance. In this way, the learner should begin to associate the relationship between the forces she produces and the resulting distances that the disc travels. According to Schmidt and Wrisberg (2000), this type of practice should help the learner develop a schema (i.e., a set of rules) for determining the parameter value (in this case for force) necessary to produce a particular outcome (in this case desired speed and distance of the disc). As the girl becomes more adept at adjusting the force parameter, she might be encouraged to set more of her own targets with the only restriction being that she vary the distance of the targets from one attempt to the next.

References:

Eichstaedt, C.B., & Lavay, B.W. (1992). *Physical activity for individuals with mental retardation.* Champaign, IL: Human Kinetics.

Schmidt, R.A., & Wrisberg, C.A. (2000). *Motor learning and performance* (2nd ed.). Champaign, IL: Human Kinetics.

Evaluation of Jane's Solution

Jane organizes and writes her solution well. She thoroughly describes the game, the performer's goal, and the basic actions of the movement. However, Jane should add a citation for her description or indicate the source from which she obtained her information about the activity.

When Jane describes the learner, she cites a reference to document the condition of mild mental retardation but does not indicate whether this condition places any particular restrictions on the learner. She mentions that the learner has good communication skills and a low level of physical fitness and is self-conscious in evaluative situations. These are characteristics a practitioner might need to consider when structuring practice experiences.

Jane states that the most obvious variable parameter of the shuffleboard movement is force, but does not discuss the theoretical notion of the generalized motor program or its relationship to parameter learning. However, Jane does suggest an interesting varied-practice activity to give the learner opportunities to adjust force level. She also discusses the concept of schema development (citing a supporting reference) and indicates how varied practice might enable the learner to develop a schema rule for relating desired distance to required force level. Jane does not offer any rationale for her decision to let the learner choose some, but not all, of the distances of disc travel. Thus, the reader is left to wonder whether this decision, which seems rather creative, is based on Jane's knowledge of the learner's capabilities or is just a haphazard choice.

Richard's Solution

The skill I have chosen for this exercise is the placekick in American football. The goal of the placekick is to project the football different distances over a crossbar (10 feet above the ground) and between two uprights (separated by a distance of 18 feet, 6 inches). Most place kickers use a soccer-style motion that consists of the following sequence of actions: pre-impact, impact, and follow-through (Adrian & Cooper, 1995). During pre-impact the kicker takes an angle approach to the ball that involves two quick steps, the second of which is a leap step ending with the plant foot firmly placed alongside and slightly to the rear of the ball. While this is happening, the shank of the kicking leg flexes so that the heel is well back. The arms are used to counterbalance the forceful forward swing of the kicking leg. The arm on the same side as the kicking leg is swung back, while the one on the opposite side is swung forward. Just before impact, the velocity of the shank of the kicking leg increases dramatically, resulting in rapid knee extension. During the impact stage, the body leans backward so that contact occurs on the upswing of the kicking arc. The center of the ball is contacted with the instep of the foot. During follow-through the speed of the kicking leg is decreased, and the player gains control for subsequent actions.

The learner is a 15-year-old male who has played organized soccer for 6 years but wants to learn how to placekick so he can try out for the position of place kicker on his high school football team. The individual is physically fit and highly motivated to practice the skills necessary to achieve proficiency at this task.

The skill of placekicking is performed with very little variation in force, but it does require subtle adjustments in foot placement to achieve the desired combination of ball distance and trajectory. The closer the ball is to the goal, the more important it is to elevate the kick. The greater the distance between the ball and the goal, however, the more important it is to trade off vertical trajectory for horizontal distance. If more vertical ball trajectory is desired, the support foot is placed more to the rear of the ball. This placement results in a greater backward body lean and contact with the ball on the upswing of the kicking leg.

In the target context (i.e., a football game), placekicks might occur at distances from 20 to 60 yards to the goal and at angles ranging from 45 degrees (about 27 feet) to either side of the center of the goal. An effective place kicker must find the optimal approach angle and determine the location of foot placement that produces the desired direction, distance, and trajectory of ball flight.

For the learner in this example, a varied-practice schedule might consist of a series of kicks attempted from 10 combinations of distance and angle to the goal. A hypothetical sequence might include the following distance–location combinations (this is using a field 160 feet wide, and hash marks located 53 feet 4 inches from either side line, dividing the field into thirds):

10-yard line/right hash mark

35-yard line/center of field

40-yard line/left hash mark

20-yard line/left hash mark

45-yard line/right hash mark

30-yard line/center of field

15-yard line/left hash mark

25-yard line/right hash mark

40-yard line/center of field

10-yard line/right hash mark

By practicing combinations such as these, the player would be learning how to make the kinds of adjustments in foot placement that produce the outcome he desires on each kick, regardless of where the ball may be located on the field when the individual is called into the game.

Reference:

Adrian, M.J., & Cooper, J.M. (1995). *Biomechanics of human movement* (2nd ed.). Dubuque, IA: WCB Brown & Benchmark.

Evaluation of Richard's Solution

Richard provides a detailed description (with documentation) of the goal of the activity and the basic actions involved. Some of the details he provides (e.g., use of the arms to counterbalance the forceful forward swing of the kicking leg) actually go beyond the scope of the assignment. All the exercise requires is enough description to suggest that the target skill is produced by a single generalized motor program with adjustable parameters.

In contrast to his detailed explanation of the kicking action, Richard describes the learner in only a general way. He proposes a varied-practice activity that is quite creative. There is little question that the exercise allows the learner the opportunity to practice adapting his kicks to meet the requirements of different situations. What is less clear is the type of relationship (i.e., schema rule) that is being developed by this experience. Is the learner attempting to determine the relationship between the location of foot placement and the trajectory of the ball? Is he developing a schema rule for relating the angle of approach and the direction of ball flight? Richard should discuss the theoretical notion of schema development or the way schema rules are developed.

The schema notion deals with the development of rules for producing variations of a movement class. While it is possible that place kickers adjust the location of foot placement by adjusting some parameter of the movement (e.g., duration), their decision about the desired angle of approach may have nothing to do with the kicking action itself. If this is the case, at least some of the learning (or schema development) that occurs when a person practices placekicking in a varied format is probably perceptual (e.g., interpreting field conditions and weather conditions, estimating the correct angle of approach), rather than motor, learning (Vernon, 1955).

Reference:

Vernon, M.D. (1955). The functions of schemata in perceiving. *Psychological Review, 62,* 180–192.

Your Solution to Exercise 9.2

Designing the Varied Practice of a Target Skill

NAME_____ DATE_____

1. Definition of problem:
2. Type of instructional assistance:
   Teaching   Coaching   Rehabilitation   Human factors
3. Description of the skill
   Goal of the movement:
   Basic actions required:
4. Description of the learner:
5. One parameter performers might adjust to produce different environmental outcomes:
6. Varied-practice experience that might facilitate the learner's ability to adjust the parameter:
7. References:

Exercise 9.3

Structuring the Random Practice of Several Consistent S-R Mapping Situations

Sometimes learners must recognize a stimulus and produce a quick response to it to perform target skills. When a particular stimulus always requires the same response (i.e., consistent mapping), performers can practice the response until it becomes virtually automatic (Shriffin & Schneider, 1977). However, in most open-skill environments (see chapter 1), stimuli occur randomly, not predictably. Here you should consider two or more consistent-mapping situations that might be found in a sport skill or movement activity and then describe how you might design a random-practice experience to promote automatic processing. Your solution should do the following:

- Describe the target skill, emphasizing the goal of the movement and two or more possible consistent-mapping situations.
- Describe the learner (a hypothetical individual or someone you know).
- Discuss a random-practice format that might promote development of automatic processing in consistent-mapping situations.

Reference:

Shiffrin, R.M., & Schneider, W. (1977). Controlled and automatic human information processing: II. Perceptual learning, automatic attending, and a general theory. *Psychological Review*, 84, 127–190.

Martin's Solution

Description of the skill:

The skill I have chosen for this exercise is the pivot of the second baseman during a double play in baseball. In a double-play situation there is an opposing runner on first base with less than two outs. If a ground ball is hit to the third baseman or shortstop, that player fields the ball and throws it to the second baseman, who is approaching the second base bag. The goal of the second baseman is to catch the ball, touch the base, and throw the ball to first base. Prior to touching the base, the second baseman must quickly notice whether the base runner is sliding to the left or right of the base or directly into the base. If the slide is to the right, the second baseman pivots by touching the base with the left foot, pushing off, and throwing to first base. If the slide is to the left, the second baseman pivots by stepping across the base with the left foot and then throwing to first base. If the base runner is very close to the second baseman and sliding directly into him, the second baseman steps on the base, jumps directly up into the air, and throws the ball to first, avoiding a collision by allowing the runner to slide underneath him (Delmonico, 1992).

Description of the learner:

The learner is a 14-year-old male who has played competitive baseball since he was 7 years old. The boy loves to play second base, and he wants to learn how to perform the three pivots to execute the double play more effectively.

Random-practice format to develop automatic processing:

As suggested in the first paragraph, the double play is a situation in which the second baseman must quickly identify the direction of the base runner's slide and then produce the most appropriate and effective pivot. This situation seems well suited for a random-practice drill that would give the learner experience selecting the appropriate response for each type of slide (i.e., automatic responding to consistent-mapping situations). Initially, the activity could be simplified by instructing the learner to catch the throw, identify the direction of the base runner's slide, and execute the appropriate pivot without throwing the ball to first base. Teammates could serve as base runners and, for each ground ball that is hit to the shortstop or third baseman, they could execute one of the three slides. Prior to the drill, the runners could be reminded to vary the type of slide so that the learner would not be able to predict in advance which slide was being executed. Once the learner shows the capability of recognizing the direction of the slide and making the correct pivot, he could be instructed to complete the double play by throwing the ball to first base each time.

Reference:

Delmonico, R. (1992). *Hit and run baseball.* Champaign, IL: Human Kinetics.

Evaluation of Martin's Solution

Martin selects three S-R mapping situations that involve the double play pivot in the sport of American baseball. His explanations of the goal of the double-play pivot and the basic actions involved are good. He further points out that the type of pivot most appropriate for a particular situation depends on the direction of the slide by the approaching base runner. Thus, the runner's slide acts as a stimulus the second baseman must quickly recognize and respond to with the most appropriate pivot. The close correspondence between the type of slide and the type of pivot makes the double play a good candidate for the practice of consistent S-R mapping.

Martin describes the learner in only a limited way. However, he suggests a consistent-mapping, random-practice activity that seems appropriate. The randomized aspects include the runner's type of slide and the infielders from whom the second baseman receives the throw. Martin contends that this drill should promote the learner's development of automatic responding. However, he provides no theoretical discussion or related literature dealing with the notions of stimulus-response mapping or automatic responding. Martin suggests that the exercise might be simplified by eliminating the throwing movement; but here, too, he does not offer any theoretical rationale (e.g., limited attentional capacity of performers).

Holly's Solution

The target skill is spiking or hitting a volleyball, which involves a goal of contacting the ball so that it is likely to hit the floor on the opponent's side of the net. In most cases, the hitter executes the spike near the net on either the left or right side of the court. The challenge for the hitter is to recognize the location of the block being executed by the opposing player(s) and then to select the type of hit that has the best chance of circumventing the block. Usually the blocker's position discourages the spiker from hitting either crosscourt in a diagonal direction or down the sideline straight ahead. Occasionally, teams commit two blockers to a hitter in order to prevent spikes in *either* direction.

Recognizing the location of the block and executing the most appropriate response seems to be a good example of a consistent-mapping situation (Schmidt & Wrisberg, 2000). When a block is set to the inside of the spiker (blocking the diagonal direction), the spiker should hit the ball straight down the line. If the block is set up to the outside (blocking the straight-ahead direction), the spiker should hit the ball crosscourt in a diagonal direction. When two opponents set a block that closes off both directional avenues, the spiker might fake a spike and "dink" the ball over the block, so that it lands on the floor just behind the blockers.

The basic components of the spiking action are the approach, the ascent (or jump), and the hit. The approach is a quick, three-step movement that enables the hitter to achieve horizontal acceleration in the direction of the net. During the ascent, the spiker transfers this horizontal acceleration into vertical height by flexing and then forcibly extending the legs. When hitting the ball, the spiker uses a basic throwing motion that travels in the intended direction of ball flight. The hitter contacts the ball as high and as far in front of the hitting shoulder as possible. For full-speed hits the spiker uses a whip-like arm motion, contacting the ball with a loose wrist and relaxed hand. For "dink" shots, the spiker contacts the ball at the same point as in the full-speed hit but stiffens the wrist and hand and opens fingers at the moment of contact to place the ball over the block (Neville, 1994).

The learner is a 19-year-old female who has recently joined her college volleyball team. She is new to volleyball, having recently been recruited by the coach because of her outstanding jumping ability. The woman is physically fit and has had extensive experience in basketball. In addition, she has good levels of two abilities identified by Fleishman (1964) that could help her learn to use the spike appropriately in blocking situations. These abilities are *response orientation* (i.e., the ability to make quick choices among numerous alternative movements) and *manual dexterity* (i.e., the ability to manipulate large objects with the hands and arms).

Defeating opponents' blocking maneuvers requires quick decisions and appropriate responses by the hitter. Since opposing players usually mix up the types of blocks they present to hitters, a drill that might help would require the learner to recognize the position of a randomly ordered series of blocks and execute the most appropriate hit for each. Teammates could serve as blockers and be instructed in advance as to the position they should assume in forming each block. Here is a randomized sequence of 10 blocking–spiking combinations:

Type of block	Desired response
Inside, one player	Straight ahead, down line
Outside, one player	Diagonal, crosscourt
Inside, one player	Straight ahead, down line
Inside and outside, two players	Dink over block
Outside, one player	Diagonal, crosscourt
Inside, one player	Straight ahead, down line
Inside, one player	Straight ahead, down line
Inside and outside, two players	Dink over block
Outside, one player	Diagonal, crosscourt
Inside and outside, two players	Dink over block

References:

Fleishman, E.A. (1964). *The structure and measurement of physical fitness.* Englewood Cliffs, NJ: Prentice-Hall.

Neville, W. (1994). *Serve it up: Volleyball for life.* Mountain View, CA: Mayfield.

Schmidt, R.A., & Wrisberg, C.A. (2000). *Motor learning and performance* (2nd ed.). Champaign, IL: Human Kinetics.

Evaluation of Holly's Solution

Holly does a nice job explaining the goal of spiking a volleyball and describing its basic actions. Holly describes three consistent-mapping situations that confront the spiker during most hitting opportunities. The challenge for the spiker is to detect the location of the opponents' block and then execute the type of spike with the highest probability of defeating the block. Holly briefly discusses (citing a source) the notion of consistent-mapping and explains its relevance to the spiking situation.

Holly also provides an excellent description of the learner, including information about the woman's previous sport experiences and underlying abilities that might help the individual as she attempts to learn the technique and strategy of the spiking movement. Here, too, Holly offers documentation for the learner's abilities that she mentions.

Holly aptly proposes a practice activity comprising a random arrangement of the three consistent-mapping situations she has described, and she includes an informative table illustrating a possible sequence of 10 blocking–spiking combinations. All in all, Holly's solution is a good application of the notion of consistent mapping. She might have improved her answer a bit by adding more theoretical discussion of the concept of stimulus-response mapping along with supporting references from the motor learning literature.

Your Solution to Exercise 9.3

Structuring the Random Practice of Several Consistent S-R Mapping Situations

NAME_____   DATE_____

1. Definition of problem:
2. Instructional situation:
   Teaching   Coaching   Rehabilitation   Human factors
3. Description of the target skill
   Goal of the movement:
   Possible consistent-mapping situations:
4. Description of the learner:
5. Random-practice format for promoting the development of automatic processing:
6. References:

CHAPTER 10

Providing Feedback During the Learning Experience

World-class athletes, such as John McEnroe, have used on-court video feedback to make adjustments in technique. Here McEnroe corrects his famed service motion with tennis coach John Yandell.

Bud Syms

◀◀◆ Key Concepts

To improve skills, learners sometimes require instructional feedback about their performance from a movement practitioner. This type of feedback conveys information about aspects of the learner's movements that deviate from the desired state of performance. Feedback from an external source (such as a movement practitioner) is referred to in the motor learning literature as *extrinsic* (or *augmented) feedback*. Feedback that occurs naturally during task performance and that learners can pick up on their own (i.e., both exteroceptive and proprioceptive information) is referred to as *intrinsic feedback*. For simple skills, such as dribbling a basketball, learners may be able to improve their performance with very little extrinsic feedback. However, for more complex skill learning, such as a high bar routine in gymnastics, most people require additional feedback from an instructor.

Chapter 10 of the textbook explains how extrinsic feedback serves several important functions during the process of skill learning. Sometimes extrinsic feedback motivates learners to continue pursuing their goals. For example, a golfer might hear that she has improved the distance of her tee shots by 10 yards during a practice session. Other times instructional feedback might reinforce learners' performances and encourage them to repeat the actions they have produced (e.g., a teacher might tell a piano student that he contacts the keys on the keyboard smoothly even though the sounds are still less than ideal). Perhaps the most important function of extrinsic feedback is providing error information that learners can use to correct or refine their movements. For instance, an observer could tell a cricket bowler about spatial errors in the release point of his throwing action.

Before providing extrinsic feedback for learners, practitioners should consider five issues. The first is whether to provide feedback at all. Some learners prefer to use available intrinsic feedback to improve their performance and to rehearse their movements without instructional assistance. As research has shown, too much extrinsic feedback can sometimes be detrimental to skill learning, particularly when learners become dependent on it.

The second issue practitioners should consider is what type of feedback to provide. For example, an instructor might present feedback in a verbal or visual form. She might give it in a descriptive (what happened) or prescriptive (what to do next) statement; she could present it in terms of the results produced by the learner's movements (knowledge of results) or the quality of the movements themselves (knowledge of performance). Practitioners might initially provide *program feedback* that assists learners in developing the *generalized motor program* that produces the movement pattern (e.g., sequencing). For example, a tennis teacher might tell a student to move her wrist faster than her arm during the serving motion. In contrast, instructors might also provide *parameter feedback* that targets the effectiveness with which the learner is adjusting parameter values of the program (e.g., force, speed, distance). As an example, a baseball coach might inform the pitcher about the speed of different pitches he is throwing.

The third feedback issue concerns how much information to provide. People are limited in their capacity to process information. In giving extrinsic feedback, therefore, practitioners should avoid overloading learners with too much information. Individuals at a more advanced stage of learning can usually handle more feedback than can beginners. Two types of extrinsic feedback that optimize the amount of information instructors might provide are *summary feedback* and *average feedback*. Both these forms of feedback inform learners about their performance tendencies during a block of practice attempts. For beginners, practitioners should summarize a smaller block of practice attempts than they would for advanced performers. This approach can provide optimal feedback assistance for learners at all stages of practice and, at the same time, decrease the individual's dependency on extrinsic information.

The fourth issue deals with the precision of feedback. One way practitioners can determine how precise their feedback should be is to set a bandwidth of performance error that they will tolerate before providing feedback. Early in skill learning the practitioner might set a wider bandwidth and provide feedback only when the beginner produces large errors. Once the learner can consistently produce the desired pattern, the practitioner might narrow the bandwidth and provide feedback only when it assists the learner in refining the movement. In this way, extrinsic feedback guides the learner in the direction of the desired movement pattern while still allowing the person to initially explore a variety of movement strategies.

The final issue practitioners should consider deals with the frequency or timing of feedback delivery. Effective practitioners know not only the types, amounts, and precision of feedback to provide but also when and how often to provide extrinsic information. Practitioners should first allow learners the opportunity to evaluate their own performance feedback following a practice attempt—and then provide extrinsic feedback. This sequence encourages learners to attend to intrinsic information sources and develop their own capacity to detect errors. Finally, the scientific evidence indicates that extrinsic feedback is more effective when it is provided at the learner's request than when it is delivered more frequently. Generally speaking, beginners require more frequent and more concise feedback than do more advanced performers.

 Key Terms

To answer the questions and complete the exercises in this chapter you need a basic understanding of the following terms or concepts:

intrinsic feedback

extrinsic feedback

knowledge of results

knowledge of performance

verbal feedback

visual feedback

motivating feedback

reinforcement

generalized motor program

relative timing

program feedback

parameter feedback

descriptive feedback

prescriptive feedback

attentional cueing

attentional focus

variable error

 Review Questions

Answer each of the following questions and *provide rationale for your answers.* If you are not familiar with the skill or activity presented in a particular scenario, you may discuss it with an expert or consult a book or training manual that contains more detailed information.

1. In most motor learning situations, learners can obtain some intrinsic feedback on their own to improve their performance. At various points, however, learners require extrinsic feedback from an instructor to achieve further performance improvements (Schmidt & Wrisberg, 2000, chapter 10). In the first scenario, two examples of intrinsic feedback and extrinsic feedback are provided (with supporting rationale). In the other scenarios, a hypothetical learner and learning task are briefly described, and you are to suggest the two examples of each type of feedback (with supporting rationale).

a. Scenario: Learning the skill of tenpin bowling.

Hypothetical learner:

A 30-year-old female with partial paralysis of the lower body wants to learn to bowl so that she can participate on a wheelchair bowling team. The woman has an average level of physical fitness but has never played any sports.

Learning task:

Bowling requires rolling a large, heavy ball down a smooth, wooden lane toward a grouping of wooden pins arranged in a triangular formation at the opposite end of the lane. The game's object is to knock down as many pins as possible on each roll. There are 10 frames to a game, and all but one frame consist of one or two rolls. If the bowler knocks down all 10 pins with the first roll, then a second roll is not necessary. A bowler who knocks down all 10 pins on the first two rolls of the 10th frame is allowed an additional roll. Learning to bowl requires developing the skill to topple pins by rolling the ball at them smoothly and at the proper angle (Agne-Traub, Martin, & Tandy, 1998).

Examples of intrinsic feedback:

The most obvious intrinsic feedback is the sight of the ball rolling down the lane and hitting (or missing) the pins. The learner can evaluate any changes she makes in her delivery by visually attending to the resulting action of the ball and pins. For example, the learner could change her angle of approach and notice how the path of the ball results in a particular type of pin action. Another source of intrinsic feedback is the feel of the weight and momentum of the ball from the beginning to the end of the pendular arm motion. Learners can experiment with balls of different weights and use this source of intrinsic feedback to determine the ball weight that is best for them.

Examples of extrinsic feedback:

Extrinsic feedback might be used to deal with the position of the ball in the hand and the follow-through motion. The most effective delivery for bowlers requires the positioning of the wrist so that when the arm is dangling at the side (for a right-handed bowler), the thumbhole is at the "ten o'clock" position and the finger holes are at the "four o'clock" position. From this position, the bowler can deliver the ball so that it travels in a slightly curving pattern toward the center of the pin formation. Many beginners adopt a less-effective hand position that places the thumbhole at "12 o'clock" and the finger holes at "6 o'clock." Second, beginning bowlers, particularly those with less arm strength (such as this scenario's learner), tend to slow down the forward arm motion before they release the ball. As a result the ball rolls more slowly and tends to deviate from the desired path. The practitioner could provide program feedback to help the learner develop the relative timing structure (Schmidt & Wrisberg, 2000, chapter 6) for the desired arm movement. That is, she could instruct the individual to exaggerate her follow-through by maintaining arm speed during the forward motion and by holding her arm and hand in the finish position for several counts after the ball's release (Agne-Traub, Martin, & Tandy, 1998).

References:

Agne-Traub, C., Martin, J.L., & Tandy, R.E. (1998). *Bowling* (8th ed.). Dubuque, IA: WCB/
    McGraw-Hill.

Schmidt, R.A., & Wrisberg, C.A. (2000). Motor learning and performance (2nd ed.). Champaign,
    IL: Human Kinetics.

b. Scenario: Learning the ceiling shot in racquetball.

Hypothetical learner:

After playing racquetball for several months, a 19-year-old male wants to learn to hit the ceiling shot. An experienced athlete in a number of ball sports, he is in excellent physical condition.

Learning task:

The racquetball ceiling shot is basically a defensive shot that involves directing the ball with an upward motion of the racquet to a point on the ceiling about one foot from the front wall. After striking the ceiling, the ball deflects downward, hitting the front wall and then descending sharply to the floor where it bounces high and travels toward the rear of the court (Kozar & Catignani, 1997).

Examples of intrinsic feedback:

-
-

Examples of extrinsic feedback:

-
-

Reference:

Kozar, A., & Catignani, E. (1997). *Beginning racquetball.* Winston-Salem, NC: Hunter Textbooks.

c. Scenario: Learning to hit a sand shot in golf.

Hypothetical learner:

A 46-year-old woman has golfed for 20 years but until now has not been able to consistently execute a successful shot out of a sand trap; the learner is physically fit and highly motivated.

Learning task:

The sand shot requires the golfer to project the ball from inside the sand trap toward a target on the fairway or green. There are two types of sand shots, depending on the lie of the ball, which is usually either atop the sand's surface or buried in the sand with only a small portion of the ball in view (Bunker & Owens, 1984).

Examples of intrinsic feedback:

-
-

Examples of extrinsic feedback:

-
-

Reference:

Bunker, L.K., & Owens, D. (1984). *Golf: Better practice for better play.* Champaign, IL: Leisure
    Press.

d. Scenario: Learning to play the piano.

Hypothetical learner:

A 10-year-old boy's parents want him to learn to play at least one musical instrument. He selects the piano. The boy enjoys a variety of team sport activities (baseball, football, basketball), but is not motivated to learn to play the piano.

Learning tasks:

Pianists execute sequences of finger movements to depress various combinations among the piano's 88 keys. They vary the tone, loudness, and pitch with the fingers, and depress key pedals with the right (and sometimes left) foot to create different degrees of smoothness, softness, or sharpness in the sounds.

Examples of intrinsic feedback:

-
-

Examples of extrinsic feedback:

-
-

2. Two types of extrinsic feedback are knowledge of results, which informs learners about the results of their movements, and knowledge of performance, which indicates something about the quality of the actions themselves. In this question, four learning tasks are briefly described. For the first task, two examples of knowledge of results and knowledge of performance are provided. You are to suggest two examples of each of these two types of extrinsic feedback (with supporting rationale) for the remaining tasks.

a. Scenario: Learning the skill of rapid-fire pistol shooting.

Learning task:

Rapid-fire pistol shooting is sometimes referred to as silhouette shooting because of the shape of the targets. From a standing position, a performer fires a total of 60 shots at 5 targets located 25 meters away. Shots are fired in groups of five, with each group being fired at a different target. Targets rapidly turn from a side-on (facing away from the shooter) to a face-on (facing the shooter) position and are exposed for only a short period of time (4 to 8 seconds). The targets are 1.6 meters high and .45 meter wide; they are divided into 10 zones, each having a different scoring value of between 1 and 10 points (The Diagram Group, 1974).

Examples of knowledge of results:

Learners might benefit from knowing the total points for a round of shots and the average deviation of the shots around the center of the 10-point zone of the target. The point value alerts the performer to the score he or she would receive during a round of competition. The average deviation value indicates the consistency of the performer's shots within the 10-point zone. A practitioner could calculate the average deviation of the performer's shots by using the formula for variable error discussed by Schmidt and Wrisberg (2000) in chapter 7 of the text (see table 7.6).

Examples of knowledge of performance:

Performers might want feedback about the postural characteristics and breathing patterns they use in pistol shooting. Significant postural characteristics for successful shooting include the horizontal positioning of the shooting arm, the vertical alignment of the upper and lower body, and the relative positioning of the head and shooting shoulder. The instructor might provide the performer with ratings of movement form (Schmidt & Wrisberg, 2000, chapter 7) for any or all of these characteristics. Research suggests that breathing activity during a firing sequence produces small body movements that affect the accuracy and consistency of shots (Wilkinson, Landers, & Daniels, 1981). Therefore, if a portable breathing apparatus were available, the instructor could provide the performer with information about respiration patterns within and between shot sequences.

References:

The Diagram Group (1974). *Rules of the game.* New York: Paddington Press Ltd.

Schmidt, R.A., & Wrisberg, C.A. (2000). *Motor learning and performance* (2nd ed.). Champaign, IL: Human Kinetics.

Wilkinson, M.O., Landers, D.M., & Daniels, F.S. (1981). Breathing patterns and their influence on rifle shooting. *American Marksman*, 6, 8–9.

b. Scenario: Learning to hit the short-and-low serve in badminton.

Learning task:

Players in the doubles game of badminton use the short-and-low serve to initiate a rally. This serve is used more frequently than others because the doubles service court is shallower but wider than the singles court, allowing the server a greater space to hit to in the front of the opponents' court (Chafin & Turner, 1988). The server must hit the shuttle so that it travels in a low trajectory, barely clearing the net. Since the short-and-low serve projects the shuttle to points immediately in front of the receiver, it can be returned forcefully if the shuttle trajectory is too high. The server keeps the wrist in an extended or laid-back position during contact, stroking the shuttle with only the forward movement of the arm. This action reduces the force with which the shuttle is contacted, sending it just over the net and into the front of the service area. Effective servers can achieve a consistently low shuttle trajectory while hitting the shuttle to a variety of target locations.

Examples of knowledge of results:

-
-

Examples of knowledge of performance:

-
-

Reference:

Chafin, M.B., & Turner, M.M. (1988). *Badminton everyone.* Winston-Salem, NC: Hunter Textbooks.

c. Scenario: Learning to pitch a softball using the windmill arm motion.

Learning task:

The softball pitcher produces the windmill motion by producing one revolution of the throwing arm that carries the arm forward, up, and over the head; down the backside; and forward again. The pitcher releases the ball at a point slightly in front of the body. The pitcher faces the batter, who stands 40 feet away (46 feet for men), and delivers the ball directly toward the plate. Whatever variation (fastball, change up, drop, rise, curve) she uses, the pitcher's primary task in the windmill pitch is to deliver the ball into the strike zone. The strike zone involves an area 17 inches wide (the width of home plate) and a height determined by the approximate distance between the batter's knees and chest (Reach & Schwartz, 1992).

Examples of knowledge of results:

-
-

Examples of knowledge of performance:

-
-

Reference:

Reach, J., & Schwartz, B. (1992). *Softball everyone*. Winston-Salem, NC: Hunter Textbooks.

d. Scenario: Learning the basketball jump shot.

Learning task:

The jump shot is the preferred shot of most basketball players. By jumping before releasing the ball, the player elevates the body above the opponent's to increase the probability of producing an unimpeded shot. A player may execute the jump shot from numerous angles and distances relative to the basket. A successful shot involves balance, control, and rhythm. During execution, the shooter jumps by extending the legs, back, and shoulders and then shoots the ball by extending the elbow and flexing the wrist and fingers (Wissel, 1994).

Examples of knowledge of results:

-
-

Examples of knowledge of performance:

-
-

Reference:

Wissel, H. (1994). *Basketball: Steps to success*. Champaign, IL: Human Kinetics.

3. Practitioners must decide what kinds of extrinsic feedback to give learners. Chapter 10 of the textbook discusses verbal, visual, program, parameter, prescriptive, and descriptive types of feedback. Four scenarios are described here that include a hypothetical learner and a learning task. The first scenario gives you two examples of extrinsic feedback that might be appropriate for skill learning. You are to provide two examples of appropriate types of extrinsic feedback (with supporting rationale) for the other scenarios.

a. Scenario: Learning to hit a forehand volley in tennis.

Hypothetical learner:

A 17-year-old female has been playing tennis recreationally for several years. She executes her serves and ground strokes at the level of an advanced beginner, but lacks the confidence in her volley to approach the net.

Learning task:

The volley is a shot that is hit with little or no backswing. The player stands 8 to 10 feet from the net with the knees bent and weight on the balls of the feet. Facing the opponent and holding the racket directly in front of the body, the player carefully watches the approaching ball, rotates the shoulders slightly to the rear, steps forward, and contacts the ball with a firm grip and a punch-like arm and shoulder action (Brown, 1995).

Examples of appropriate types of extrinsic feedback:

Many beginners experience two problems when attempting to volley: (1) hitting the ball with little or no power and (2) failing to hit the ball on the center of the strings.

1. If the learner's volleys lack power, likely she is not stepping forward to hit the ball or is blocking the ball instead of "punching" it (Brown, 1995). Prescriptive, verbal statements ("Step forward to hit the ball" or "Follow through in the direction you want the ball to go") would be appropriate types of extrinsic feedback to correct this mistake. Prescriptive feedback (what to do) is usually more helpful than descriptive feedback (what you did) for beginners who may not know how to correct their errors (Schmidt & Wrisberg, 2000, chapter 10). A combination of prescriptive program feedback could help: visually demonstrating the timing of the correct volley action while verbally emphasizing that the swing should be executed with a forward motion of the hitting shoulder (rather than with the elbow or wrist).

2. Players who consistently fail to hit the ball on the center of the strings are probably not watching the ball carefully enough. You can determine this by watching the learner's eyes as she executes her volleys. A verbal prescriptive feedback statement, such as "Watch the ball all the way to the strings" or "Look for the seams on the ball," should encourage the learner to narrow her attentional focus (Nideffer, 1995) on the approaching ball.

References:

Brown, J. (1995). *Tennis: Steps to success.* Champaign, IL: Human Kinetics.
Nideffer, R.M. (1995). *Focus for success.* San Diego: Enhanced Performance Services.
Schmidt, R.A., & Wrisberg, C.A. (2000). *Motor learning and performance* (2nd ed.). Champaign, IL: Human Kinetics.

b. Scenario: Learning the fireman's carry in wrestling.

Hypothetical learner:

A 14-year-old male enjoys intense physical activity requiring strength and power. The boy approaches his high school wrestling coach for help in learning some basic moves of the sport. He is physically fit and has several abilities that should help his learning, including response orientation, explosive strength, static strength, and speed of limb movement (Fleishman, 1964).

Learning task:

A wrestler uses the fireman's carry to take the opponent down to the mat. Beginning in a standing position facing the opponent, the wrestler quickly grabs the opponent's left triceps with his right hand (assuming the learner is right-handed). The wrestler then thrusts both his legs forward and under those of his opponent. One leg should be on either side of the opponent's left leg. Next he quickly thrusts his left arm between his opponent's legs and takes a deep crotch hold. At the same time, the wrestler plants his feet and forcefully extends the legs, driving hard off the mat, and pulling down on the opponent's left arm. With his left arm the wrestler lifts his opponent and throws him over his body and down to the mat. The key to the fireman's carry is using the right hand to keep pressure on the opponent's left arm (Mysnyk, Davis, & Simpson, 1994).

Examples of appropriate types of extrinsic feedback:

-
-

References:

Fleishman, E.A. (1964). *The structure and measurement of physical fitness.* Englewood Cliffs, NJ: Prentice-Hall.
Mysnyk, M., Davis, B., & Simpson, B. (1994). *Winning wrestling moves.* Champaign, IL: Human Kinetics.

c. Scenario: Learning to target-cast a fishing lure.

Hypothetical learner:

The learner is a 20-year-old male who has been blind since birth. The individual has no other physical handicaps and has lived a reasonably active life, enjoying recreational archery, bowling, and dancing.

Learning task:

In target casting, the performer usually stands and directly faces the target, though some individuals turn slightly sideways, one foot positioned a bit forward of the other. After lining up the rod with the intended target, the person moves the rod's tip slowly and smoothly to a vertical position above the head and stops. He then produces a forward motion of the rod's tip by sharply flexing the wrist and extending the forearm. During the backward motion, he holds the line in place by depressing the reel button or the reel spool. During forward motion, the performer releases the thumb's pressure, allowing the line and plug to carry toward the target (Adams & McCubbin, 1991).

Examples of appropriate types of extrinsic feedback:

-
-

Reference:

Adams, R.C., & McCubbin, J.A. (1991). *Games, sports, and exercises for the physically disabled* (4th ed.). Philadelphia: Lea & Febiger.

   d. Scenario: Learning to juggle three beanbags.

Hypothetical learner:

The learner is a 40-year-old female who wants to learn juggling to impress her teenage children, who consider her incapable of performing any type of skilled motor activity. The woman has no physical handicaps and seems to have better-than-average levels of multilimb coordination (Fleishman, 1964), which should help her achieve her goal.

Learning task:

Beginning with two beanbags in one hand and one in the other, the performer tosses one of the two bags in an arc toward the hand holding the single bag. When the airborne bag just begins to descend, she tosses the single bag in the other hand in the opposite direction. The juggler repeats this sequence of tossing the bag in one hand at the instant that an airborne bag coming from the other hand begins to descend. The key to successful juggling is making great tosses, not great catches (Cassidy & Rimbeaux, 1994).

Examples of appropriate types of extrinsic feedback:

-
-

References:

Cassidy, J., & Rimbeaux, B.C. (1994). *Juggling for the complete klutz.* Palo Alto, CA: Klutz.
Fleishman, E.A. (1964). *The structure and measurement of physical fitness.* Englewood Cliffs, NJ: Prentice-Hall.

   4. In giving extrinsic feedback, practitioners must determine the optimal degree of feedback precision, which depends on factors such as the individual's stage of learning and the complexity of the task (see Schmidt & Wrisberg, 2000, chapter 10). In the first scenario, two examples of extrinsic feedback that vary in precision are provided. You are to suggest two examples (with supporting rationale) of feedback that vary in precision for the other scenarios.

a. Scenario: Learning to perform a two-footed spin in ice skating.

Hypothetical learner:

A 25-year-old female who has been ice skating for about a year has attempted the two-footed spin a few times—with little success. She feels more comfortable doing the movement counterclockwise.

Learning task:

The two-footed spin is executed as the skater glides forward. To initiate the counterclockwise spin, the skater places her left foot slightly in front of the right and shifts her weight to the inside blade of the right skate. Leaning slightly toward the middle of the spiral, the skater extends her arms to point the right arm forward and the left slightly to the rear (in the direction of the upcoming spiral). Essentially, the skater positions the arms as if to embrace an imaginary circle located at the center of the spiral. When the skater arrives at the center of the spiral, she performs a three-point turn on her left skate that shifts the direction of her skating from forward to backward and leaves an etching on the ice in the shape of a backward number "3." The right leg then follows the left, wrapping around it in a spinning motion. During the transition from the three-point turn to the actual spin, the skater shifts her weight from the inner blade of the left foot to the middle of her body in order to maintain balance throughout the spin (Kunzle-Watson & DeArmond, 1996).

Examples (varying in precision) of extrinsic feedback:

Since the learner in this scenario has had experience ice skating, she can skate both forward and backward and produce crossover movements (i.e., cross one leg over the other to execute turns in the oval ice rink). Her biggest challenge is getting a general idea of the basic movement pattern of the spin. Common problems in learning the spin include a slumped posture and failure to keep the weight centered in the middle of the action.

1. Less precise feedback: General prescriptive feedback statements, such as "Head high," "Arms outstretched," and "Weight centered," might help her achieve the feel of correct timing. They would direct her attention to aspects that contribute to learning the generalized motor program for the spinning action (Schmidt & Wrisberg, 2000, chapter 6).

2. More precise feedback: Once the learner can produce an approximation of the correct movement, visual feedback (using a portable camcorder and video monitor) might assist her seeing how her pattern deviates from the desired spatial and temporal pattern (Seat & Wrisberg, 1996). An instructor could also encourage the learner to check the quality of the backward-3-shape etchings on the ice cut during her three-point turns. Such visual knowledge of results can be a useful source of intrinsic feedback that the skater can repeatedly use to evaluate and refine her turns.

References:

Kunzle-Watson, K., & DeArmond, S.J. (1996). *Ice skating: Steps to success.* Champaign, IL: Human Kinetics.

Schmidt, R.A., & Wrisberg, C.A. (2000). *Motor learning and performance* (2nd ed.). Champaign, IL: Human Kinetics.

Seat, J.E., & Wrisberg, C.A. (1996). The visual instruction system. *Research Quarterly for Exercise and Sport, 67,* 106–108.

b. Scenario: Learning to dance the fox trot.

Hypothetical learner:

A 20-year-old female wants to learn the fox trot to add this dance to several others she already knows (the swing, waltz, and rumba) when she visits a local dance club.

Learning task:

In dancing the fox trot, the two partners stand facing each other. The woman positions her right foot between the man's feet and shifts her weight to the balls of her feet. The man holds his right hand under the woman's left shoulder blade, and the woman rests her left hand on the man's right shoulder. The man then takes the woman's right hand in his left, and both partners extend their arms out to the side just below the height of the shoulders. In the fox trot, the woman performs this sequence of steps:

1. Step back on the right foot; slow.
2. Follow through with the left foot and step to the left side; quick.
3. Close the right foot against the left foot, transferring the weight; quick.
4. Step forward on the left foot; slow.
5. Follow through with the right foot and step to the right side; quick.
6. Close the left foot against the right foot, transferring the weight; quick.

The fox trot has a 4/4 meter and rhythm and involves a "slow, quick, quick" tempo. Slow steps are performed to two beats of music, and quick steps are performed to a single beat (Smith, 1995).

Examples (varying in precision) of extrinsic feedback:

-
-

Reference:

Smith, D.L. (1995). *Dance at a glance.* Boston: American Press.

c. Scenario: Learning the forward dive in the pike position.

Hypothetical learner:

A 12-year-old male has just learned the standard forward dive and now wants to learn to dive in the pike position.

Learning task:

The forward dive in the pike position involves pushing the hips up while reaching for the toes. The diver keeps the legs straight and bends only at the hips. After touching the toes, the diver extends the arms laterally to prepare for entry into the water. By swinging the arms directly forward, the diver causes the legs to lift (American Red Cross, 1992).

Examples (varying in precision) of extrinsic feedback:

-
-

Reference:

American Red Cross. (1992). *Swimming and diving.* St. Louis: Mosby-Year Book, Inc.

d. Scenario: Learning to throw a ball.

Hypothetical learner:

The learner is a 7-year-old female who wants to learn how to throw a ball effectively to play in various ball games. She is physically fit and motivated to achieve a high level of throwing skill.

Learning task:

Throwing is a fundamental movement produced by this general sequence of actions: (a) forward step with the foot opposite that of the throwing arm; (b) forward rotation of the pelvis; (c) backward and then forward rotation of the upper spine; (d) forward rotation of the throwing shoulder; (d) swinging and inward rotation of the upper arm; (f) elbow extension; (g) ball release; (h) follow-through (Haywood, 1993).

Examples (varying in precision) of extrinsic feedback:

-
-

Reference:

Haywood, K.M. (1993). *Life span motor development* (2nd ed.). Champaign, IL: Human Kinetics.

 ## Problem-Solving Exercises

In Exercise 10.1 you discuss and provide examples of three types of extrinsic feedback that a practitioner might provide for a learner. In Exercise 10.2 you describe how a practitioner might provide program feedback and parameter feedback to assist a person in developing a skill that is perhaps governed by a generalized motor program. In Exercise 10.3 you explain one aspect of an individual's performance that might benefit from the person's getting verbal feedback and one aspect for which visual feedback might be of more assistance.

Exercise 10.1
Choosing Appropriate Extrinsic Feedback

Practitioners consider several issues before providing extrinsic feedback for learners. In this exercise you are to briefly describe a motor skill you are familiar with and then discuss three examples of extrinsic feedback you might give a learner to promote the individual's goal achievement. Your solution should do the following:

- Describe the target skill, emphasizing the goal of the movement and its basic actions.
- Describe the learner (a hypothetical individual or someone you know).
- Discuss three examples of extrinsic feedback you would provide, giving supporting rationale for each.

Spencer's Solution

The skill for this exercise is high hurdling. In the 110-meter race, runners must clear a series of 10 hurdles en route to the finish line. The goal of the hurdling action is to approach and clear each hurdle in a smooth, relaxed fashion while running at near maximal speed. Thus, correct form in hurdling should be thought of as a type of correct sprinting. The key ingredients include maintaining continuous leg action from takeoff to landing, straightening without locking of the lead leg, delaying of the trail leg to make the action smooth, and combining a rapid snap-down of the lead leg and forward-pull of the trail leg in a single action (Cooper, Lavery, & Perrin, 1970).

The best hurdlers use a good sprinting action when approaching the hurdle. They thrust the lead leg upward and forward while keeping it relaxed and unlocked. They focus the eyes ahead to the next hurdle, achieve a pronounced forward body lean and elevation of the knee of the trail leg, and land on the toes of the lead foot. They then return quickly to good sprinting form.

The learner is a 16-year-old male sprinter on a high school track team. He wants to learn the hurdling action to qualify for the 110-meter hurdles event at the conference championships. The boy demonstrates excellent sprinting speed and seems to have dynamic flexibility (Fleishman, 1964), which should help him achieve the degree of leg extension he needs to clear the high hurdles.

The learner's first challenge is to understand the general hurdling action. One way to assist his grasp of the action is to set up a single hurdle and instruct him to perform several repetitions of the hurdling movement. Watching him attempt the movement, I would particularly note the relative timing of his arm and leg actions. Then I would provide him with verbal program feedback that points him in the direction of the correct timing structure.

Once the learner can do the correct hurdling action fairly well, I would add two or three more hurdles and instruct him to run through the series of hurdles at near top speed. The hurdler needs to identify the optimal distance from each hurdle from which to begin his takeoff. After several repetitions of this activity, I would provide him with general directional feedback instructing him to take off closer to or farther from the hurdles. Extrinsic feedback is practically essential in helping the learner identify the correct takeoff point. This is because the athlete must keep his eyes on the hurdles and not watch the placement of his feet.

When the athlete demonstrates that he can successfully navigate most of the hurdles in a 110-meter event, I would begin videotaping his actions to provide him with visual feedback regarding more subtle errors in his movements. When videotaping, I would consider which visual perspective provides the best view of the feature(s) I am targeting for his attention. For example, I might decide to videotape the athlete from the side if I wanted to show him how the rear action of his lead arm is so pronounced that it is forcing his shoulders to turn too far to the side.

References:

Cooper, J.M., Lavery, J., & Perrin, W. (1970). *Track and field for coach and athlete* (2nd ed.). Englewood Cliffs, NJ: Prentice-Hall.

Fleishman, E.A. (1964). *The structure and measurement of physical fitness.* Englewood Cliffs, NJ: Prentice-Hall.

Evaluation of Spencer's Solution

Spencer selects an appropriate activity and provides a good description of the movement's goal and the basic actions involved. His description of the learner is adequate, noting the learner's previous experience as a sprinter, his dynamic flexibility, and how the ability might be helpful in achieving the degree of leg extension he needs to clear the hurdle.

Spencer proposes three examples of extrinsic feedback, but fails to document the sources of motor learning literature from which he obtained this information. He correctly pinpoints the initial challenge of identifying the appropriate relative timing pattern for the hurdling movement. Although he indicates that he would provide verbal program feedback to assist the learner, he offers no specific examples.

Spencer next suggests that he would provide general directional feedback to assist the learner in identifying the correct takeoff point for his hurdling movements. However, he does not indicate what form this feedback would take (e.g., visual, verbal), nor does he provide any specific examples of the feedback. Finally, Spencer suggests that he would administer videotape feedback to help the learner fine tune his actions. Though Spencer does not provide a specific explanation of how he would introduce this feedback, he does indicate that he would carefully consider the positioning of the camera to provide the learner with the best visual perspective. In summary, Spencer offers several interesting suggestions for extrinsic feedback but he needs to provide additional discussion and rationale in places, along with more specific examples and documentation.

Lyle's Solution

I have selected the *ogoshi*, or basic hip throw, in the sport of judo. The ogoshi is one of the first throws students learn because it is simple and fun to perform. The throw can originate from several positions, but should initially be learned from an upright position. Facing the opponent, the learner uses her left hand to grasp the opponent's sleeve just above the right elbow and uses her right hand to grasp the opponent's left lapel. Once she secures both grips, the learner releases her grip on the opponent's lapel and moves her right hand forward and under the opponent's arm to a position on his back. The student then pulls the opponent's right arm forward, bends at the waist and knees, and spins her body counterclockwise so that her back is against the opponent's chest. Now that her center of gravity is below her opponent's, the learner extends her legs while keeping her waist bent so that her body forms a 90-degree angle. With the opponent now on his back, the student pulls on his right elbow and rotates his body counterclockwise over her shoulder and lands him on his back on the mat (see the photos at the bottom of this page for the steps in the ogoshi).

The learner in my example is a 20-year-old female who is 5 feet 4 inches tall and weighs 120 pounds. She participates in a variety of fitness activities and is learning judo for self-defense. Before learning the hip throw, the student masters the various forms of falling to minimize the risk of injury when her opponent throws her.

Initially, I would tell the learner's opponent to remain passive and to allow her to attempt her hip throws unimpeded. The two keys to a successful hip throw are a firm grasp above the opponent's right elbow and a body position that results in a lower center of gravity than that of the opponent (Watanabe & Avakian, 1970). Therefore, I would watch the learner's left hand and waist as she attempts her throws. Examples of verbal feedback statements to assist the learner in correcting errors in her performance are "Grab quick and pull!" and "Spin and bend." According to Schmidt and Wrisberg (2000), beginners benefit from feedback statements that are simple and prescriptive in nature. If practitioners keep their feedback statements simple, they reduce the possibility of overloading learners with too much information. Prescriptive statements alert learners to specific changes they might make in their movements to increase their chances of successful goal achievement.

Once the learner can produce the basic hip throw action, she can try situations with the opponent more actively resisting. The secret of most judo moves is to counteract an opponent's movements by using the opponent's momentum—rather than by resisting it. For example, if the opponent grabs for the learner, he would make himself more vulnerable to a hip throw because his momentum is already in the direction of the learner. Therefore, I would tell the learner's opponent to vary his movements occasionally. I would then watch the learner's countermovements and give summary feedback that informs her about the appropriateness of her responses. An example of an inappropriate response would be if the learner tries to throw the opponent when she should be trying to avoid him or hold him. By providing summary feedback after a series of movements, I would encourage the learner to also evaluate her own errors (Schmidt & Wrisberg, 2000).

After several practice sessions, I would videotape the learner's movements and provide visual feedback for her to use in refining the hip-throw action. To encourage her own error detection, I would ask the learner to tell me if she sees any errors in her movements before offering my own comments. If she identifies a particular error, I would ask her to tell me how she might perform the movement differently the next time.

References:

Schmidt, R.A., & Wrisberg, C.A. (2000). *Motor learning and performance* (2nd ed.). Champaign, IL: Human Kinetics.

Watanbe, J., & Avakian, L. (1970). *The secrets of judo.* Tokyo: Charles E. Tuttle Company.

Evaluation of Lyle's Solution

Lyle provides a nice description and an illustration of the ogoshi action sequence. He does not specifically mention the goal of the movement, although it seems to be implied in his task description. Lyle needs, however, to reference his discussion of the task.

The description of the learner seems adequate. Lyle goes on to explain and document two keys to successful performance of the hip throw. The rest of his solution and his examples of feedback are good, although he might have provided a bit more theoretical discussion of the concept of error detection capability and of the factors practitioners should consider when providing videotape feedback.

Your Solution to Exercise 10.1

Choosing Appropriate Extrinsic Feedback

NAME_____   DATE_____

1. Definition of problem:

2. Type of instructional situation:
   Teaching   Coaching   Rehabilitation   Human factors

3. Description of the skill
   Goal of the movement:
   Basic actions required:

4. Description of the learner:

5. Three examples of extrinsic feedback (with rationale):
   a.
   b.
   c.

6. References:

Exercise 10.2
Providing Program Feedback and Parameter Feedback

Some types of skill learning include developing generalized motor programs (Schmidt & Wrisberg, 2000, chapter 6) that performers can *adjust* to achieve different goals in the target context. For example, a tennis player develops a general program for serving and learns to adjust it by selecting various parameter values for force to produce different types and speeds of serves during a match. By providing learners with program feedback and parameter feedback (Schmidt & Wrisberg, 2000, chapter 10), practitioners can enhance the performer's development of generalized motor programs and parameterization capabilities. In this exercise you pick a class of tasks that a performer might control using a generalized motor program. Then you provide one example of program feedback and two examples of parameter feedback you might give the learner to promote program learning and parameterization capability. Your solution should do the following:

- Describe the target skill, emphasizing the movement's goal and basic required actions.
- Describe the learner (a hypothetical individual or someone you know).
- Give one example of program feedback.
- Give two examples of parameter feedback.

Ellen's Solution

The skill is the soccer pass, the goal of which is to deliver the ball to a teammate in such a way that it is easy for the person to receive the ball and control it. The soccer pass is an appropriate skill for this exercise because it is governed by a generalized motor program that the player can adapt to produce different types of passes. Its basic action includes the passer's keeping her head steady and eyes on the ball, placing the kicking foot alongside the ball while allowing room for the kicking leg to swing freely, contacting the ball with the instep of the kicking foot, and following through in the direction of the target (Pronk & Gorman, 1991).

The learner is a 9-year-old girl who wants to learn to play soccer with her friends. The only kicking experience she has had is in occasional kickball games in her physical education class at school.

Observing the learner during a few of her kickball games, I notice that she tends to lock her ankle and knee and use a pendular action of her entire leg to kick the ball. I also notice that she contacts the ball with the toes of her foot. Since this movement pattern is inappropriate for a soccer kick and since the learner might be tempted to use the pattern because it is familiar, I might need to provide program feedback that encourages her use of the proper kicking action. For example, I might say "Your lower leg is moving too slow." This comment could help the girl realize that she needs to move her lower leg faster than her upper leg. Sometimes when beginners are instructed to increase the force of their kicks, they naturally increase the speed of their lower leg. Therefore, a more effective program feedback statement for this young learner might be "Kick the ball as hard as you can."

Practitioners can also provide parameter feedback to help learners correct errors in the values they select to make their movements meet environmental requirements (Schmidt & Wrisberg, 2000). The generalized motor program for the soccer pass can be modified to produce different types of passes. For example, the push pass is the most reliable pass a player can use to accurately deliver the ball along the ground at a moderate pace to an open teammate. It is produced with a smooth action of the lower leg and a follow-through in the direction of the target. The chip pass is another type of pass that a player can use to play the ball over an opponent's head to a teammate a short distance away. The player produces this pass by contacting the undersurface of the ball with a "stabbing" action of the lower leg.

If I saw the learner execute a push pass that was too fast for her teammate to control, I might make the parameter feedback statement "That was too hard." If I saw her produce a chip pass that resulted in a ball trajectory that was too low, I might say, "You kicked the ball too high." By alerting the learner to errors in the parameter values she is selecting, I hope to assist her in learning how to adjust parameter values of the generalized motor program more effectively.

References:

Pronk, N., & Gorman, B. (1991). *Soccer everyone* (2nd ed.). Winston-Salem, NC: Hunter Textbooks.

Schmidt, R.A., & Wrisberg, C.A. (2000). *Motor learning and performance* (2nd ed.). Champaign, IL: Human Kinetics.

Evaluation of Ellen's Solution

Ellen does not actually present any theoretical discussion (or documentation) of the concept of the generalized motor program. She provides a general description and referencing of the goal of the movement and the basic actions involved, but might have added a figure illustrating the key components of the kicking sequence.

Ellen's description of the learner is brief and general. All the reader knows is that the individual is young, female, and brings little previous kicking experience with her to the learning environment.

To Ellen's credit, she observes the learner's kicking skill prior to providing instructional assistance; she heightens her awareness of the type of program feedback that might help the learner acquire the proper fundamental kicking action. Unfortunately, Ellen provides little theoretical discussion of the concept of program feedback. In addition, her examples of program feedback are vague (particularly the example of descriptive feedback) and likely difficult for the young learner to interpret.

Ellen decides to promote the learner's development of parameter adjustment capability by instructing her to attempt to produce different variations of the soccer pass (e.g., the push pass and the chip pass). While varied practice has generally been shown to facilitate parameterization development (Schmidt & Wrisberg, 2000, chapter 9), it is sometimes an ineffective practice structure to use with younger learners who may need a period of repetition with one movement variation before attempting another (Wrisberg & Mead, 1983). Even if varied practice were an appropriate strategy for assisting a 9-year-old child, Ellen's feedback examples offer little information for parameterization development. The statements are worded descriptively, rather than being prescriptive (see Kernodle & Carlton, 1992, for an example of why prescriptive feedback is more helpful). Moreover, Ellen's first example ("That was too hard") seems quite vague (what does "that" refer to?) and her second example ("You kicked the ball too high") only gives information the learner should be able to pick up for herself.

In short, Ellen's solution lacks a clear connection with the motor learning literature. Ellen may need to reread chapter 10 in the textbook (particularly the section on program feedback and parameter feedback) to establish a more solid theoretical rationale for her solution.

References:

Kernodle, M.W., & Carlton, L.G. (1992). Information feedback and the learning of multiple-degree-of-freedom activities. *Journal of Motor Behavior, 24*, 187–196.

Schmidt, R.A., & Wrisberg, C.A. (2000). *Motor learning and performance* (2nd ed.). Champaign, IL: Human Kinetics.

Wrisberg, C.A., & Mead, B.J. (1983). Developing coincident-timing skill in children: A comparison of training methods. *Research Quarterly for Exercise and Sport, 54*, 67–74.

Sam's Solution

The target skill I have chosen for this exercise is the overhead shot in badminton. A skilled badminton player uses the overhead motion to hit a clear, a smash, or a drop. By using the same motion to produce different outcomes, the player makes it difficult for his opponent to predict the variation of the shot he is going to hit. Thus, the overhead badminton motion is a good example of a skill controlled by a generalized motor program (Schmidt & Wrisberg, 2000, chapter 6), which the performer parameterizes to produce variations of the movement (i.e., the clear, smash, or drop).

The basic action of the overhead motion starts with the player turning his body so that the left side (for a right-handed player) faces the net. The player then draws the racket back into the full backswing position. As the shuttle approaches, the player extends his hitting arm forward and upward to contact the shuttle well above his head and slightly in front of his body (see figure at the bottom of this page). The player determines the specific shot he is going to hit by varying the wrist action at the moment of impact. For the clear shot, the wrist is flexed *rapidly* and contact is made with an *open* racket face (i.e., the racket face points upward at about a 45-degree angle). For the smash shot, the wrist is flexed *rapidly* and contact is made with a *closed* racket face (i.e., the racket face points downward at about a 45-degree angle). For the drop shot, the wrist is flexed *slowly* and contact is made with a *closed* racket face (Chafin & Turner, 1988).

The learner is a 19-year-old male learning to play badminton to compete against members of the badminton club at his college. He is physically fit and experienced in tennis and racquetball.

Schmidt and Wrisberg (2000) define *program feedback* as extrinsic feedback about the timing or sequencing of the movement pattern that leads to changes in the fundamental structure of the generalized motor program. Many beginners have problems in producing the overhead motion because they fail to extend the arm upward when hitting the shot. They initiate the swing with the elbow bent and make shuttle contact at a point only slightly above the head. This pattern of relative motion consists of a rapid wrist action and little or no arm and shoulder movement. If I noticed this type of overhead motion, I would give prescriptive, verbal feedback statements, such as, "Reach and hit" or "Upward and forward" to encourage the learner's extension of his arm more before contact with the shuttle. Such feedback should also help him adjust the relative timing pattern of the overhead motion by increasing the speed of shoulder and arm movements.

a   b   c

Reprinted, by permission, from T. Grice, 1996, *Badminton: Steps to success* (Champaign, IL: Human Kinetics), 35.

The learner should get considerable intrinsic parameter feedback by watching the shuttle flight characteristics and the location of shuttle landing. If I noticed the learner having difficulty correcting a particular type of error, I might provide him with an occasional parameter feedback statement suggesting an adjustment he could try. One statement of verbal, prescriptive parameter feedback is "Faster wrist snap," leading to his increasing the value of the wrist force parameter for the smash or clear shots. A second is "Hit down more sharply," leading to his decreasing the value of the wrist angle at impact for the drop shot, making the racket face more closed.

References:

Chafin, M.B., & Turner, M.M. (1988). *Badminton everyone.* Winston-Salem, NC: Hunter Textbooks.

Schmidt, R.A., & Wrisberg, C.A. (2000). *Motor learning and performance* (2nd ed.). Champaign, IL: Human Kinetics.

Evaluation of Sam's Solution

Sam's solution is nicely organized and written well. He provides theoretical rationale for and documentation of the task and points out how the performer might modify the generalized motor program to produce several variations of the pattern. His description of the basic overhead action and adjustments necessary to produce variations of the movement is good, and he supplements his discussion with a figure.

Sam's description of the learner is not very detailed. Obviously, the less a practitioner knows about a learner prior to the learning experience, the less effective the practitioner can be in providing assistance.

Sam offers a good theoretical discussion of the concept of program feedback and the way it functions to assist the learner in developing an effective generalized motor program for the target skill. Sam's examples of prescriptive verbal feedback are straightforward and simple, and he explains how each feedback statement might assist the learner in developing the correct relative timing pattern.

Sam correctly points out that the learner can receive intrinsic feedback about his accuracy by watching the flight characteristics and landing location of the shuttle. For situations in which the learner appears unable to correct parameterization errors, Sam offers two nice examples of extrinsic parameter feedback he might provide and suggests rationale for why each might be effective.

Your Solution to Exercise 10.2

Providing Program Feedback and Parameter Feedback

NAME_____ DATE_____

1. Definition of problem:
2. Type of instructional situation:
   Teaching   Coaching   Rehabilitation   Human factors
3. Description of the skill
   Goal of the movement:
   Basic actions required:
4. Description of the learner:
5. Example of program feedback:
6. Two examples of parameter feedback:
7. References:

Exercise 10.3

Providing Verbal Feedback and Visual Feedback

Most extrinsic feedback comes in either a verbal or visual form. Sometimes instructors simply give descriptive feedback, telling learners what they are doing incorrectly, or prescriptive feedback, telling them how they might improve their performance. At other times instructors *show* learners what they are doing wrong. Occasionally, they provide a combination of verbal and visual feedback to assist learners in achieving their performance goals. In this exercise, you select a skill you are familiar with and discuss two circumstances for which an instructor might provide verbal or visual feedback (or a combination) for a learner. Your solution should do the following:

- Describe the target skill, emphasizing the movement's goal and basic actions.
- Describe the learner (a hypothetical individual or someone you know).
- Discuss an aspect of an individual's performance for which a *verbal feedback* statement might be appropriate and give one specific example of verbal feedback.
- Discuss an aspect of an individual's performance for which a *visual feedback* presentation might be effective and give one specific example of visual feedback.

Mark's Solution

The target skill of pole vaulting requires the vaulter to propel the body as high as possible and successfully over a horizontal bar mounted on two uprights. Vaulters use a flexible pole to achieve this goal.

The vault's basic components (for a right-handed person who takes off on the left foot) are as follows: the run; pole plant; takeoff and hang; swing-up; rollback; vertical extension; pull and turn; and push-up, clearance, and landing (Cooper, Lavery, & Perrin, 1970). The sequence of actions is shown in the figure on the next page. During the run, the vaulter carries the pole slightly above the head in a horizontal plane. The vaulter uses a relaxed grip, the hands spread comfortably. The length of the run is usually determined by the skill of the vaulter and the time it takes him to achieve maximum speed. After several practice runs, the vaulter places a mark on the track at the intended point of foot takeoff. During the last third of the run, he points the pole in the direction of the vaulting box.

The pole plant and takeoff are the two most important components of the vaulting action (Cooper, Lavery, & Perrin, 1970). The vaulter begins the pole plant about two strides from the box by rotating the right shoulder to the rear and bringing the pole to the side and above the head. Simultaneously, the vaulter supports the pole with the left hand as he directs it toward and plants it firmly in the box. During the takeoff, he pushes with the left foot and hangs briefly in an extended position. During the swing-up, the vaulter's body remains extended until it achieves a horizontal posture, at which point he flexes both knees and brings them back toward his shoulders. This flexing action causes the pole to bend and the hips to be aligned with each other. The rollback is a continuation of the swing-up and is achieved by rolling the head and shoulders backward. By rotating the hips upward and past the shoulders, the vaulter gains the vertical extension. He then pulls on the pole and rotates the hips so that the body assumes a prone position for clearance. The vaulter performs the push-up by pressing down with both hands, then releasing the left followed by the right. The head remains facing down during clearance as the vaulter focuses his eyes on the landing area.

The learner is a 16-year-old male who has participated in other high-risk activities, such as gymnastics and springboard diving. He wants to learn how to pole vault to compete as a member of his high school track team. The learner has high levels of multilimb coordination, manual dexterity, explosive strength, and trunk strength (see Fleishman, 1964). This combination of abilities is probably important because pole vaulting requires coordinating arm and leg movements precisely, manipulating the pole during the pole plant and pull phases, using the arms explosively during the swing-up and push-up phases, and contracting the trunk muscles to flex the knees during the swing-up and vertical extension phases.

An importance difference between gymnastics or diving and pole vaulting is the vaulter's having to manipulate an external object (i.e., the pole). While gymnasts perform stunts on various types of apparatus and divers attempt their dives on a board or platform, these athletes are not required to manipulate these objects as a vaulter must manipulate the pole. Therefore, considerable initial practice of the run and pole plant would be necessary for this learner to successfully acquire a general idea of the task (Gentile, 1972).

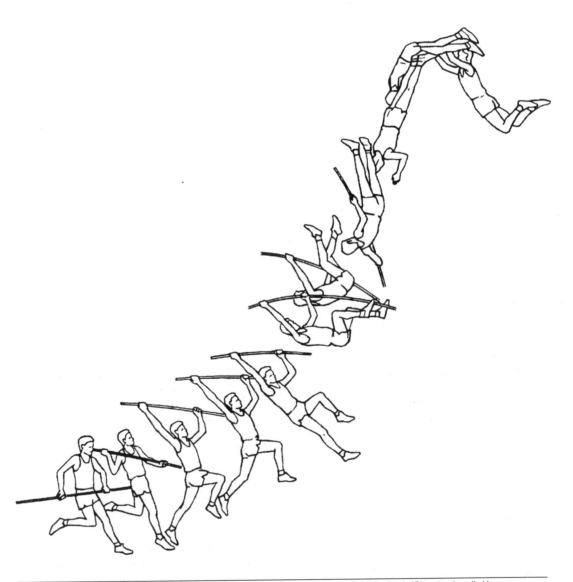

Reprinted, by permission, from G. Carr, 1999, *Fundamentals of track and field*, 2nd ed. (Champaign, IL: Human Kinetics), 176.

Verbal feedback would be appropriate during practice of the run and pole plant for correcting errors in the feeling of the action, such as the acceleration of the run or the hand grip on the pole. If the instructor notices a uniform speed during the last half of the run, he might tell the learner to "build speed" as he approaches the box. If the learner demonstrates less speed during the run or a lack of coordination during the plant, the instructor might say, "Relax your grip" or "Cuddle the pole" to instill images of a relaxed pole carry.

Visual feedback might best demonstrate errors in form (Schmidt &Wrisberg, 2000). During the early stages of practice, it would probably be helpful to provide split-screen videotape feedback that shows the learner how his form deviates from that of an accomplished vaulter. Research by Newell, Carlton, and Antoniou (1990) has revealed that beginners benefit more from visual feedback that includes a depiction of the correct action in addition to their own movement than from visual feedback that shows their actions in isolation. The learner could use visual feedback to improve the position of the hands relative to the head and shoulders, the spatial orientation of the pole relative to the ground during the run and pole plant, and the moment of pole plant relative to the moment of takeoff.

References:

Cooper, J.M., Lavery, J., & Perrin, W. (1970). *Track and field for coach and athlete* (2nd ed.). Englewood Cliffs, NJ: Prentice-Hall.

Fleishman, E.A. (1964). *The structure and measurement of physical fitness.* Englewood Cliffs, NJ: Prentice-Hall.

Gentile, A.M. (1972). A working model of skill acquisition with application to teaching. *Quest Monograph* XVII, 3–23.

Newell, K.M., Carlton, L.G., & Antoniou, A. (1990). The interaction of criterion and feedback information in learning a drawing task. *Journal of Motor Behavior*, 22, 536–552.

Schmidt, R.A., & Wrisberg, C.A. (2000). *Motor learning and performance* (2nd ed.). Champaign, IL: Human Kinetics.

Evaluation of Mark's Solution

Mark's solution is well conceived and nicely written. For example, he provides a detailed description of the action sequence and later relies on some of those details to build a rationale for the verbal and visual feedback he proposes.

Mark provides a thorough description of the learner, adding a discussion of how each ability the learner has might contribute to a particular component of the vaulting movement. He also offers a nice rationale for emphasizing the run and pole plant components of the vault during initial practice sessions. Mark argues that verbal feedback is more appropriate for aspects of the vaulting action that emphasize the feel of the movement (e.g., a relaxed pole carry) since "feel" would be a difficult thing to convey with a visual image. Mark's examples of verbal feedback are simple and to the point.

Mark makes a good case for using visual feedback to convey form characteristics of the pole-vault movement and for using split-screen videotape so the learner can spot differences between his form and that of an accomplished vaulter. Mark also includes primary-source research evidence.

Jackie's Solution

The target skill is the breaststroke, one of the oldest swimming strokes in recorded history and one used in both competitive and leisure swimming (American Red Cross, 1992). Some instructors consider it the best stroke to teach beginners because they can keep their head out of the water to see and breathe more easily. The goal of the breaststroke is to propel the person forward in the water.

Basically, the breaststroke action has a power and a recovery phase. During the power phase the swimmer begins with the arms outstretched in front of the head (the glide position) and pulls the hands outward (the catch position) and downward toward the feet (propulsion). The swimmer then sweeps the hands inward and upward along the front of the body until the palms are facing each other just below the chin. Elbow position is important for good propulsion. Throughout the power phase, the swimmer should maintain the elbows in a position higher than the hands and lower than the shoulders. During the glide phase, the swimmer squeezes the elbows together and extends the arms forward (glide position). To kick, the swimmer brings the heels up toward the buttocks during the glide phase and then presses the feet outward and downward during the power phase (American Red Cross, 1992).

The learner is a 12-year-old female with cerebral palsy and spastic diplegia. The girl has enjoyed aquatic activities for several years but until now has not attempted to learn any of the basic swimming strokes. Like many individuals with cerebral palsy, her greatest movement potential is in the horizontal plane (Adams & McCubbin, 1991). Because the breaststroke is performed primarily in the horizontal plane and consists of identical bilateral movements, it is a good target skill for the learner. Having spasticity, the girl should also find the "frog-type" kick more conducive than the flutter kick (which would induce increased rigidity of the hips, trunk, and back). The inflatable arm supports the learner has used in the past should help her in learning the breaststroke. The devices allow full range of movement, work effectively in the prone position, and work well on individuals who have adequate head control.

Schmidt and Wrisberg (2000) emphasize the importance of two-way communication between the movement practitioner and the learner. This is essential when teaching individuals with cerebral palsy because their speech is often difficult to comprehend. Some time should be devoted to developing an adequate communication system before commencing instruction. In addition, the therapist should attempt to create a nonthreatening, relaxed learning environment. Using background music and a soft tone of voice could help reduce any muscle hypertonus due to anxiety.

In providing feedback, the therapist must be aware of the individual's information-processing limitations (Schmidt & Wrisberg, 2000) and attempt to present feedback that remains within the learner's processing capabilities. In this scenario, verbal feedback might best take the form of reinforcement for desired bilateral movement or increased range of motion. Comments such as "You look like a beautiful snow angel" or "You look like a butterfly stretching its wings" are affirming phrases that conjure images of expanded movement in the horizontal plane.

In a similar vein, visual feedback might take the form of a visual model of the desired action, since videotape feedback of the learner's own movements may contain excessive information for her to process. By giving the learner the opportunity to request to view a model (either the therapist or perhaps a videotape of another child), the therapist might help her come closer to the desired horizontal action and, eventually, the achievement of her movement goal: independent mobility in the water.

References:

Adams, R.C., & McCubbin, J.A. (1991). *Games, sports, and exercises for the physically disabled* (4th ed.). Philadelphia: Lea & Febiger.

American Red Cross. (1992). *Swimming and diving.* St. Louis: Mosby-Year Book.

Schmidt, R.A., & Wrisberg, C.A. (2000). *Motor learning and performance* (2nd ed.). Champaign, IL: Human Kinetics.

Evaluation of Jackie's Solution

Jackie's solution is quite creative and represents a nice application of the motor learning literature to instructional situations involving a person with physical handicaps.

Jackie succinctly describes the movement goal and explains in some detail the basic components of the breaststroke sequence and the learner's condition. However, she might also have provided a visual illustration of the action. Jackie builds a strong therapeutic case for teaching the girl the breaststroke. In addition, she documents the need for the instructor to establish open, two-way communication with the learner and to create a nonthreatening learning environment.

Jackie's verbal feedback examples are sensitive to the learner's information-processing capabilities, therapy needs, and self-esteem. She emphasizes the reinforcing properties of extrinsic feedback and documents her use of verbal feedback as a type of reinforcement for the learner. Jackie suggests a form of visual feedback that technically departs from the standard definition of feedback but that may be appropriate for this learner. While her suggestion may have potential merit, Jackie needs to provide more theoretical rationale from the motor learning literature for its implementation.

Your Solution to Exercise 10.3

Providing Verbal Feedback and Visual Feedback

NAME_____ DATE_____

1. Definition of problem:
2. Type of instructional situation:
   Teaching   Coaching   Rehabilitation   Human factors
3. Description of the target skill
   Goal of the movement:
   Basic actions required:
4. Description of the learner:
5. Discussion and example of verbal feedback:
6. Discussion and example of visual feedback:
7. References:

About the Author

Craig A. Wrisberg, PhD, is a professor of motor behavior and sport psychology at the University of Tennessee, Knoxville (UTK), where he has taught since 1977. During the past 25 years he has published numerous research articles on the topics of anticipation and timing in performance, knowledge of results and motor learning, and warm-up decrement in sport performance. He has received the Chancellor's Award for Research and Creative Achievement (1994) and the Brady Award for Excellence in Teaching (1982).

A past president of the North American Society for the Psychology of Sport and Physical Activity, Dr. Wrisberg is a fellow of both the American Academy of Kinesiology and Physical Education and the Association for the Advancement of Applied Sport Psychology.

In addition to his teaching and research, Dr. Wrisberg supervises the provision of mental training services for student-athletes in the Departments of Men's and Women's Athletics at UTK. In his work with athletes, he applies many of the important concepts and principles covered in this edition of *Motor Learning and Performance*, using the problem-based learning approach on a consistent basis.

Dr. Wrisberg enjoys several outdoor activities, including tennis, canoeing, and hiking in the Great Smoky Mountains.